ALL OF ME

ANNE MURRAY

with Michael Posner

ALL OF ME

ALFRED A. KNOPF CANADA

PUBLISHED BY ALFRED A. KNOPF CANADA

www.randomhouse.ca

Grateful acknowledgment is made for
permission to cite lyrics from the following songs:
"A Little Good News" Words and Music by Tommy Rocco,
Rory Bourke and Charlie Black. Copyright © 1983 UNIVERSAL—
POLYGRAM INTERNATIONAL PUBLISHING, INC. and
CHAPPELL & CO. All rights reserved. Used by Permission.
"It's Alright, Ma (I'm Only Bleeding) © 1965;
renewed 1993 Special Rider Music

GRAMMY and the gramophone logo are registered trademarks of
The Recording Academy ® and are used under license.

Pages 329 to 330 constitute a continuation of the copyright page.

LIBRARY AND ARCHIVES CANADA CATALOGUING IN PUBLICATION
Murray, Anne
All of me / Anne Murray with Michael Posner.
ISBN 978-0-307-39844-4
1. Murray, Anne. 2. Singers—Canada—Biography.
I. Posner, Michael, 1947– II. Title.
ML420.M86A3 2009   782.42164092   C2009-902611-2

Printed and bound in the United States of America

4 6 8 9 7 5 3

This book is dedicated to Leonard Rambeau,
whose faith in me never faltered.

CHAPTER ONE

My mother had prayed for a little girl.

Every day during her fourth pregnancy, Marion Murray entreated Saint Anne, the mother of the Virgin Mary, to deliver a girl to join her three young sons. This was not an idle request. Mom took her prayers—and her Catholicism—very seriously. She lit candles, said novenas and promised Saint Anne that if she were to be blessed with a girl, she would call her Anne. In the end, when I was delivered by Dr. Harold Simpson on the morning of June 20, 1945, at All Saints Hospital in Springhill, Nova Scotia, I was named Morna Anne—Morna after my paternal grandmother. Morna came first because Morna Anne Murray flowed a lot better than Anne Morna Murray—my first lesson, perhaps, in the importance of rhythm. My mother had no doubt that it was prayer alone that had been responsible for my arrival. Such was her gratitude that virtually until the day she died, she stayed in touch with priests at the Sainte-Anne-de-Beaupré shrine in Quebec, sending regular donations.

With three older brothers—David, Daniel and Harold—and later two younger ones—Stewart and Bruce—my childhood fate was largely predetermined. I didn't have a chance. Even before I could walk they had laced a pair of boxing gloves onto my hands for a family photograph. I never actually donned them for a fight, but they are an apt metaphor. I was a tomboy and relished the role, wanting to do everything my brothers did, stubbornly resisting the repeated well-intentioned efforts of my mother to transform me into a model of junior femininity. I did have dolls and I did play with them, but they were never a major part of my childhood. Only years later, long after I had left home, did my mother succeed in decorating my bedroom as she had long envisaged it, with frilly pinks and whites replacing my posters of Hollywood heartthrob James Dean and Tony Dow (*Leave It to Beaver*'s older brother, Wally). I had it bad for Tony Dow.

Taught by my older brothers, I learned to catch, throw and hit a baseball with proficiency. Along with them I rooted for the Brooklyn Dodgers and the Toronto Maple Leafs, though my loyalties shifted from time to time to Dad's favourite team, the Montreal Canadiens. The boys owned a vast baseball card collection that we stored in gallon ice-cream pails. In time I memorized the batting and earned-run averages of every major-league player. My brothers liked to quiz me—they would cover up most of the card and, from the portion that remained visible, I had to identify the player and what team he played for and recite all his relevant numbers.

Outdoors I was recruited for neighbourhood games and, because I had a good arm, later played centre field for our girls' softball team, the Top Hats. We won the town championship, but my contribution to our victory was minimal. Despite my training, I was never a confident player, either at bat or in the field. I rarely swung at pitches and in the field I was often thinking, *Please, don't hit it to me.*

I would never be able to compete seriously with my brothers on the sports field, and I knew it. This is just a theory, but it's possible that when I discovered in my early teens that I could sing reasonably well, I worked hard at it precisely because it was one thing that I could do better than they could. I couldn't get enough of singing; it was a tonic for my otherwise deflated sense of self-esteem. But that was later. In my early years we were a sports-mad family. We swam, played baseball and hockey (Dad would rent the local skating rink for an hour on Sundays after church), and on Saturday nights during the winter and all through the Stanley Cup playoffs, watched hockey games religiously around the family TV. It was a nineteen-inch black-and-white Westinghouse with chrome legs that sat in my parents' bedroom; all eight of us and assorted friends sprawled in awkward configurations on the bed or the floor to watch it. (In his later years, whenever the Canadiens were playing, Dad would don his official Guy Lafleur number ten jersey.)

They were an active bunch, my brothers; they loved to box and wrestle with each other, and often roughhoused with me as well. Until Harold went off to college, I don't think he ever missed an opportunity to slug me in the arm if I was within his considerable range. He was merciless with all of us—on the day he left, Stewart, Bruce and I cheered lustily from the back porch of our big Main Street home. On my sixteenth birthday two of the older boys administered the traditional sixteen slaps to my butt with such enthusiasm that

I was brought to tears. I would fight back—writhing, wriggling, flailing, screaming and complaining frequently to Mom, but usually without results. The precise circumstances of one incident are lost in the mists of memory, but Harold had pushed me a little too far, and in a moment of anger I picked up a small rock and hurled it at him, nicking his ear (I think I was eight or nine at the time). He put his hand to his ear, felt the blood trickling down and flashed me a big, wicked grin—not because he was proud of me for fighting back, but because he knew he would need a few stitches to sew it up. And, since I had drawn blood, he knew that some form of parental wrath would be expressed and that I, for once, would be its recipient. He was going to savour that moment.

Much of the time, I'm sure, I was either a nuisance or a burden to my brothers—or both. Once when I was an infant, the boys wheeled me down the street in my pram and left me while they went inside a store. One small problem: they had neglected to put on the brake—and Springhill is built on a cluster of steep hills. So down the hill I went, gathering speed, until an alert neighbour spotted the careening carriage and raced out to save me. But for that timely intervention, my music career might have been aborted very early. On another occasion, while I was still a toddler, I was again consigned to the less-than-scrupulous care of the older boys. They wanted to play baseball. These two imperatives—play and supervision—conflicted, so they cleverly arrived at a solution that would keep me from wandering off: they thoughtfully tied me to a nearby tree and the game continued. At other times I was a victim of their pranks. Walking home at night from movies at the community hall in Northport, where we spent our summers, they would run ahead and hide in ditches and behind trees, leaving me alone in complete darkness. Then they'd jump out and scare me half to death.

In turn, when I was charged with their care, I often regarded my younger brothers as an unwelcome responsibility. I was three years older than Stewart and six years older than Bruce, and I could be as inattentive as my older brothers had been. Once when I was ostensibly babysitting four-year-old Bruce, he decided he wanted to use the record player. To do so he had to move a lamp, which he laid down on a foam pillow, which then caught fire—while I was busy playing cards downstairs with a boyfriend. I smelled burning rubber and, Dad being at work and Mom out, my boyfriend ran to get his father. The local newspaper, the *Record*, reported the story of menacing Master Murray, the four-year-old arsonist, but no serious damage was done.

My brother Daniel was the family tease. He enjoyed pinning me to the floor, his knees firmly pressing down on my shoulders so that I was immobilized, and then threatening to lick my face, inching ever closer. He denies these accusations today, but his memory is clearly flawed. Daniel had other idiosyncratic methods of torture as well. With a doctor for a father and a nurse for a mother, their six germ-carrying kids were repeatedly instructed never to drink from each other's glass or eat food the others might have touched. Daniel exploited these instructions ruthlessly. Typically Mom would have us all sit at the kitchen table while she rushed back and forth with plates of food. Even before we'd finished the main course, she'd set out the dessert as well. One of our favourites was date squares. She'd be fussing with something, her back turned, and Daniel, slowly and methodically, would take each square and carefully lick both sides, effectively claiming them as his own. After that we couldn't and wouldn't touch them. But, if we knew what was good for us, we also couldn't snitch on him to Mom. So Mom would ask, "How come no one but Daniel is eating the squares?" and we could say nothing—Daniel's withering glare warning us of dire consequences if we dared. That kitchen table, incidentally, contained a small drawer in which Bruce and I hid bread crusts, which we hated. I'd been told they put hair on your chest, and I didn't want any part of that.

To be completely candid, I should confess that my treatment of my younger siblings occasionally reflected the treatment I had been accorded by the others. I once teased Bruce to the point where he threw a pair of scissors at me. At other times I had a tendency to treat both him and Stewart as living dolls, dressing them and coiffing their schoolboy hair as I—and sometimes my friends—pleased. (Hair, in fact, became something of an avocation. I used to cut Dad's hair at our cottage at Northport in the summer, and at university I ran a virtual salon, offering trims and dye jobs to my dorm-mates.) Later my attentions to Bruce and Stewart became more practical and well-intentioned: I taught them both to dance.

Afraid of being ridiculed by the others, no one really expressed their fears. I certainly didn't. I vividly recall hearing, either through some fundamentalist proselytizers at our door or on the radio, that the world was coming to an end on a given day. Somehow I took this warning very seriously, but instead of articulating my mounting fear, I took refuge under my bed on the appointed day. Only when it became clear to me that the forecast had failed did I reappear.

Having five brothers, I should add, was not without its benefits. They taught me far more than just how to read a box score. I had to learn self-reliance because they had better things to do than cater to me. They taught me by example how to recognize and cut through spin and bullshit, a skill that would come in handy more than once during my life in the music industry. And they made sure that whatever success I might achieve, in school or elsewhere, wasn't going to swell my little head. I wasn't inclined that way in any event, self-confidence being in short supply, but they'd have cut me down to size quickly if I had been. When, years later, I walked onstage at Radio City Music Hall to a rousing standing ovation, my brother Harold looked around in some astonishment, as if to say, "What's going on? It's just Anne."

MY PARENTS' MARRIAGE WAS, first to last, a script lifted from a fable. My mother, Marion Burke, was a nurse in training at All Saints Springhill Hospital when, in 1934, James Carson Murray arrived. He was a handsome young Dalhousie medical school grad who had just completed a year of surgical training at St. Luke's Hospital in Cleveland (later the Cleveland Clinic) and a year's practice with his father, a country doctor in nearby Tatamagouche. The nursing corps of Springhill Hospital was then administered by a group of strict and sober Church of England nuns, and they ranked doctors as not far below the angels. More importantly, perhaps, they were advised by Dr. Simpson, the chief of staff, to turn a blind eye to the courtship developing in front of them, between the handsome Presbyterian from Tatamagouche and the comely young Catholic coal miner's daughter with deep Acadian roots from nearby Joggins. In a sense, you might say that Dr. Simpson twice facilitated my birth.

My grandparents, on the other hand, took a decidedly more jaundiced view of this romance. Both sides were initially opposed to the union on religious grounds, such were the entrenched prejudices of the day. It was probably family pressure that led my mother, after they had been dating for a while, to ask for a time out. Three weeks went by; then Dad, who was always very quiet and shy, turned up at the nurses' dorm and asked my mother whether she might be interested in buying a set of encyclopedias. Mom declined the books but accepted his proposal. Not long after, they were married, although even then they could not be married in a church. In 1937 they exchanged their vows before Monsignor Currie in what was known as the Glebe, an annex of St. Thomas Aquinas parish in Joggins. None of their parents was present; Mom's sister, Erma, and John Burbine, Mom's first boyfriend, stood as witnesses. Although the laws of the Church kept them from the ceremony, Mom's parents did host a luncheon reception at their home. The honeymoon was a weekend in Saint John, New Brunswick, at the Admiral Beatty Hotel. The parental frostiness did not linger; in fact, it melted as soon as the first grandson, David, arrived about a year later.

Growing up, we didn't see much of Dad. His work ethic was legendary. On a typical day he'd be up at dawn to start surgery, delivering babies (4,500 over the decades) or tending to the dislocated or broken limbs routinely sustained by the city's two thousand coal miners, the mainstay of Springhill's principal industry. Then he'd do rounds at the hospital and return home for lunch. He took lunch, as he took breakfast and dinner, in bed; the only times the family gathered all together for a meal were Thanksgiving, Christmas and Easter. After lunch he'd take a short power nap, then go to his office above Wardrope's drugstore and see patients for three or four hours. Then he'd come home for dinner—again in bed (we kids would have eaten already)—take another twenty-minute nap, and then set off to see more patients at his office and make final rounds at the hospital. Dad did this every day except Saturday and Sunday, although he was always on call and worked one Sunday in four in rotation with other doctors. He also made house calls. In the summers, when we were at the family cottage at Northport, it was not unusual for people to pull up to announce that he was needed (we had no phone). He'd then drive to the nearest telephone office for a consultation or back into town for an emergency procedure.

Dad kept up professionally by reading exhaustively, often late into the night, from medical journals he kept stacked beside the bed. And his dedication was matched by his extraordinary surgical skills. To cite just one example, I received a letter a few years ago about a man who, as a child of two or three, had managed to get his forearm stuck in the rollers of an old wringer washing machine. Muscle and bone had been badly damaged, and the medical consensus was that amputation would be the best and most efficient course. Dad had disagreed, saying there was no way he was going to allow the little boy to lose an arm without trying to save it—which is exactly what he proceeded to do. The surgery was successful and the little boy grew up to become a welder, a profession that would have been virtually unthinkable with one arm. When Dad died in 1980, dozens of people came forward with stories like this, about how he had saved this or that part of them. And, quite frequently, I think, he refused to charge poorer families for his services.

Dad didn't waste a lot of time on religion—that was Mom's domain—and so we were raised Catholic; in fact, his consent on that point had been a condition of the Church's sanction of their marriage. Four out of five brothers served as altar boys, and Bruce played the church organ from the time he was eleven. We said the rosary every night on our knees, attended Mass during the week and on Sundays, gave up candy for Lent, and I went to catechism on Friday night, right through Grade 10. I sang in the church choir and, as a girl, said my prayers every night, kneeling beside my bed while a crucified Jesus (and Tony Dow) gazed down at me. On my dressing table was a glow-in-the-dark miniature chapel with the Virgin Mary standing behind a gate.

But it wasn't long before a certain doubt and disillusion-ment began to set in. In Springhill the Protestants outnumbered the Catholics ten to one, and our local priest, Father Buchanan, regularly and confidently informed us that all Protestants were going to hell. Now, my father was a Protestant, and in my eyes at least, he was a veritable saint. It wasn't possible that he could be going to hell. And I had any number of Protestant friends, none of whom seemed like wastrels destined for the fiery furnace. So there was something about this dogma that began to strike my adolescent brain as terribly wrong. The narrow-mindedness extended even to extra-liturgical matters—we were not allowed to sing in non-Catholic churches. In fact, I often had to turn down invitations to sing at non-Catholic weddings.

I never really warmed to the ritual part of Catholicism either, the elaborate vestments and the incense. It just seemed over the top. Nor could I ever really get a handle on confes-sion. At his first confession, Bruce, who must have been about seven, spent what seemed like an hour in the confessional booth, clutching his copy of something called the *Baltimore Catechism*. Notwithstanding his accidental flirtation with arson, I couldn't imagine how his little seven-year-old life could have been so terribly warped and misspent as to require so much atonement. Nevertheless, I continued to sing in church and attended Sunday Mass all through my college years, and even later, while I was living in Halifax.

By my early teens I was no longer very comfortable in church, for reasons that had nothing to do with spiritual misgivings. As a family we were almost always late for services—getting six kids scrubbed, brushed and dressed took forever—and by the time we walked down the aisle to our pew I was already anxious, feeling like I was going to faint or throw up. I could feel people watching me, and that made me uncomfortable to the point of panic. After about five minutes I'd get up and go outside, just for some fresh air. Around that time I was something of a nervous wreck, riddled with an assortment of strange neck tics and bad habits. I bit my nails and gnawed a few of my knuckles until they were raw. I never talked about it, and Mom, who must have noticed, never said a word. Eventually the tics and habits went away, as these things generally do.

Looking back, I think those early adolescent years were very hard for me—the awkward transition from girl to young woman made all the more difficult by living among five brothers. The more like them I could be, the happier I was— so much so that when I first started to develop breasts at twelve or thirteen, I began to carry myself hunched over to avoid drawing attention to this emergent, rather fundamental anatomical difference. Mom was often on my case about that. "For heaven's sake, Anne," I can still hear her saying, "stand up straight!" (In fact, she was still reminding me in her nineties.)

It must have been during that period of terrible self-consciousness, complicated by the arrival of my first period, that Mom took me to buy my first brassiere. I hated these bumps that I had developed; they made manifest what I was most in denial about—the differences between me and my brothers. Having made the purchase, I actually had to wear it; I had to sit down at lunch with the boys, all of whom were acutely conscious of my dramatically altered form. I remember Bruce turned to stare at me—he would have been about six or seven—and said, "What are those things? What are those bumps?" And bumps they were—bras in those days created a very pointy look. Daniel and Harold, sitting adjacent, were busy elbowing him and saying, "Shut up, Bruce." Of course, all my girlfriends were going through similar trials, but they didn't have to cope with five brothers. I thought it was so unfair that boys were spared the ordeal of protruding breasts and crampy periods. Mom had prepared me for that, but that didn't mean I had to like it.

WHEN HE WASN'T WORKING, Dad was a keen outdoorsman. He loved to be active, often saying, "Never sit if you can stand" and "Never lie down if you can sit." He was a strong advocate of fitness long before it became fashionable. He loved to snowshoe—sometimes to work. From the house my mother would carefully watch him crossing the fields, because Dad suffered from asthma; if he had an attack she would see him collapse and rush over to him with a hypodermic needle prepared for just that contingency. Dad also cross-country skied. Some of my favourite times alone with him were on ski outings, the sweat dripping from his nose, his layers of clothes discarded and hung on tree branches along the route as his body temperature rose. He taught us to swim, played catch with us in the big field adjacent to our house, and loved to hunt. Occasionally at the cottage my brothers would lure him into a game of bridge, but he was a reluctant player. He always wanted to be outdoors.

Once when I was a young teen, he took me rabbit hunting. It was freezing cold and I was bored and miserable. After about three hours of what seemed like pointless wandering, he said to me, "There's one over there. Shoot there." I couldn't see anything but I fired the gun; to my great surprise and greater regret, I actually hit the rabbit. I heard it whimpering and I felt awful, and felt worse when Dad had to put the poor thing out of its misery. We may have taken it home, but I've repressed the memory. I did tell Dad, "Don't ever ask me to go hunting again."

On occasion he'd take all of us kids fishing, lining us up beside the brook with our rods, while he went off to find some trailing arbutus (mayflower), the wonderfully aromatic provincial flower of Nova Scotia, to take home to Mom. I still remember the fragrance of those pink and white blossoms filling the car, an old Meteor, on the drive home. We never caught any fish, mainly, I think, because Dad was less interested in fish than in the flowers. He took us to where he knew the mayflowers were; fishing was simply a way to distract us while he collected them in peace.

And Dad relished adventure. He loved nothing more than getting himself stuck in some muddy rut on the Casey Road, a prime, unspoiled hunting area about twenty miles away, and then figuring out how to dig himself out. He carried an old beaten-up rucksack in his trunk, filled with hatchets, knives and other survival gear, just for these occasions. Mom hated that bag, especially when we had a station wagon and it was visible in the back. "Carson," she'd exclaim, "you are not taking that rucksack!" But of course he did.

Much to my mother's annoyance, he would also look for opportunities to experience manageable risk. Once he took Stew, Bruce and me on a boat ride when, I am convinced, he knew that a big storm was brewing on the Northumberland Strait. When the storm hit, we were cruising down the Shinimicas River and had to take cover. There just happened to be an overturned lobster boat on the shore, so we pulled over, took refuge under the lobster boat and ate our picnic lunch. When the storm had passed, we were on our way again. We got back to find Mom rooted to the bank, furious, arms folded. "Carson," she bellowed, "what were you thinking?" She always called him "Cars," except when she was angry; then it was "Carson!" And he called her "Mummy the Dummy," affectionately, of course. They adored each other. She was feisty and fun, full of life, a perfect complement to his calm reserve. When he pulled one of his stunts, she'd light into him verbally for a few minutes. When she was finished, he'd just say, with a little grin on his face, "Pardon?"

One day he went duck hunting and, just as dusk approached, he finally shot one. He had to wade out into the water to retrieve it, so he decided to strip down to his shorts, leaving his clothes on the bank. By the time he got back, however, night had fallen and he couldn't find his clothes in the dark. So he found a farmhouse and, in his underwear and freezing cold, knocked on a stranger's door. They kindly lent him some clothes—and a flashlight.

Dad had a dry and wry sense of humour. Once he was summoned to a nursing home where a senior citizen had died.

"She's not dead," he declared, after conducting a brief examination.

The presiding nurse glared at him. "Well, she was dead five minutes ago!"

"Well, then," said Dad. "I guess it's a good thing for her that I didn't get here earlier."

Even as a disciplinarian, Dad was taciturn. He never lectured or sermonized—he didn't have to. One look, one glance, was enough to tell us kids that we had offended and had better stop, pronto. He spanked me only once, when I was about four. Mom had asked me to go upstairs and fetch the toothpaste and I had refused, more than once, I think because I was afraid of the dark upstairs. She promised punishment when Dad came home, but he'd never hit me before, so when he asked me to get the toothpaste, I said no to him as well. He put me over his knee and probably slapped me about three times. I never said no again, at least not to him. All he had to do was look at us.

However, Dad was usually absent, so it fell to Mom to impose some modicum of discipline on the boys. She did this well for the most part, sometimes carrying a narrow strip of linoleum, a kind of whip that she wielded as an instrument of intimidation. But there were times when she simply closed the bedroom doors and let the lads go at it on their bunk beds, pounding the daylights out of each other, the walls fairly reverberating with the raucous symphony of fraternal warfare. My father's mother, Nanna Murray, once opined that it was unlikely Mom would see her sons as adults; she was sure they would kill each other off in battle before that.

Nanna couldn't have been more wrong. All grew into responsible adults, successful in their chosen fields. David became a nephrologist; Daniel a geologist; Harold a gastroenterologist; Stewart, the only one who stayed in Springhill, a program manager for Corrections Canada; and Bruce a singer and later a teacher. Mom was generally lenient and fair, and none of the boys ever posed a serious behavioural problem. She was equally relaxed with me. She seldom imposed a curfew and it never really occurred to me to rebel. Apart from some experimentation with marijuana in university, neither did the boys. We had an innate sense of what was right—or at least of what was wrong.

My mother doted on my father, and spoiled him. As a couple they never had much of a social life—Dad's work habits didn't allow it—but she seemed untroubled by that. She was with the man she wanted to be with. She baked and cooked; she volunteered with the Catholic Women's League and the hospital auxiliary; and once a week she played bridge with a group of friends. When Dad finally came home at night, she'd already be in bed, sitting up half asleep but dressed to the nines—the best-looking woman in bed. She was happiest when there were people around and mouths to feed, the more the merrier. My brothers would sometimes bring their baseball teams to the cottage and she'd feed them all for an entire day, thinking that was the greatest thing. In Springhill she was aided by Dena Vienneau, a remarkable woman who came to work for us in 1946, when she was sixteen, and stayed fifty-eight years, until Mom's death. Dena had no children of her own, so we were it. Her husband, Alfred, was a great friend of Dad's, and when Dad retired, the two of them (sometimes accompanied by Stewart) went hunting almost every weekend.

More than in most other houses, I suspect, language was important. Both my parents were sticklers for good grammar, but Dad had a particular way of correcting us. If we slipped up on something, he'd stare at us and say, very coolly, "Pardon?" And he'd keep saying "Pardon?" until we got it right. And Dad loved poetry, particularly the English Romantics—Keats, Shelley, Wordsworth, Byron, as well as Sir Walter Scott's *The Lady of the Lake*—and among the moderns, Robert Frost and the playful Ogden Nash. He could recite many of their poems and, often without warning and sometimes for no apparent reason, would launch into a recitation. I recite some of those poems today, much to the embarrassment of my children.

Neither of my parents swore. Dad never did, and the worst thing I can recall hearing Mom say was "Oh, damn" after she discovered that her cake in the oven had fallen, likely because the boys had been running around the house. Among the brothers and me, there was frequent invocation of the word *frig*—friggin' this and friggin' that. But even now none of us really swears, although our kids, I think, more than compensate.

Having put my father on a substantial pedestal, as a child I was not able to see how hard Mom worked and how much she contributed to the family's cohesion. It was only years later, when I became a mother myself, that I realized how selflessly she had laboured on our behalf. I'm sure I must have disappointed her at times. I was not remotely the girly girl she had wanted. Once, invited to help her at a tea and wearing a new dress, I ended the affair by climbing a tree with the neighbourhood kids. Quite frequently we sparred verbally, usually for the most trivial of reasons, arguments that sometimes descended into yelling matches. Though I regret it now, we argued about everything. I loved her dearly, but the truth is that I was in many ways your classic pain-in-the-ass adolescent. For all that, Mom always made me feel special. When I was fourteen, she took me out of school early and we rode the train across Canada to visit Dad's sister, Ethel Livingstone, and her family in Vernon, B.C. We were gone a month—a great trip that brought us closer.

In addition to his medical practice, Dad owned an equity share in Wardrope's drugstore. But while we were comfortable, we were not particularly affluent and we lived quite modestly. In the heyday of the coal industry, Springhill miners were well paid, and the homes of my friends whose fathers worked in the mine were as well appointed as our own. Our family never ate in restaurants and owned only one car; while the boys were always outfitted with sporting equipment, it was always the hand-me-down variety. After Daniel and David begged for months for bicycles, they got one—to be shared between them. I got my first bike when I was twelve. It was second-hand and cost ten dollars.

Both parents had tasted the Depression and had trouble spending money. As recently as the 1990s, Mom had resolved to buy some new juice glasses but, when she discovered they were selling at the inflated price of $1.50 each, decided she could make do with what she had. There were no extravagant family vacations. In the late 1930s Dad had paid $500 for the cottage at Northport, a white, three-bedroom structure with an outhouse (at least for a few years) and a verandah (later screened in). It was right on the water in the best part of Nova Scotia weather-wise, and we spent the better part of every July and August there. It was an idyllic time, the long summer days full of sport and frolic, clam digs and lobster dinners, playing on the broad sand flats that, when the tide was out, stretched for what seemed like miles.

⁓

ALTHOUGH MY CHILDHOOD was mostly untroubled, the town of five thousand in which I grew up seemed to have been blighted by some dark curse. Springhill, nestled in the Cobequid Hills, sat over vast deposits of black coal, some of them a mile underground, among the deepest seams in the world. Mining had been not just the main industrial activity for more than eighty years; it had been virtually the only one. In fact, the town was originally known as Springhill Mines.

In Springhill's west end, so-called duff banks (slag heaps) of coal lay exposed. At night, people too poor to afford conventional delivery would come to dig for coal in these banks. The digging stoked smouldering fires that seemed to burn continuously. During the day, when the wind was westerly, the town's air was tinged with sulphurous fumes rising from the mines. Climbing the stairs at high school, I often had to stop to catch my breath. Homes were heated by coal, which left residues of soot. As a result, only the affluent in Springhill could afford to live in a white house, because it had to be repainted every year. And everyone had to wash their walls and ceilings once a year; wallpaper was rubbed down with something called Smokey City, a playdough-like product that absorbed the soot, turning absolutely black.

The work in the mines was dangerous, every trip down a silent roll of the dice. On November 1, 1956, when I was eleven—only a few days after the Soviet invasion of Hungary— there was a powerful explosion 5,500 feet underground at the mines. I was at Elizabeth Calder's house across the street, sitting on a couch reading, I think, when we heard and felt the explosion. I remember being thrown off the couch and then running out to the street to see a cloud of black smoke rising from the mine area a mile away. Several buildings had been flattened and dozens of miners were trapped a mile below the surface. Most were rescued, but there were thirty-nine deaths, many of them the fathers of childhood friends. I could scarcely imagine what that must have been like.

The following December a fire swept through what passed for Springhill's downtown, reducing a row of fifteen businesses and five apartment houses to ashes in slightly more than three hours—a loss representing 20 percent of all tax revenues. That same evening I'd been skating at the rink and had passed those buildings on my way home, only minutes before the fire began. The town's then mayor, Ralph Gilroy—the unlucky thirteenth in its history—said at the time, "Everything's happened now that can."

He was, alas, wrong. Less than a year later, on October 23, 1958, a third disaster struck—a so-called bump, or underground earthquake, at the mine. It was even more lethal than the first one, killing seventy-five men—one of the worst disasters in Canadian history, commemorated in songs, poems and books. On this occasion as well, several girlfriends lost their fathers. I physically remember the shockwaves as they registered in our house, more than a mile away from the pithead. It happened just after 8:00 p.m. I'd been home watching television, again with Elizabeth Calder; my brother Harold and my friend Donna Smith were appearing as part of a singing quartet on *High Society*, a high school show broadcast live out of Moncton, New Brunswick. They had done a song

Patti Page had made famous that same year, "Left Right Out of Your Heart," written by Mort Garson, a native of Saint John. The show had ended and I was bidding Elizabeth good night at the door; the bump occurred at the precise moment that I closed the door. I heard my mother calling from her room, "Anne, what happened?" She thought I'd fallen down the stairs.

We knew soon enough what had happened, but not the scale of the tragedy. Everyone rushed into the streets and headed towards the mine, then owned by the Dominion Steel and Coal Corporation. For a week school was cancelled and, alongside my friends, many of whose fathers were trapped below us, we kept vigil at the pithead for hours every day while frantic rescue efforts proceeded. Mom dusted off her old nursing skills and went to work in the armoury, where they brought the injured initially and which also served as a temporary morgue. Dad worked around the clock and slept at the hospital. We were back in school by the time the first group was rescued—it was announced over the PA system and greeted with jubilation. At the end of the ordeal the Queen's husband, Prince Philip, came to town to offer moral support. Dad, then chief of staff at the hospital, was assigned to lead him through the wards full of injured men. Typically, not wanting to be in the public eye, he deputized a colleague for the honour.

One of the heroes of the day was Maurice Ruddick, a black miner and the father of twelve children, including Sylvia, Valerie and Ellen, three friends who regularly came to our house and taught me gospel songs. Maurice sang too; in fact, singing helped save him. Trapped without food or water four thousand metres underground with seven other men, his own leg broken, he refused to relinquish hope that they would be rescued. Maurice led them in song for the next eight and a half days, singing gospel hymns and folk tunes and, once, "Happy Birthday," because one of the men had turned twenty-nine. When they staggered out, they were hailed as heroes, invited to appear on the *Ed Sullivan Show*, and offered free vacations at luxurious Jekyll Island off the coast of Georgia, courtesy of its governor. But a public relations furor ensued: eighteen survivors and their families were white, but Maurice Ruddick was black, and Georgia was then a fiercely segregationist state. The other miners wanted to refuse the gift, but Maurice insisted; he went as well, staying alone at a blacks-only hotel.

Springhill was never quite the same. The mine closed in 1962 and never reopened; it was converted years later into a geothermal heating facility. Many families moved away, including several of my friends, and never returned.

⁓

BOTH SIDES OF MY FAMILY carried the musical gene. My maternal great-grandfather, Damien Belliveau, was a natural tenor well known in the region (during the Prohibition era he was also a rum-runner). Mom's mother, Mary, played the piano and was a church organist. Her sister Erma and brother Harry both played the piano for silent movies, playing in sync with the action and sometimes enduring aerial assaults of popcorn and peanuts from patrons. And Mom herself could certainly carry a tune, though she preferred to sing quietly.

On the paternal side, my grandfather sang regularly in the church choir and Dad himself liked to sing while he shaved; he had a big, wide vibrato, much like mine when I started. He had played the clarinet as a young man and had a very discerning musical ear. On Wednesday nights we'd often watch Perry Como's TV show together in his bedroom and he'd point out who was singing sharp and who was singing flat. Soon I found that I could do that too. His brother, Don, was a fine pianist and excellent musician; he wrote "Dalhousie Dream Girl," a university song that is still occasionally performed. Later he won a songwriting contest sponsored by the Tommy Dorsey Orchestra with a song that the orchestra recorded.

Dad's sister, Betty, made an enormous contribution to choral music in the province and founded the Nova Scotia Festival of the Arts in Tatamagouche. One year my brother Daniel and I went to hear the incomparable Maria Callas sing there. We had no tickets and the event had long since been sold out, so we sat outside, listening to her magnificent voice through the open windows. Later Betty started annual three-week summer music camps at New Annan, near Tatamagouche, where she'd direct Gilbert and Sullivan operettas. I was in the chorus of *The Gondoliers* the summer I turned nineteen, and doubled as the camp's recreation director. Bruce, who was just thirteen, played one of the leads: Luiz, drummer to the Duke of Plaza-Toro (played by our cousin, John Livingstone) and secretly heir to the throne of Barataria. My God, Bruce could sing. It was shocking to hear that big tenor voice coming out of that little boy.

Aunt Betty was something of a taskmaster. We rehearsed six hours a day—two hours each in the morning, afternoon and evening—although there was also time for swimming and games. She was something of a paradox, at times somewhat reserved, like Dad, at others quite gregarious. And like Dad again, her work ethic was remarkable. But when she conducted, she was transformed, a completely different personality, intense and vibrant, as if she were on the podium of the New York Philharmonic.

In their general outlook and thinking, my parents were both small-l liberals, politically and culturally. They never denigrated the sometimes strange musical and literary choices their children made, however different those might have been from their own. When we watched Elvis Presley gyrating his hips on the *Ed Sullivan Show* in September 1956 like no one had ever done before, Dad just smiled. There were no dismissive judgments of rock 'n' roll, the Beatles or any of the other music we brought home. Mom voiced some objections to the longer hair that Stewart and Bruce wore in the seventies, a look inspired by the Beatles, but Dad just shrugged it off. "It's only hair," he'd say. "What difference does it make?"

My father probably learned this tolerance from his father, Dr. Dan Murray. As a medic in the First World War, he'd been the only doctor willing to treat members of Canada's Black Battalion, a group of black non-combatants sent overseas in 1917 to do construction; they would ultimately build 125 hospitals along the Western Front. His best friend in the war was Captain William White, a black Baptist minister and chaplain to the construction corps who kept a journal of their experiences. Coincidentally, I sang with Reverend White's son, Lorne, on *Singalong Jubilee* for several years in the late 1960s and celebrated my twenty-first birthday at Lorne's house in Halifax. (Lorne's sister, Portia White, became an internationally acclaimed contralto concert singer.) I knew nothing of this history at the time and Lorne, though he had read his father's journal and had heard all the stories about Dr. Dan, didn't know then that I was Dr. Dan's granddaughter.

It was years before we made the connection. Anthony Sherwood, a cousin of Lorne's, was making a TV documentary about the Black Battalion and wanted to interview me about Goula (the nickname we used for my grandfather). I invited him to my home north of Toronto for the interview and Anthony arranged to bring Lorne in from Halifax the same day. When Lorne arrived at the house, he just about fell over when he saw me, because he had no idea whose house he was coming to. It was only then that we realized our shared history. Sadly, Lorne passed away in April 2008 at the age of seventy-nine, while visiting Texas. They flew his body home to Halifax for the funeral. That same day, as it happened—what were the odds of that?—I was scheduled to perform at the Halifax convention centre as part of my final Canadian tour, so I was able to go to the visitation at the church. The lineup to pay final respects extended down the street, a tribute to the esteem in which Lorne was held. The whole *Singalong Jubilee* group held a final singalong in his much-deserved honour. He was one of the nicest, kindest people I ever met, and a fine singer in his own right.

GROWING UP WITH FIVE BROTHERS, I was introduced quite early to our anatomical distinctions. But I had no awareness of what one did with his or her equipment, no idea of what sex was or how babies were made. It was a neighbourhood friend, Paul Merlin, who took it upon himself to put an end to my ignorance. I might have been about nine years old, or perhaps ten; Paul would have been about twelve. We used to play in a loft above his grandfather's garage, right next to our house. His grandfather, Hally Brown, was the town's under-taker, and his garage floor was filled with rough boxes, vertical wooden containers for coffins, in and around which we played hide-and-seek. But somewhere in the loft Paul kept a collection of books and magazines of uncertain provenance that must have contributed to his superior education in this area.

At any rate, one day he proceeded to teach me about the birds and the bees, and I knew immediately that he was lying. He had to be lying. I said, "I'm going home to ask my father. He's a doctor. He'll know the real story."

So off I went to find Dad, who of course was in bed. I said, "Paul Merlin told me this is how babies are made and I don't believe him."

Dad asked, "Well, what exactly did he say?"

I can't remember what words I used, but I found some delicate way to communicate what Paul had described.

And then my father just shook his head and said, "Well . . . Paul is right."

All I could think was, *That is so gross, so disgusting*, although I didn't say that. But I was horrified. I hated the idea, and more than anything I hated the idea that Paul had been right. Anyway, the very next day, out came a book I had not seen before, *The Stork Didn't Bring You*, by Lois Pemberton, placed conspicuously by Mom next to the telephone in the family den, where I wouldn't miss it.

When, at about twelve or thirteen, I started going on little dates—to the local movie theatre (the Capital) or the skating rink—I was careful never to say or kiss good night anywhere near the house, for fear my brothers would be lying in wait, itching to tease me or the boy mercilessly. My first boyfriend, Brian Fuller, lived across the street. His family had one of the first television sets in Springhill, and I can still remember climbing the dogberry tree in our yard to get a better look inside his house, scarcely believing that you could watch moving pictures on a machine in your living room. My romance with Brian Fuller was adolescent puppy love, but it was intense for its time. We went to the movies, held hands and kissed behind the barn on his property. I had no doubt that I loved him. I'm told that I even helped him carry equipment to his hockey games.

Then one day I was at the movies, and he sat down right in front of me with Donna Smith, who, like Brian, was two years older. (Donna later married my brother Harold—they've been happy together for forty-three years.) At the time I was totally crushed, and it took me a year to get over the hurt. About five years later, in university, we had a few more dates, but the old spark was gone. I never felt the same about Brian, and the truth is I never felt that way about anybody until I met Bill Langstroth, who would become my husband in 1975. These were the two great loves of my life. After Brian's betrayal I became very protective of myself. Although I dated extensively at university—an active social life that took its toll on my grades—I wouldn't let anybody get too close.

My best friend when I was growing up was Sharon Cameron. We did just about everything together—skated, sang in choirs, joined cheerleaders and went to movies. Her grandfather owned the theatre and her uncle Lloyd ran it, so sometimes we'd get in for free. I remember being taken upstairs behind the balcony and seeing the projector and huge 35-millimetre reels.

Sharon and Richard Calder, whom she later married, were at my sixteenth birthday, at Northport. Eight girls stayed overnight; we smoked a thousand cigarettes (putting the butts in the pot-bellied stove—I don't know why we thought Mom wouldn't see them), did each other's hair and danced into the wee hours. The boys we had invited showed up on the next day for a bonfire, and we sang and danced all night.

Until university I was a grade A student. It wasn't that I worked especially hard or I was a particularly keen reader (though as a child I did love *Peter Pan* and the Nancy Drew and Hardy Boys mystery series). The work simply came easily to me. And I actually liked it, especially history, English literature and grammar. My main academic competition came from Helen Elizabeth Gilroy, the mayor's daughter. She always got higher grades—sometimes, maddeningly, by mere fractions of percentiles—until the provincial exams in Grade 11, when I placed first.

I had two favourite teachers in high school. One was Lillian Matthews, who taught English in grades 10 and 11. I was fascinated by grammar and Lillian knew her stuff. But she was more than a bit eccentric. For example, she would rap underneath her desk, pretending that someone had knocked at the door, then get up to see who might be there and carry on a conversation with the imaginary visitor. On one occasion she went to an open window and had a conversation with Owen Hartigan, the manager of the coal mines, on whom she was said to have had a crush. We were convinced that the conversation was entirely imagined—that Hartigan was almost certainly not standing in the schoolyard in the middle of the day talking to her. For all that, she was a dedicated professional; in a school with no gymnasium and no resources for drama or other extracurricular clubs, she took it upon herself to organize choirs, in which I always sang, often rehearsing in her home.

The other major influence and by far the best teacher I ever had was Catherine Ward, who taught me both history and geometry in Grade 10. Her class preparation was phenomenal; you could see the hard work that had gone into it. She had the ability to make geometry a matter of simple logic. Whereas I struggled in algebra and had to be tutored, learning it all in the final week, geometry came as naturally as speech. In the combined Grade 11 math final, geometry and algebra, I scored the highest mark in the province that year.

At age eleven I started private piano lessons and continued for six years. I wasn't a model student, although I did stay with it longer than most of my brothers (except Bruce, who still plays), and long enough to learn Rachmaninoff's Prelude in G Minor for my final recital. I practised just enough to get away with it. We played on a Willis and Company upright piano that Dad had bought after the Second World War. His brother, Don, who knew his pianos, had gone with him to try out the models available. At recitals my older brothers often played duets, but they operated on the assumption that the faster the piece was played, the better it sounded, regardless of the specified tempo. Artistic finesse was not their forte.

There was always music in the house, either from the radio or from the record player—at first a tabletop model that played 78s (I remember *Peter and the Wolf*, Bing Crosby, the Mills Brothers and Doris Day) and then a cabinet RCA on which we played 45s—Elvis Presley, the Everly Brothers, Pat Boone, Buddy Holly and Connie Francis, among many others. Later David came home from university with a portable that played LPs. He loved Broadway musicals but we also listened to Dixieland jazz, Mahalia Jackson, Alice Babs and the Swe-danes (an early forerunner of groups like the Manhattan Transfer) and film scores from *The Five Pennies* and *High Society*. There was music playing constantly and we were always singing along.

Still, my first ambition was to be a movie star. I was a regular at the Capital Theatre, pored over issues of *Photoplay* and other movie magazines with the same passion that my brothers evinced for *Sports Illustrated*, and watched scores of black-and-white movies on television at home. Among my favourites were *Mrs. Miniver*, with Saint John native Walter Pidgeon and Greer Garson, and *The Greatest Show on Earth*, with Cornel Wilde, but the films that are still at the top of my all-time list are *The African Queen* and *Random Harvest*, again with Garson. This dream of Hollywood was a complete fantasy. I had never acted and had no prospect of training; there were no drama clubs in school. By my early teens I had let this go, without regret, as music had taken on greater importance.

I think I was nine when, riding in the car one day, we heard Gale Storm's "Ivory Tower" on the radio. My mom's future sister-in-law, Kay, heard me singing along in the back seat and said, "My God, Marion, Anne has a beautiful voice." And I thought, *I do?* We later learned that Aunt Kay was tone-deaf. The next year, however, I had a more official assessment of my talent, and it was not auspicious. In Grade 5 my music teacher, Mrs. Ritchie, administered singing tests. We were each instructed to sing a few lines from a song, and I was told to sing from Stephen Foster's "Swanee River." I had sung less than a line when she told me to stop—that was enough. Later she gave me a C, as low a mark as I'd ever had in anything.

I was shocked. Here I had thought I could sing, but this evaluation gave me pause, however briefly.

Still, I kept on singing. At fifteen Mom and Dad suggested I take singing lessons. I don't think they harboured any specific ambitions for me; they simply knew my interest and believed that I could and should develop whatever potential I had. And as in so many other aspects of my life, I reacted reflexively, without protest, assuming that if my parents thought it was a good idea, it must be a good idea. So, every Saturday morning for the next two school years, I got on the bus in Springhill at 8:00 a.m. and went to Tatamagouche, a ninety-minute ride away, where my paternal grandparents lived. I'd spend part of the day visiting them, have my private lesson with Karen Mills, sing with other students as part of her Northumberland Girl Singers (a nonet) and then ride the bus back again at night. I didn't love the music we sang, which was principally Italian arias, German lieder and other material from the world of classical music. I was much more interested in contemporary sounds, both rock 'n' roll and folk. But I was reluctant to stop for fear that I might miss something. And the lessons did prove useful, more than I ever realized at the time. I learned sight-reading, proper phrasing, when and how to breathe, and how to sing in a group—skills that would later prove invaluable.

In high school, with two other friends, Geraldine Hopkins and Catherine Ross, we formed a trio, the Freshettes. We'd rehearse for hours singing three-part harmony, and I would accompany us on a ukulele I had taught myself to play. We performed several concerts at various Springhill venues—the Miners' Hall, the Baptist church, the Knights of Pythias Hall—and once on TV, in Moncton. Our material included everything from folksongs such as "The Lion Sleeps Tonight" and "Cotton Fields" to pop material like "In the Still of the Night."

My first complete solo performance was at a festival in Tatamagouche when I was fifteen. I sang "The Primrose," from a poem by Robert Herrick, competing against two other girls, and won with a mark of 85. I was so nervous I was astonished that any sound at all came out of my mouth. At about the same time I also sang as a soloist in church, singing "O Holy Night" at midnight Mass.

Even more memorable for me was my high school graduation, at which I sang "Ave Maria." It was a kind of epiphany. There on stage at the Capital Theatre, for the first time I was completely conscious of the audience, and, in a sense, of performing. I was nervous, as always, and nervousness can sometimes blind you; you're so focused on the fear that you can't absorb the externals. Here I had the fear sufficiently in check to allow my eyes to move around the room, identifying my mom, friends and classmates, and their parents. It wasn't singing as an exercise or singing for sheer fun. This was different. And when I had finished, I noticed that I had somehow managed to bring some people to tears.

CHAPTER TWO

CONVENTIONAL WISDOM HOLDS THAT one's basic character is formed in the first five years of life, and I have no reason to argue the point. But in terms of shaping my own life—my most enduring friendships and, ultimately, my career path—university experience and the years immediately afterwards would prove equally important. In the fall of 1962 I waved goodbye to Springhill, drove with Mom to Halifax and moved into Evaristus, a residence at Mount Saint Vincent College, an all-women's institution run by Catholic nuns from the Sisters of Charity, just outside the city. I knew that I eventually wanted to study physical education at the University of New Brunswick in Fredericton and that MSV, as it was known, would simply be a preparatory year. Any number of other schools would have been acceptable, but my parents had recommended it. Although we did discuss the choice at length, I once again deferred to their wishes without protest, my governing assumption being that they always knew best.

There were two good reasons for choosing MSV. The first was music. I wanted to continue singing lessons, and my Tatamagouche voice teacher, Karen Mills, had referred us to a Halifax-based coach, Charlie Underwood. He drove out to the campus once a week to give private singing lessons to a group of students. Although there was no campus choir, we sang Gregorian chants in chapel, and there was no shortage of that. Father Mills used to tap the tuning fork on the pew beside me and ask me to provide the starting note.

Because of those lessons with Charlie I ended up in the school's annual production of *Broadway Bubbles*, an evening of song from American musical theatre. I chose to sing George Gershwin's "Summertime," from *Porgy and Bess*. After several rehearsals, one of the nuns asked to see me in her office. A couple of black women involved with the show had complained that my rendition of the song sounded "too black." Could I try a different approach? I was devastated— as I explained to her, I was just singing it the way I heard it. My first impulse was to pull out of the event, so stung was I by this completely unfounded criticism. In the end I sang the song exactly the way I wanted to, and, in the old cliché of show business, it brought the house down. Nobody said anything more to me on the subject, but it took a long time to recover from that incident. I didn't really understand the complaint. My voice sounded more nasal then than it would later—I had not yet had my tonsils removed—but I could still sing pretty well. I certainly wasn't trying to imitate any particular sound, black, white or anything in between.

The second reason for MSV was religious. Mom's Catholic ties were genuine and meaningful to her, and I respected them. I think she secretly hoped that the good nuns might succeed where she, in her own eyes at least, had failed—at turning me into some facsimile of a lady. She also hoped to pass on something of that sacred connection to her children. Thus all my brothers completed their under-graduate studies at St. Francis Xavier University, which is also affiliated with the Catholic Church. Today, while my level of formal religious observance is minimal, I do consider myself spiritual. I have faith and I still pray, though not nightly and not on my knees.

Although I had worked summers and holidays at Wardrope's drugstore, that job had mainly supplied pocket money. Dad looked after the cost of tuition, which ranged from about $300 to $500 a year. In fact, he paid for all our schooling, believing that if you had children, you assumed responsibility for the cost of their education.

The nuns at Mount Saint Vincent constituted a formid-able sisterhood. Levity, shall we say, was not the order of the day. I can still hear their rosary beads rattling as they paced the halls; I would think to myself, *Oh-oh, what have I done now?* Some of them were lots of fun, among them Sister Alice Michael, who taught us the bawdier parts of Chaucer. She later left the sisterhood, reverting to her given name, Catherine Wallace. She became president of MSV for nine years, was made a member of the Order of Canada and was a major force in the national women's movement. Some of the other nuns had an accusatory way of looking at you, as if you were transparently guilty of some heinous offence. On more than one occasion I'd be running down the long corridors in my high heels, only to be stopped by one of the nuns.

"Miss Murray?"

"Yes, Sister?"

"Would you mind going back to where you started and trying that again?"

"No, Sister."

"Only this time, would you do it walking?"

"Yes, Sister."

We were allowed out only two nights a month, and only on a Friday or a Saturday. On other nights the doors were locked at 6:00 p.m., making us de facto inmates of an educational prison. Our rooms were subject to cursory spot checks virtually every day, and bedroom doors had to be left open except when we slept. We had to wear skirts to dinner, as well as high heels. I think I wore the same dinner skirt every night for the entire year. Once they held a three-day retreat in which we retreated mainly to our rooms or the chapel. We were to remain silent—an injunction widely but discreetly ignored— to meditate on our spiritual development and to immerse ourselves in a book, something suitably uplifting. Anticipating the event, I went to the library, took out *Gone with the Wind*, and hid it in my room. Lying open on my bed I left *Lives of the Saints*, a book I still haven't read. I can't say *Gone with the Wind* was a religious experience, but I certainly was immersed in it.

My escape hatch from this minimum security facility was weekend passes, duly signed and authorized by Mom. These allowed me to spend a couple of days in the agreeable company of her youngest brother, Wilfred, and his wife, Kay, as well as my cousins and my brothers David and Harold, who were already studying or practising medicine. Without the imposition of absurd curfews, I was also able to date. One date was with a handsome young man named Scott Moore. When I met him, I guess my outfit must have left something to be desired; he asked me out to a dance, but he also asked if I wanted to borrow a dress from his sister. That relationship did not last long.

We all chafed a little at the tight leash on which we were held, but I wouldn't say I was unhappy at Mount Saint Vincent. I enjoyed the experience of meeting and living with a group of lively, intelligent women. And the nuns did manage, eventually, to instil some ladylike habits, teaching me, for example, how to sit properly in a chair while wearing a skirt. Academically, I took a potpourri of subjects, including history, English, French, biology and religion, and my grades were quite good. My extracurricular activities extended beyond music: I was elected president of the class and also managed the women's basketball team. In winter a pond behind the residence became a skating rink, and we'd play pickup hockey during our free time. When Mom arrived to drive me home for Christmas, I came through the doors lugging my skates on a hockey stick. She must have despaired.

After my year at MSV, I spent the summer of 1963 at Keltic Lodge, a spectacular resort in Ingonish, on Cape Breton Island. My brother Daniel had worked there a few years earlier as a desk clerk, so I applied and was accepted as a staff maid, which meant one week cleaning the staff quarters and the next preparing the dining room for meals and cleaning up afterwards. I earned the handsome salary of $20 a week. We spent the first few weeks scrubbing and waxing hardwood floors in the main lodge before the seasonal guests arrived. I'd never scrubbed floors before, but I was well taught by Mrs. Weaver and I was a diligent worker. If someone gives me a job, I do it. I can still make a bed with the best of them and, to the chagrin of more than one Las Vegas hotel chambermaid, I'm happy to demonstrate the proper method. To this day a poorly made bed is a pet peeve of mine. Many times I'd return to my room after a show, sometimes even at 3:00 a.m., and, exhausted as I was, remake the bed—properly.

In fact, I made beds so well at Keltic that Mrs. Weaver wanted to promote me to guest maid, which would have meant an opportunity for tips. But it also would have meant longer hours. I had most of my afternoons free to go to the beach and, there and in the staff lounge, I was having so much fun with the other kids that I declined. One of those kids was a boy named Dave Chisling. He, Roger Young and I formed an impromptu trio and sang for guests in the Keltic recreation hall. Roger must have been a pretty fair guitar player, because I remember singing the Kingston Trio's big hit "Scotch and Soda" to his accompaniment, and it's a demanding piece instrumentally. I had a big crush on Dave but it was, alas, unrequited. He later became a minister. Spurned by Dave, I turned my attention to another young man, Finlay MacDonald.

Of all the men I dated in those university years, the one who lingers in my memory is Finlay. The son of a senator who was also president of the federal Progressive Conservative Party, he eventually took a law degree and then went into broadcasting. He became the first Canadian journalist to interview Cuban president Fidel Castro, and later he established a very successful communications consulting practice. But when I knew him, he was just a bright, witty young man. I don't think I was in love with him, but he was fun to be with, and more than a bit of a renegade. I'm not sure whether the stories are true or apocryphal, but Finlay is said to have once thrown a TV set out a hotel room window and to have mooned passengers on a train. Some of that might have been done while under the influence, as they say, because Finlay liked to drink. At Keltic, where he was a desk clerk, he used to call me Morna Middlehead because I'd often go walking on dates along forest trails on the Middlehead Peninsula. He later wrote me letters with the same salutation. The other preferred hangout was the resort's magnificent golf course, one of the finest in the world, but used by staff for different scoring purposes. We all went there after dark for grassin'—a euphemism for necking.

In February 1964, about the same time the Beatles were landing in New York and playing the *Ed Sullivan Show* for the first time, Finlay came up to UNB, where I had transferred for second year, for Carnival, our annual winter festival. That particular visit did not go well, however. He had promised to call me and then didn't, and when we finally connected, he said he wanted to skip the Carnival events and attend a house party with his friends, among them Thor Eaton and Dave Bassett. I acquiesced but was annoyed when he and a Toronto friend picked me up at 9:00 p.m., already drunk. They continued drinking at the party, of course—everyone there was pretty far gone—and I eventually decided that I'd had enough, and left. After that we lost touch for a while, but I saw him again, on and off, in Halifax for a couple of years in the late 1960s. Once, in the wee hours of the morning, I insisted that he leave my apartment. He was quite drunk at the time, and the next morning I opened the front door to find him lying in the hallway. He'd been there all night. He looked up at me with a grin and said, "Just delivering your paper."

WHEN I REGISTERED in the fall of 1963 at the University of New Brunswick, I was wearing a sailor-style top and skirt. It was an ensemble I liked until, standing in line to get my room assignment at Lady Dunn Hall (we lovingly called it the Dunn Inn), I met Joanne Taylor and Nancy Webster, two Montreal women who were taller, much better dressed and clearly more sophisticated than I.

"You're in Room 201," the registrar said to me.

"Oh," said Joanne, "so am I."

My heart sank. *She looks so cool,* I thought. *She must think I'm a real hick.*

I was wrong, and not for the first time. Both women became good friends and have remained so. Joanne was my roommate for the next three years and eventually matron of honour at my wedding. She was quiet and a good student, and how she tolerated and found a way to work through the constant noise of my radio, ukulele and impromptu sing-alongs, I don't know. But she did. I crashed with Nancy in Toronto when I recorded my first album in 1968. And she later worked for me, handling the Anne Murray Fan Club. I'm not sure which of them started to call me Mur, but that nickname stuck all through those college years and is still used by many friends today.

UNB's phys. ed. program wasn't the only drawing card for me. At Mount Saint Vincent there had not been much opportunity to date. In Fredericton, although the residences were segregated, there were seven men for every woman, a ratio rather more to my liking. Curfews were less restrictive as well; we could be out until 11:00 p.m. during the week and until either midnight or 1:00 a.m. on the weekends. I still have an old diary listing all the guys I dated; it's an absurdly long list, evidence of just how little attention I was paying to my courses. And if the list is not persuasive, my poor marks clearly indicate just what a good time I was having. In second year I flunked history and French and earned a bare 50 percent on a third subject. One percentage point lower and I'd have been expelled. So either the gods of academe conferred their grace or someone knew my situation and took pity on me. I skipped classes all the time, stayed up half the night socializing in the residence and slept in a lot. Joanne maintains that I seldom rose before noon. In short, I was a slug. I hardly recognize that person today (now I'm up at the crack of dawn). But I loved university life, loved everything about it. I even loved summer school, which I had to attend to make up for the failed courses. I took psychology and sociology, buckled down and made good grades. I roomed with Nancy Webster in a co-ed dorm, men and women on alternate floors, and we partied a lot, with some memorable singsongs at the lake.

I think I resisted drinking beer until the second semester. The first one tasted awful, but not awful enough to deter me from having a second. Soon I was drunk as a skunk. A little unsteady on my feet, I slipped as I was walking outside. My left leg banged against the edge of a car and went under it. I was hobbling for days and still have a bump on my shin, a tangible memento of my first waltz with inebriation.

That fall, convinced that all the other singers would be better than I, I decided not to audition as a soloist for the *Red 'n' Black Revue*, the campus's annual variety show. Instead I ended up in a choral number and a square dance. I was returning from class on the afternoon of November 22 when I heard the news that President John F. Kennedy had been assassinated. One of our performances was scheduled for that night;

while neither the performers nor the audience felt up to it, the show went on. Of course, I quickly discovered that the soloists' voices were no better than mine, and auditioned the next year. In that show I sang two numbers, "Unchained Melody," one of the most popular songs ever written, and "A Little Bit of Soap," which had been a one-hit wonder for the Jarmels in 1961. The latter was written by Bert Berns, who, before he died at the age of thirty-eight, also wrote "Twist and Shout" (which I sang thirty-two years later, karaoke style, while celebrating my fiftieth birthday with twelve close friends in a Chinese restaurant in Scotland).

Although I had no premonition of where I was ultimately headed, it's clear in retrospect that music was occupying an increasing proportion of my life. The urge to sing was like some insatiable hunger, always present. I was strumming relentlessly on my ukulele, singing in the glee club, performing in *Red 'n' Black* and listening addictively to (and harmonizing with) pop music on the radio, on either Radio UNB or commercial stations, including many from New England that I was able to pick up in my room. The residence halls fairly reverberated that year with the music of the Mamas and the Papas, the Beach Boys and the Beatles, whom I loved. "She Loves You" was playing morning, noon and night. I remember watching their first *Ed Sullivan Show* performance on the common-room TV set, completely absorbed by the scene. I had my first professional gig that year, at a curling club in Fredericton, and was paid the royal fee of $35.

As I had at MSV, I also managed the UNB distaff hoopsters, the Red Bloomers, who won their eighth Maritime Intercollegiate Championship with a record of 26 and 0. I loved the camaraderie, and it was another opportunity to take along my guitar and sing on the bus. I had a captive audience.

My courses at UNB included English and history but increasingly were devoted to kinesiology, anatomy and other sports-related subjects. One day in kinesiology lab in third year, I was dressed in a leotard, and someone pointed out that my spine appeared to be curved. I quickly became a specimen—Exhibit A. Upon further examination it turned out to be scoliosis. It might seem strange that a doctor's daughter with this condition went undiagnosed for so long, but with five brothers, I was always careful about modesty. As Dad said to Mom when she asked why his surgeon's eye had failed to notice it, "I never saw her without clothes." It was only with my first pregnancy that I began to feel its effects; regrettably, they have worsened through the years.

In another class, rhythmical gymnastics, our teacher, Mrs. Bird, told me, "There's nothing wrong with you except that you have no rhythm." My friends got a good laugh out of that. In 1976, when I went back to UNB to open the Aitken Centre, I told that story to the audience. I was pregnant with my son, Will, at the time, so I turned to show my bulging profile and then said, "I guess Ms. Bird was right about my having no rhythm."

I had a second health-related issue to deal with at that time: my tonsils. They were huge and filled my throat, which led to chronic colds, strep throat and ear infections. I was on a first-name basis with the UNB infirmary nurse, whom I called Nursie. But I'd had the condition as a child too, described by Dad as acute bilateral otitis media. In the summer of 1965 we decided to have them removed, courtesy of Dad's cousin Dr. Doug Murray, in Halifax. I remember trying to hum as soon as I emerged from the anesthetic, because I was concerned that something might have gone wrong. A little slip of the hand and my singing days would have been over. But everything was fine. In fact, sans tonsils, I was now able to fully open my throat for the first time. The sound that emerged was almost magical.

I was still a virgin in those days, but sex, not surprisingly, was a frequent subject of discussion. One year a few of my friends and I did not get invited to Carnival, so someone illegally brought a mickey of rum into Lady Dunn Hall and we drank it—my first taste of hard liquor.

"Here's what to do," said one of the girls. "Take a swig and then stand on your head. It works faster."

So we four young women, all phys. ed. students more than capable of standing on their heads, took a swig of rum and stood upside down in the hall, our feet splayed up on the walls. It worked, all right. We didn't need dates after all. Then the talk turned to sexual etiquette. Two of the girls said that after you'd had a few dates with a decent guy, it was perfectly acceptable to have sex. Naïf that I was, I was shocked and appalled. I was of the mind that you should probably be engaged or ready to marry someone before you had sex, and I may have said as much. My friend Jenny Adam was of the same view. Our reaction, of course, was a mark of the times, of just how innocent many of us were. Walking back to my room, Jenny and I could not even look at each other, such was the state of our moral outrage. When we had closed the door, I remember saying, "Do you believe that?"

The next year I did have a date for the Carnival events— Tom Rogers, who drove a pretty spiffy sports car. We went to a Brothers Four concert and then repaired to Ontario House for the after-party. The Brothers Four, mainly folksingers who had scored success with the ballad "Greenfields" and the up-tempo novelty song "Frog Went a Courtin'," came too and led a long singsong. I sang with them for at least two hours, almost totally ignoring Tom. He wasn't terribly happy, quite justifiably, but I was. I don't think I could have been happier. The only blot on an otherwise perfect evening was that some drunken fool on an upper balcony dropped a beer bottle on one of the Brothers' heads. Fortunately he was not seriously hurt.

In my final year my roommate, Joanne Taylor, was elected Carnival queen. To celebrate, we decided to violate the school's prohibition against alcohol in the residences, and smuggled a twelve-pack of Alpine beer into the building. We consumed it, but then had a problem: where to stash the evidence of the crime. We stuffed the cans into our closet but later concluded that we needed to get rid of them. In the middle of the night I carried the cans down to the laundry room, where the trash was placed, and left them there. After they were discovered, a royal furor ensued, because the administration was growing increasingly concerned about drinking in the dorms. Someone had flagrantly dared to flout the no-drinking rule, and they decided to make an issue of it. With a long weekend in the offing and many students planning ski trips, a formal assembly was called and the question sternly put: who had put the beer cans in the laundry room? Until the administration had a satisfactory answer, they insisted, no one would be allowed to leave the campus. It was like that scene in *The Caine Mutiny* in which the demented Captain Queeg (played by Humphrey Bogart) repeatedly demands to know which member of the crew has stolen a quart of his frozen strawberries.

At the assembly no one said anything—what could they say? *We* were the guilty parties. But later, Joanne and I, not wanting to be responsible for aborting the plans of so many, went to the dean and confessed. The look of shock on her face is still with me. At first she said she'd have to inform the university's president, Dr. Colin Mackay, and we feared we might be expelled. In the end nothing came of it. Years later, when I was awarded an honorary degree from UNB, I reminded Dr. Mackay, by then the chancellor, about the incident, but he knew nothing of it and laughed when I told him. Later that semester, with graduation assured, Joanne and I drove her motorbike to a nearby beer store, bought six cans of Alpine, sat on a hill overlooking the campus and drank them all. By the time we returned to residence we had a pretty good buzz on. I stood at the top of the stairwell that looked over the dining hall and, still feeling no pain, loudly demanded the floor.

"Excuse me," I said, "I have an announcement to make. We put the beer cans in the laundry room." Everyone applauded. It was a great moment. I had my degree, and they couldn't take it away.

⁓

IT WAS DURING MY SECOND YEAR AT UNB that I applied to audition for *Singalong Jubilee*, the Canadian Broadcasting Corporation's summer replacement show for its popular prime-time Don Messer series. A nursing colleague of my brother David sang on the show and somehow arranged for me to get the application form. I filled it out and, one spring weekend, flew on a Viscount aircraft with two girlfriends, Jenny Adam and Liz Gurholt, from Fredericton to Halifax for my audition. It was my first time on an airplane and I was a nervous wreck. At the CBC studio there were about eighty-five people competing for jobs. I sang with the altos in a workshop format and had the option of returning the next day for a solo audition. Jenny pushed me to go and, having come all that way, it seemed stupid not to try. I sang "Oh, Mary, Don't You Weep," a Negro spiritual written before the American Civil War, which I knew from Pete Seeger and other folk albums of the time. I thought I'd done reasonably well but, not long after returning to Fredericton, I received a letter from the show's producer, Manny Pittson, saying their complement of altos was sufficient and my services would not be needed. The word *devastated* does not do justice to how I felt.

Years later I learned that the show's key decision makers—Pittson, Ray Calder, Graham Day (later Sir Graham, who had sung on the show for four seasons) and Bill Langstroth—had agreed in advance not to replace an experienced known singer with someone essentially untried. Since no one was leaving, we had all wasted our time, though the CBC had an obligation to audition all aspirants. But I must have made a positive impression on its young music director, Brian Ahern, and on Langstroth, the show's host. Certainly they didn't forget me. Two years later Bill got the CBC radio station in Fredericton to call me at UNB, relaying a message that he wanted to talk to me. Still smarting from their rejection, I ignored it. Then he somehow found the number of the pay phone on our residence floor, called it and had whoever answered it summon me from my room.

"Would you consider coming down for another audition?" he wanted to know.

"No, I don't think so," I said. "I'm not going through that again."

And then he said, "Well, what if I pretty much guarantee that you'll be given the job? We just need you to go through the motions with the audition, for the sake of the process."

"Oh," I said. "That's different."

For the second audition, accompanied on guitar by Brian Ahern, I sang "You've Lost that Lovin' Feelin'," which apparently went on to become the most played song of the twentieth century, and nailed it. Sometimes you just know when you've delivered the song bang on, and I had—an impression confirmed years later by Athan Katsos, a young production assistant on the show and later producer of my first national CBC special. Athan said that I seemed perfectly relaxed, sang with emotional intensity and knocked it out of the park.

Offered a contract for the summer, I signed, earning $71.50 per show or, if I worked as a soloist, $99. The *Singalong* brass weren't entirely thrilled when I notified them that I'd have to miss four shows. I had a condition known as chondromalacia patellae, which involves an accumulation of cartilage on the kneecap. I'd had chronic problems with my knees for years (at one point in high school I had to be pulled to class on a toboggan), and finally had surgery on the left knee at seventeen, spending the summer recuperating before starting university. Now it was time to have the other leg done. Even when I made my first TV appearances, I had a full bandage on the leg and had to be seated at the front so I could keep it stretched out.

That summer I bought my first car, a standard maroon Envoy Epic, made by GM Vauxhall. My father lent me the $1,850 it cost and I repaid him from my earnings from

Singalong. I had never driven a car with standard transmission, but the salesman at Letcher's Garage in Springhill gave me a quick lesson on the spot, and off I went to Halifax.

The *Jubilee* family was a close and welcoming one. My first performance coincided with my twenty-first birthday, so the company ordered a cake and helped me celebrate at Lorne White's house. It was the show's sightless guitarist, Fred McKenna, who taught me to fully appreciate country music for the first time, lessons that would have an enormous effect on my later career. Guitarist Georges Hébert worked with me patiently on my limited guitar skills and later spent years on the road touring with me. Bill Langstroth coached me on overcoming nervousness, which TV cameras can all too readily detect. Catherine McKinnon was there that summer as well. I remember meeting her for the first time. She blustered into the dressing room one afternoon, just back from London, laden down with bags. Rummaging through one of them to find something, she pulled out a cartridge of birth control pills, shook it and declared, "Greatest invention ever!" Her candour left me a little stunned. My closest friend from the show was Karen Oxley, a year younger than I but with more TV years to her credit, and she took me under her generous wing. Although we were thrown together for only a few months, we became good friends, so much so that the next year she asked me to stand for her at her wedding.

By then I had graduated from UNB and was teaching phys. ed. and health to four Grade 9 and four Grade 10 classes at Athena Regional High School in Summerside, Prince Edward Island. The classes were labelled A, B, C and D—the D standing, the students told me, for Dumb. That struck me as unfair, because many of the so-called dumb kids were, in my judgment, anything but stupid. I had some lively arguments with other teachers in the staff room about students they thought lacked intelligence. "I beg to differ," I'd say. "You come and see her on a basketball court. I'll show you who's smart." Many of the students had been told they were dumb for so many years that they'd given up trying academically.

I loved teaching and I loved the kids, most of whom were from rural P.E.I. and had to be bused to school. The vast majority had an innate sense of respect for teachers that, sadly, seems to have gone out of fashion. There were no discipline problems and we got on famously. I remember laughing so hard in health class once that the principal came to the door to see what the matter was. On occasion I'd take a few girls to my home in Springhill for the weekend. And on bus trips to inter-division games, I'd bring along my guitar or ukulele and we'd sing. After we won the provincial basketball champion-ship (we also won the volleyball title), I bought cigars and we smoked them on the bus back to Summerside.

I was hired at Summerside with my classmate and good friend Larry Wright because the recruiters preferred male-female tandems. I liked the idea of teaching at a rural school, one that might not have the best athletes with the highest expectations of their coaches—a thought process that reflected my lack of confidence. The problem was that there had been no gym, track or sports of any kind available to girls in Springhill schools. Therefore, I had to learn volleyball, bas-ketball, track and field and other sports from the ground up as part of UNB's phys. ed. curriculum. I knew how to teach the basics, but I wasn't very good at coaching any of them and had to rely on the kids to remember what they'd been taught previously. Fortunately the teacher whom Larry and

I replaced, Stu Burbine, had done a phenomenal job. The girls' basketball and volleyball championships that we later won were really to his credit. I also had Larry, who knew a lot more, to lean on. I was paid $4,550 for the year, enough to trade in the Epic and buy my first gem of a car, a Mustang fastback in midnight blue. Again I borrowed the money from my private banker, Dad, and paid him back. In those days I had a real interest in cars. Two years later I traded in the Mustang for a new Cougar convertible.

In Summerside I rented a room and boarded with Borden and Marion Connell, a couple whose children were already grown and gone. They spoiled me terribly. Borden even made sandwiches for me for lunch, every day, and did my tax returns. I think my only contribution was making my bed. I went back to visit them a decade later with my son, Will, and they laughingly recalled how useless I had been around the house, compared to other girls who had boarded there. I'd been doted upon at home and they essentially picked up where Mom and Dena had left off. I get embarrassed even thinking about it. I was twenty-one and domestically useless. I learned, though; they should see me around the house now.

Many weekends that year, I'd grab the early Friday afternoon ferry from Borden, P.E.I., to Cape Tormentine, N.B., and then make the three-hour drive to Halifax to do radio shows for the CBC. I had no reason to think it would lead anywhere, but I enjoyed singing and wanted to keep doing it whenever possible. And the extra money was more than welcome. I also found two Athena students, sisters Susan and Carol Perry, who could sing, and formed a trio with them; we sang three-part harmony at school assemblies. By then I was already a minor celebrity, having had TV exposure from *Singalong* the previous summer.

In February 1967 I faced a major decision. Almost every month that year I'd received special-delivery letters—long-distance telephone calls were too expensive—from Brian Ahern, who had left *Singalong Jubilee* and moved to Toronto. He was working with a company called ARC Records and he wanted me to quit teaching, join him in Toronto and start recording. He held out the youthful promise of fame and fortune. When I finally did agree, Brian was doing so well that the first thing I had to do upon arriving in the city was visit a Church Street pawn shop and get his guitars out of hock— surely the best investment I ever made. But that was a year later. In 1967 I wasn't ready and I simply ignored his letters. The school, however, wanted to know whether I planned to return for a second year of teaching. I'd had a good experience on *Singalong* the previous summer, done several solos and been invited back. I also had another carrot dangling: a slot on *Let's Go*, a national TV music show that hired singers to cover the current hit parade. On Mondays it originated in Halifax, the next day it was broadcast from Montreal, then moved to Toronto, Winnipeg and Vancouver. If I was ever going to take a stab at a show business career—though I had no idea at the time what that even meant or what such a life would be like—now perhaps was the time.

But I was, as ever, uncertain. I'd been wrestling with the issue for weeks and suddenly it was the night before I had to give the school my answer. I was at my wit's end. I called several friends, and their opinion was split. I called my parents in Springhill and they were as ambivalent as I. Finally I called Bill Langstroth, who had been instrumental in hiring me on

Singalong. And Bill said straight up, "There's no doubt at all what you ought to do. You should sing. You should give up teaching and move to Halifax and give it a shot." This consultative approach was typical of the way I later ran my career, canvassing opinions from people I trusted and trying to sort through the sometimes conflicting perspectives in search of a consensus. Making decisions that way was always a lot easier for me. At 7:00 a.m. the next day my parents called. They'd been up half the night discussing it and had decided that I should give it a try. I had arrived at the same conclusion. The school officials were disappointed, but understanding.

In the meantime I confronted a couple of serious health problems. The first was stomatitis, an inflammation of the mucous lining of the mouth. I went home to Springhill, uncertain of what the ailment was, and Dad diagnosed it. I had to drink out of a straw for a week. Then, around Easter, I was feeling sluggish and complaining of pain in the intercostal muscles between the ribs; I thought it was just a phys. ed. injury. I returned home for the holiday and, after taking in my car for servicing, was walking up the hill towards home when I was suddenly gripped by a stabbing pain in my back and keeled over. I couldn't breathe. Mom, driving down the hill into town, spotted me and took me home. I went to Dad's car, found the stethoscope in his medical bag, put the tubes in his ears and made him listen to my chest.

"Oh," he said. Then he listened some more. "Oh," he said again. And then a third time.

We went immediately to the hospital for X-rays. The diagnosis: pneumonia and pleurisy. I was out of school for seven weeks and bedridden for most of that time, being treated with antibiotics and 292s to stop the coughing. My old teacher Lillian Matthews emptied the local library on my behalf and I read voraciously. In retrospect, between those two illnesses and my early Friday departures for Halifax, I can see that I did not give Athena High School the attention it deserved. Poor Larry Wright had to pick up the ball that I kept dropping. He stayed on for years and became a school principal, and I still see him every summer.

———

THE FATEFUL DECISION MADE, I moved to Halifax that summer. Life on the set of *Singalong Jubilee* was fun, but hard work. Bill Langstroth was a taskmaster, and we were always rehearsing. I'm not sure how widely known this is, but virtually all the singing on the show was lip-synched, including what would become a famous black-and-white clip of me singing Gene MacLellan's "Snowbird." We sang during the taping but there were no microphones; everything had been pre-recorded. I worked hard at lip-synching and became very good at it. Bill, on the other hand, was notoriously inept, always forgetting the words. He needed cue cards, and the running gag whenever he began to sing was "The parimutuel windows are now open for betting"—as in, how soon would it be before he screwed up the lyrics?

I had not foreseen how busy I would be. My first year as a professional set a pace that didn't let up for almost a decade. There were four *Sounds '68* shows (fifteen minutes each, all produced and directed by Bill) as well as weekly appearances on *Let's Go* and *Singalong*, which started around the middle of May. Toronto producer Ross McLean heard me cover Bobbie Gentry's "Ode to Billie Joe" on *Let's Go* and had me tape it again for *Where It's At* (formerly *This Hour Has Seven Days*). Then I flew to Toronto for another show, *In Person*. And somewhere in there I also appeared on a Wayne and Shuster comedy special. One reviewer said I was the high point of the show but, comparing me to another CBC singer of the time, Mary Lou Collins, added, "Unfortunately she does not possess Miss Collins' deep breathing apparatus, and consequently can be expected never to be heard from again."

In between all the tapings, Bill was booking me on week-long live gigs at small clubs across the Maritimes—at the Monterey in Halifax, the Prince Edward Lounge in Charlottetown, the Grand Hotel in Yarmouth, Henry Wong's in Antigonish and the Colonial Inn in Amherst. I sang and played guitar, accompanied by Robbie MacNeill, who in addition to being a fine guitar player was a wonderful song-writer. To this day his "A Million More," which I recorded on the album *Keeping in Touch*, is one of my favourite songs (along with "You Needed Me" and "Song for the Mira"). His melodies were out of this world, although the lyrics were sometimes opaque and forced you to work too hard to figure them out. But my kids and I still sing his songs more than any others.

At the March break, in search of a quick holiday, my girl-friend Jenny Adam, who was a teacher, and I booked a flight to where we thought the action would be—Fort Lauderdale, Florida. We were deeply disappointed. Most of the younger people were too young and most of those staying at our motel were senior citizens. The only consolation was a Beach Boys concert, for which we managed to snag front-row seats. I was a huge fan of their music. We spent a couple of days serenad-ing the old folks—I'd brought my trusty ukulele—and then, since our tickets included an optional flight to Nassau, in the Bahamas, decided to exercise the option. It turned into a memorable trip. On Paradise Island we'd spend the day at the beach, then spruce ourselves up for cocktail hour. After ten minutes in the lounge we would invariably be approached by a couple of cute young American guys.

One night we had dinner with two of them and the following day the four of us explored the nearby islands in a rented boat. The next night was even more interesting. We had drinks with two other guys, then we took a cab to a magnificent oceanside restaurant. One of the boys had money and wasn't averse to parting with it, so we ate well and drank liberally under a full moon. Intoxicated in more ways than one, we walked on the beach and held hands with two guys we'd known for about three minutes. We eventually returned to the restaurant for nightcaps and at the bar met the famous trumpeter and composer Herb Alpert. It was so late when we were ready to call it a night that the taxis had stopped running. The bartender, who was closing down the bar, kindly offered to drive us back to our hotel. So we had more drinks and then finally headed out to his car, a small Mustang convertible. There were six of us—Jenny and I, our two instant boyfriends, the bartender and Alpert—all squeezed like sardines into this tiny car. I ended up sitting on Herb's lap in the front seat. There we were driving down the road, the wind blowing in our hair, laughing to beat the band at the absurdity of the situation and, lest we forget, amply fortified with liquor. In fact, I laughed so hard that I proceeded to pee on Herb's pants. Imagine my embarrassment. (Years later I bumped into him again at a Grammy ceremony, where we were co-presenting an award. I reminded him of my moment of Bahamian incontinence; he recalled the evening, but he had no memory of my name.)

The next night brought a new adventure, much less amusing. I had a terrible headache but we went to the bar anyway and were quickly hit on by a couple of very nice young men. The one I paired off with was a doctor; he had some Darvon capsules in his room and suggested I take one for my pain. He was quite drunk and not thinking clearly; when he got to his room, he became very aggressive, pushed me back onto the bed and got on top. He was a big guy and at first I couldn't move. I can't remember the details—I know I struggled—but I was saved from a potentially ugly incident by Jenny and the other guy, who wondered what was taking us so long and came knocking on the door. When Dr. Darvon got up to see who was there, I took the opportunity to flee to my own room. Later, feeling properly contrite, he tried to apologize, but I refused to see him. He banged so hard on the door that he injured his hand and had to go to the hospital. I saw him again the next day, his hand swaddled in bandages, and he was profusely apologetic. And that was the end of it.

Back in Halifax I picked up where I'd left off. In June I took two bookings on the same night—a Progressive Conservative rally in Amherst from 8:00 to 8:45, then a Liberal rally in Oxford, about half an hour away, at 9:00. We put the pedal to the metal and were only a little late, and neither party had any idea that I was working for the other. I wanted the money. The Tories paid me $100 and the Liberals paid $125, expenses included. I don't recall exactly when, but around that time I met a young man from Smelting Brook, Cape Breton, named Leonard Rambeau, a career placement officer at St. Mary's University. He booked me into a youth club at St. Peter's Church in Dartmouth and, both there and at a later gig he booked at St. Mary's, I was overwhelmed by his attention to detail in preparing for the events. There was not a single stone, as they say, that he'd left unturned. I remember walking down a flight of stairs with him, praising his work and saying, "You know, Leonard, if I ever need a manager, I'm gonna give you a call."

From time to time the *Jubilee* gang would be invited to perform at other Maritime venues; depending on what the sponsor could afford, Bill would take two, three or five of us along. That summer we were in Charlottetown, P.E.I., for a gig, staying at the Charlottetown Hotel. Crossing the street, Bill suddenly reached out to take my hand. It was with that modest gesture, in that single moment, that the light went on for the first time. *Oh-oh*, I thought. *What's this?* We went back to my room in the hotel and he asked if I wanted to smoke his stash of marijuana, and we did. We kissed, but nothing more. After a while he left, the perfect gentleman. But as I closed the door, I thought, *Oh, my God. What just happened? What have I done?* He had kissed me and I was done for. Nothing between us was the same after that day—the first stirrings of a passionate love affair, hidden for years, that would culminate in our marriage and two beautiful children. Ironically, exactly forty years later, while I was touring Canada to promote my last album, *DUETS*, my daughter, Dawn, and I were staying at the same Charlottetown Hotel. Late one night she called me from her room, complaining that there was so much marijuana being smoked in the adjacent rooms that she could barely breathe. I had a good laugh over that and told her the story of her father and me smoking pot all those years ago. And then we found her another room.

Those early years with Bill, while exhilarating as all new love affairs are, weren't easy. I was in an awful spot. It's true that his thirteen-year-old marriage was in trouble long before I arrived on the scene, but I felt very uncomfortable, to say the least. However unhappy he might have been in his marriage, he was still married (with two young children), almost fifteen years my senior and also my boss. But I was falling in love, fast, and powerless to do anything about it. It was like a train hurtling down the track—I don't know what I could have done to stop it. Emotional chemistry is often hard to explain, but we had it. I couldn't get him out of my mind and then I had to work with him. The sometimes goofy character Bill played as co-host of *Singalong* disappeared as soon as you got to know him. What emerged was a warm, very bright and wickedly funny man. He was outgoing, social, charming, well-spoken and confident, a classy guy. Born and raised in Montreal but with Maritime roots, he'd studied fine arts under the great realist painter Alex Colville at Mount Allison University in Sackville. He'd even met my Uncle Don, who lived and taught school there, and had sung with my cousins Dawn and Pam Murray. After graduation Bill had gone straight to work for the CBC in Halifax.

Bill was good for me in so many ways. I was reticent and he was a dreamer. He believed that you can make things that seem impossible happen, and he made me believe that too. Very early on he articulated a vision of a compound for the wider Murray family, somewhere on the Cumberland Shore, where the extended clans would each have their own place and gather every summer. My brothers and Dad were rather skeptical of the idea at first, but of course it eventually happened—in 1982, when we subdivided a 32-acre tract of land at

Pugwash, a mere kilometre, door-to-door, from the oceanside Northumberland Links Golf Club. We've been gathering there for more than twenty-five years. David, Daniel and Stewart have cottages on the property; Harold's summer place is twenty minutes away. Bruce inherited the family cottage at Northport.

But the whole love affair was bottled up inside me. It had to be. I couldn't tell my family; they would have taken a very dim view of this burgeoning relationship. The only one I told was my best friend from the *Singalong Jubilee* gang, Karen Oxley, though she had already sensed it. Perhaps it was obvious to others on the show as well. In love with Bill but forced to meet him almost clandestinely, I had to keep other suitors at arm's length, including my old beau Finlay MacDonald. He was a law student at Dalhousie and he was obviously still serious—at least about me—because he asked me to marry him. He took me home for dinners to meet his parents, both charming people. But by this time I was already more than a bit smitten with Bill. Finlay sensed it. He'd say to me, "What about this Langstroth fellow? Is anything going on there?" I, of course, denied any interest. He was concerned too, I think, about my budding music career. "I don't want to be a stage-door Johnny," he'd say, and he seldom came to my little gigs. But I wasn't remotely ready, intellectually or emotionally, for marriage, and I must have made that clear. There were other guys—for a brief time Brian Mulroney courted me. He came around to the apartment I shared with Simone Cottreau, whom I'd met at Mount Saint Vincent (she and I have been friends now for more than forty years). But I wasn't attracted to him and I didn't share his interests. On at least one occasion I had Simone answer the door and tell

Brian I wasn't home. The truth is, I wasn't interested in anyone except Bill.

Dating was an act of deflection. Eventually, two years into the relationship, I gave Bill an ultimatum—either leave your marriage or leave me. In 1970 he finally left the matrimonial home, though he still wasn't divorced. He lived briefly with Karen Oxley, who by then had married Jack Lilly, the drummer on *Singalong*. Then, in 1971, he followed me west to Toronto, moving into my tiny one-bedroom midtown apartment. But he was still married, and our relationship, while known to friends, continued to remain hidden from public view. In those early years, when reporters asked about my love life, I said I was too busy to have one. In fact that wasn't far from the truth; I was so busy there wasn't even much time for Bill.

BRIAN AHERN, the soft-spoken Maritime musical genius, produced and orchestrated—literally and figuratively—my first record album. He was an excellent guitar player, as innately musical as anyone I've ever met. And he was ambitious. He wanted to be a producer, so a few years earlier he'd left *Singalong* and joined ARC Records, a small Canadian label that specialized in East Coast talent, including Catherine McKinnon, at that time the biggest female artist in the country. ARC had also recorded a couple of *Singalong* albums—compilations of audio tracks from the show—and I'd sung on one of those.

There were obvious problems with ARC. They'd given us only $3,000 to cover the costs of the album—not nearly enough—and paid me a small honorarium of about $300. The company had no substantial distribution or promotional network that would give me broad North American exposure. Still, we had complete creative control, and the opportunity to make my own record was exciting. So in the summer of 1968 I flew to Toronto and recorded ten tracks, among them songs by Joni Mitchell ("Both Sides Now"), Bob Dylan ("Paths of Victory"), Henry John Deutschendorf Jr.—much better known as John Denver—("For Baby") and Scott McKenzie (the album's title track, "What About Me"). The Canadian folk duo Ian and Sylvia had recorded "What About Me" in 1964, and Athan Katsos suggested I sing it. Some years later I received a letter from McKenzie, who possessed one of the most beautiful tenor voices I've ever heard, thanking me for recording his song and saying that the royalties from it had been a salvation of sorts. The man who also wrote that anthemic sixties song "If You're Going to San Francisco (Be Sure to Wear Flowers in Your Hair)" had become a drug addict and hit rock bottom; the money, he said, had helped him turn his life around.

After the album was released, ARC proposed a five-year contract. Brian and I thought that was too long, but we eventually signed for a three-year period. As time passed, however, it became increasingly clear to us that three years with ARC was unlikely to advance either of our careers. Brian suggested and I readily agreed that we test the waters and see what other, bigger record labels might be prepared to do for us. As it happened, only one was willing to do better than ARC— Capitol Records Canada, then run by Arnold Gosewich and his artists and repertoire man Paul White. Capitol was a worldwide organization, and its stable of artists included a few obscure names such as Frank Sinatra, the Beatles, Peggy Lee and Nat King Cole. With nothing to lose, Brian asked for carte blanche and, to our utter astonishment, they said yes to everything. The final cost of that first Capitol album would come in at $18,000.

Except—one small detail—we were already contractually bound to ARC for the next three years. At my Aunt Ethel's house in North York, where I was staying, Brian and I pondered what to do. The essential problem was that we had no faith that ARC could or would nurture us properly. I would become just another relatively minor artist with limited exposure. This judgment, by the way, was to some extent unfair, since ARC later did expand its reach into the United States and did very well with a number of groups, including Ocean, who recorded Gene MacLellan's "Put Your Hand in the Hand" and sold a million copies. But that's a story for later.

At which point, I take no delight in admitting, Brian and I engaged in a bit of morally dubious subterfuge. We went back to ARC's two principals, Bill Gilliland and Phil Anderson, and with a straight face told them that instead of a three-year contract, we wanted the five-year deal they had proposed initially. I'm not sure how exactly we sold that to them, but they bought it; it was in their interests, after all. And, pending the drawing up of the necessary papers, we asked for all four copies of the original contract. These were promptly handed over and Brian and I drove immediately back to my aunt's house and started a small blaze in her fireplace, to which we committed the four contracts. We then made the deal with Capitol and signed within a week, committing to two albums within eighteen months. We were in the studio the next month.

At the time my conscience was largely untroubled, perhaps because we hadn't yet signed with Capitol. But the whole affair bothers me more now than it did then. It feels like a form of betrayal, which in some ways it was. I'm not sure ARC was ever fully aware of what transpired. I know that Bill Gilliland kept trying to reach us, telling us the five-year contracts had been drawn up and were ready for signing, but we just ignored his calls. Legally he might well have had a claim on me, regardless of my little bonfire at Aunt Ethel's, or, at a minimum, negotiated a share of future royalties with Capitol. That he chose not to make an issue of it speaks well of him. And, after I scored success with "Snowbird" and Capitol, ARC more than recouped its original investment through subsequent sales of *What About Me*.

⟶

ONE DAY IN 1969 Bill Langstroth called, raving about a singer-songwriter guesting on the Don Messer show that week. His name was Gene MacLellan. Bill arranged for me to meet him in a small conference room in the CBC studios on Bell Road in Halifax. He'd only started writing songs a year earlier, and we sat there while he played and sang a few of them, including "Snowbird." I couldn't believe my ears. Even then it had that signature five-note trill at the end, the rising notes corresponding to the ascending flight path of a bird. He said he'd written it in twenty-five minutes and had sung it at political rallies in P.E.I., but it had never been recorded and wasn't widely known. Until then I'd been singing covers of popular material. Here was a fresh new song and I knew instantly it was a good one, though I would never have predicted the impact it would have on my career. And there were several other good songs, one of which, "Just Bidin' My Time," Gene said he'd written expressly for me. At the end of our meeting he said, "If you like the songs, you can have them"—so typical of Gene, who was generous to a fault.

"I can?" I said.

"Sure."

So I took them home, learned to play them on the guitar, and then spent the rest of the summer singing them for anyone who'd listen. Everyone who heard them loved them. I knew I was on to something.

In August I flew to Toronto for three weeks to record my first album for Capitol, *This Way Is My Way*. Again Brian and I had complete creative control. Among the eleven tracks on the album were three by Gene MacLellan ("Snowbird," "Just Bidin' My Time" and "Hard as I Try"), as well as an upbeat Lovin' Spoonful tune ("Sittin' Back Loving You") and "I'll Be Your Baby Tonight," by Bob Dylan. Despite our control of what went into the album, Capitol had the right to decide which single to release, and its first choice had been "Thirsty Boots," a lovely folksong by Eric Andersen about a civil rights worker. But it didn't do much. The second single was "Just Bidin' My Time," with "Snowbird" the so-called B-side. It was in the spring of 1970 that a DJ in Pittsburgh, or perhaps it was Cleveland, decided to flip the 45. It's interesting, if academic, to ponder what might have happened (or not happened) if he hadn't done that. But once "Snowbird" started getting serious radio play, it took off like a rocket—and took me with it. All of a sudden the record was in demand. And so was I.

I had heard that "Snowbird" was climbing the charts in the United States, but when Capitol sent me to New York to schmooze with the folks at Billboard and Cashbox, it was still at 102 and "bubbling under," as they used to say (I didn't even know what that term meant). I couldn't understand their excitement—it hadn't even reached the Top 100. No big deal, I thought. But it kept moving up, and by July, when I joined the family at Northport for a brief vacation, someone called to say it was 45 with a bullet. That I understood. And that was when my twenty-five-year-old heart began to flutter. Within months the song had been recorded by thirty artists, including Elvis Presley, Al Martino, Andy Williams and the piano duo Ferrante and Teicher (it would eventually be covered by more than a hundred artists, making it one of the most recorded Canadian songs ever). By the end of the summer I'd sold 900,000 copies in the United States. Suddenly the phone in my apartment was ringing with an invitation to perform on the *Glen Campbell Goodtime Hour*, a CBS television show with an audience of 34 million—the audiences for the Canadian TV shows I'd been performing on were a mere fraction of that. When I boarded a plane for Los Angeles on September 7 to tape the first show, "Snowbird" was closing in on the 1 million mark—the first gold record ever by a Canadian solo female artist—and two hundred people turned up at the airport to see me off. I didn't know it then, but my life would never be the same.

CHAPTER THREE

How does a whirlwind start? If I knew the answer, I'd know the origins of the overnight phenomenon that I became.

In many ways, I think now, it didn't have a lot to do with me. I'm not affecting modesty; I sang well from the beginning and improved as the years passed. It's just that the attention I received, especially in those early years—the tsunami of media coverage that cascaded over me, almost all of it favourable; the constant demand for me to appear on TV, in nightclubs, at state fairs and other venues; the creation of the meta-entity known as Anne Murray, Canada's Snowbird—speaks to something larger.

My timing could not have been better. I came along in the late 1960s, at precisely the moment when Canada as a nation, and Canadians individually, was seized with a new sense of identity and possibility, the final shucking off of the hard legacy of the Second World War, and the optimism that attended the birth of our second century. We had recently celebrated our centennial with a six-month-long party at Expo '67 in Montreal, arguably the moment of conception of the new Canada. We had adopted a new flag and a national anthem and had finally begun to think about patriating the constitution. In those years we were also beneficiaries of a tidal wave of new immigration from both the Old and the Third World, ethnicities and cultures that vastly changed and enriched our country.

Coming of age in the late sixties, our baby-boom generation had helped elect a young, smart, energetic, cosmopolitan and attractive prime minister, Pierre Elliott Trudeau, who dated celebrities and cut a dashing figure on the world stage. Overnight, it seemed, he had transformed the long-ingrained image of Canada as a boring, still Victorian, no-liquor-on-Sundays country of wood-hewers, water-drawers and coal miners. And all of this prepared and conditioned us, made us eager to embrace new cultural icons perceived as being in synch with the new Canada.

Music was a central part of this emergent identity, in part because Pierre Juneau and the CRTC had recently mandated what then seemed to be stringent Canadian-content regulations (30 percent) for AM radio stations. (It's Monsieur Juneau for whom Canada's music awards, the Junos, are well named.) To meet the quotas, programmers and DJs were suddenly eager, even desperate, to find new Canadian music. And record companies, recognizing the demand, were keen to provide it, signing up new talent with sometimes reckless abandon.

The results were remarkable. In five short years, Cancon sales for Capitol Records in Canada went from 3 to 15 percent. The technology in Canadian recording studios leapt ahead as well—it had to. When we recorded "Snowbird," we did it in a six-track studio; there was nothing more sophisticated around. By 1972 there were five sixteen-track studios across the country, a twenty-four-track venue in Toronto and a thirty-two-track facility in Montreal. And while many radio station owners initially complained about the Cancon quotas, saying it would cost them money, not one volunteered to surrender the licence. The appetite was there and growing; they merely had to feed it.

It did not hurt, of course, that I was already a known commodity, had already had four or five years of national TV exposure via *Singalong*, *Let's Go* and other shows. Also, of course, there was Gene MacLellan's two-minute-and-nine-second rhapsodic ballad "Snowbird," which had soared to near the top of the charts in not only Canada but the United States, the foreign vote always being more important than the domestic one, and confirming evidence that Canadians might actually have some talent.

And I'm sure it helped to be painted as a straight-talking, clean-living, fresh-faced country girl who liked to sing in her bare feet. Realness, declared the *Toronto Star*'s critic Patrick Scott in 1970, was the essential factor in my rise to stardom. But even without Gene's song, something like the Anne Murray phenomenon would have occurred. Someone else would have emerged or been developed to capitalize on the new cultural ethos. I just happened to get there first.

In the summer of 1970, just as "Snowbird" was starting to take flight on the U.S. charts, the CBC made me an almost unprecedented offer: a two-year exclusive contract for all my radio and TV appearances in Canada. Until that time the public broadcaster had prided itself on never having succumbed to the temptations of the star system that applied in the United States, where a few elite performers were given disproportionate attention and money—the premise being that they would boost ratings and, by corollary, advertising revenues. With me, the CBC took a modest step in that direction. There were to be four Anne Murray TV specials, a weekly radio show, a continuing presence on *Singalong Jubilee* and eight guest appearances on the prime-time *Tommy Hunter Show*. The CBC was probably less than amused that the exclusivity part of the arrangement was weakened by the fact that I'd already taped four shows for *Nashville North*, later renamed *The Ian Tyson Show*, which aired on the competing network, CTV. Worse, from the corporation's viewpoint, two U.S. shows on which I'd been invited to appear—Glen Campbell's and Johnny Cash's— aired on the CBS and ABC networks respectively.

When the CBC announced the signing, I'd already shot the first special, produced by Athan Katsos, with other old friends as musical guests, including Gene MacLellan, Patricia Anne McKinnon (Catherine's sister) and Brian Ahern. It was a show that blended concert performance, music video, animation and documentary footage. At the press screening, then CBC entertainment czar Thom Benson surprised me by presenting the contract for me to sign—purely a photo op, since we'd already made the deal. I sat down at the desk and, unable to resist a little cheek, signed it *Alice Smith*.

The other appearances followed and soon, along with the onerous workload they entailed, I felt overexposed on Canadian television. A Vancouver newspaper headline opposite my photo blared, "In the air, everywhere, 24 hours a day." One critic called it the dawn of the Age of Anne. Less would certainly have been more. Again, however, I was unable to do much about it—although I did manage to reject a weekly Anne Murray show the CBC was proposing. And I was making good money—about $5,000 per special, and the same for any repeats.

In that first special, aired in October 1970, we shot a number of sequences in Springhill and Northport. There, perhaps for the first and last time in my career, I encountered someone who resented my sudden celebrity. We were filming at the Liar's Bench in Springhill, once a gathering place for the town's coal miners and Maritime yarn-spinners—hence the name. A crowd gathered and I heard a woman shout, "Who does she think she is, goddamned Elvis Presley?" That negativity was typically small-town, and it stung me. But it was also the old Canada speaking, the reflexive voice insisting that stardom, and everything it entails, is somehow incompatible with the way we Canadians see ourselves. I have some sympathy for that view. Idolatry can be an ugly thing—I would come to know this first-hand. But frankly I'm surprised that I didn't encounter more of that sentiment along the way. Or perhaps I did, but by then I had thoughtful colleagues who insulated me from it.

That I came to represent something more than Anne Murray—just another woman in love with singing—is clear from the way I was treated in the press. I read the old clippings and reviews now and, while there is no shortage of criticism, almost none of it is aimed directly at me or my talent. One delightful exception: "She moves," one critic wrote, "with all the sureness of a doe approaching a stream at the peak of hunting season." Sometimes the stories were about how bizarrely the CBC wardrobe department had dressed me for the specials, which was valid. I had some fun with this, however; on one show I said, "How do you like these things

I'm wearing? They're either long pedal-pushers or short bell-bottoms. I dunno, I just wear what they tell me."

Sometimes the press complained that I looked and talked like a high school gym teacher and walked like a football player, and that was entirely valid too—I did. More typically the criticism either focused on how boring and unimaginative CBC producers were or attacked CBC executive brass for not knowing how to exploit my talent. First they were accused of underexposing me, and then of smothering me and putting my nascent career at risk of overexposure. And my record company was criticized for not picking the right single to follow "Snowbird."

Had they gone after me as well, they would have been justified. The truth is, I wasn't ready for the burden being imposed—not ready vocally and not ready as a performer—by the weight and responsibility attached to being Canada's designated superstar. I feel that it took me ten years to earn my sea legs and really feel comfortable onstage. People who expected me to dress like a star and to carry myself with the poise and grace of a star were expecting too much. I still had a lot to learn.

Even cynical, often feared entertainment critics like the *Star*'s Scott seldom went after me directly, and I have to think it had something to do with not wanting to deflate the brave new mythology into which I had been drafted. In some ways I was the show-business equivalent of Canadian hero and 1968 Olympic gold medal–winning skier Nancy Greene—except that Nancy didn't have songs on the radio night and day and her face wasn't on television every week or her name in the newspapers every day. It was about this time that Elton John declared that the only two things he knew about Canada were ice hockey and Anne Murray—at once a commentary on Elton's skeletal knowledge of the postcolonial world and a reflection of the absurd speed with which an unknown young woman had become imprinted on people's minds. Had I been a pilot program to test how swiftly and how effectively the tools of media could be deployed to shape a national consciousness, I would have passed with flying colours.

And it wasn't just Canada. Once on a flight to Moncton, I sat beside a young man reading *The City of Yes*, a novel by Peter Oliva. He had come to a part in the book where a student asks the central character, a Canadian teaching in Japan, if he knows who "Ahnmura" is. The teacher is momentarily at a loss—he can't comprehend the question. Then it dawns on him. "Oh . . . you mean Anne Murray, the singer?" What a coincidence it was—he was reading that passage as he was sitting right next to me. But that's how it was; I had become somehow identified with Canada in the same way that Nana Mouskouri is associated with Greece or Julio Iglesias with Spain.

No doubt it had something to do with being the first Canadian woman to receive a star buildup. There was no shortage of other female talent around, to be sure—I'd performed with many fine singers on *Singalong Jubilee*—but few, apart from Catherine McKinnon, seriously pursued solo careers. Joni Mitchell had long since gone to the United States. Canada's pet, Juliette (Sysak), had never been more than a TV personality, excellent singer though she was. Susan Jacks and her husband, Terry, professionally known as the Poppy Family, had scored a gold record (for "Which Way You Goin', Billy?") even before "Snowbird." And though she was born in Canada, Buffy Sainte-Marie, a remarkable composer and wonderful performer—she wrote the haunting and oft-covered "Until It's Time for You to Go," among many others—had been raised in the United States. The only other woman attracting much attention at the time was Ginette Reno, who won Junos for Outstanding Performance of the Year in 1971 and 1972 and who has enjoyed a long and successful bilingual career.

In any case, in a matter of weeks after "Snowbird," I was swept up like Dorothy in *The Wizard of Oz* by some cyclonic force and catapulted into a strange new universe, at once thrilling and frightening and filled with its very own Munchkins, wicked witches, tin men, cowardly lions, scarecrows and backstage wizards. Those first few years were a whirlwind, and if I thought for a moment that I was in control of events, I was deluded. And I did convince myself for a time that I was in control. Repeatedly, in interviews from that period, I'm quoted as saying things like "I can do anything I want to . . . I'd rather get married and have kids and go back to teaching than get stuck on a show business treadmill . . . I'm going to go back home and build a house on my land near Peggy's Cove . . . I don't need to move to Toronto; I can continue to live in Halifax . . . And I'll know when it's time to stop."

I meant all of it when I said it; I simply failed to understand not only that the rocket ship I was riding was infinitely more powerful than I, but also that I was just a passenger, not the captain. In those years the career was all I had. I was not free to do anything I liked, and I was soon stuck on the showbiz treadmill I had declared I would avoid. I never did build on that precious Nova Scotia land, although in that case it was largely because I preferred to be closer to my family on the Northumberland Strait, which has better weather and nice beaches. And I did move to Toronto—only months after maintaining that I wouldn't. A few years later I told one reporter, "I've always insisted that my career would not become my life, but strangely enough, it's happened."

―――

WALKING INTO THE CBS TV studios in Los Angeles that September afternoon for the first Glen Campbell show was more than a little intimidating. Capitol had lobbied for the guest slot but I could detect a degree of apprehension—not so much from Glen, who was warm and friendly, but from his team. Glen, in fact, had championed the idea, but he had clearly put himself somewhat out on a limb in recommending me; after all, however widely exposed I was back home, Americans knew very little about me. For them I was a largely untried Canadian and, maybe they feared, a one-hit wonder with no real ability to sing. That first meeting wasn't exactly an audition—I'd signed a contract to appear—but in a sense it was. Almost as soon as we met in his dressing room, Glen invited me to sing with him; directors, producers, writers and other members of the entourage were standing around watching intently. And I was game; if I felt confident about anything in those days, it was my singing ability.

Glen asked, "Do you know 'Break My Mind'?"

"Sure," I said. "Do you want me to sing the melody line or the harmony?"

He looked at me, a little surprised, and said, "You can sing harmony?"

I could indeed. I'd been able to sing harmony—a gift you either have or you don't—since I was twelve. I was pretty proud of that, until my musically precocious daughter, Dawn, started harmonizing at the age of eight.

A few bars into the song I could see smiles starting to form and could feel the whole room starting to relax as if it had made one collective exhalation. That relaxed me too. Glen was obviously pleased. He'd staked some equity on me, rolled the dice and been vindicated; he was raking in the chips—the woman could actually sing. We sang a few more songs and the mood continued to brighten.

"Oh, yes!" he said. "This is such a treat. Anne, you have no idea what I have to deal with here, and the number of people who can't sing harmony." (Shortly thereafter Glen began calling me Annie; he and Bill Langstroth were two of the very few people who did so.)

When we finally got around to taping the actual show, we sang the uptempo number "I Wonder How the Old Folks Are at Home" as a duet. Feeling pretty comfortable by then, I started mugging at Glen every time the camera focused on him for a close-up. He loved my irreverence. He ultimately became one of my biggest professional fans, often saying that of all the stars who had made guest appearances on his show, I was his favourite.

When I returned from L.A., I went into the studio again with Brian Ahern to record another album for Capitol, rehearsed and taped another CBC special, and opened a ten-day run at the Royal York Hotel's Imperial Room, long Toronto's marquee venue for A-list talent. I broke virtually all attendance records—astonishing, given how new I was—save for one set by the incomparable Ella Fitzgerald. The cover charge was five dollars. My opening-night performance was mediocre, but we improved after that. When I sang, waiters with tape machines stood off to the side, recording me as if it were a historic event. I was barefoot but otherwise fairly well dressed in an outfit inherited from the CBC wardrobe department. The long-haired band, on the other hand, looked like a bunch of reprobates. My pedal steel guitarist, Buddy Cage, wore a vest with no shirt—a radical ensemble at the time and something of a revelation, I'm sure, to the room's long-time tuxedo- and gown-encased patrons.

I can't recall exactly when I started to perform barefoot. Growing up, I had always been barefoot in the summer, but I don't know when I adopted that "look" for the stage. I don't even know precisely why. It must have started on *Singalong Jubilee* in the late 1960s, but it continued for several years. I'd even travel on planes barefoot, a style that airport security officials today would no doubt welcome. I wore a full-length dress to the 1970 Grey Cup banquet in Toronto and was barefoot for that as well. I was even married, in 1975, at the age of thirty, in bare feet. I suspect it had something to do with a form of youthful protest against convention, some sort of rebellion that my so-called hippie generation was acting out— deeply meaningful at the time, ridiculous now. Looking back, it is a mystery to me why I did it, and something of an embarrassment. But at the time, I suppose, in a strange way it did help brand me, even though there was no deliberation or strategy on my part. It just felt right, so I did it.

I had attended the Grey Cup banquet as part of my official but entirely honorary role as Grand Marshal of the annual parade. The day before the game, I rode in a convertible past the throngs lining Toronto's Yonge Street. Somewhere along the parade route I heard someone in the crowd calling my name. I turned to see a bearded, long-haired young man, about my age, whom I knew I had never met before. "It's me," he shouted, coming up to the car and running along beside it. "It's John Beck! From Timmins!" John Beck had been my pen pal since not long after the second Springhill coal mine disaster. His teacher in Timmins had encouraged the class to write letters of support and condolence to students in Springhill. I ended up with his letter and we began a correspondence that lasted four or five years, including annual exchanges of school pictures. So I had seen the face, but I could barely recognize it through the layers of hair.

I scarcely remember anything else about what should have been a memorable day. I'm told, for example, that at the game I sat beside Prime Minister Trudeau, who was dressed rakishly in a stylish cape and theatrical hat, as if preparing to conjure up a rabbit, but I don't recall it. The Beck incident, however, did stay with me. Years later John and some of his family came backstage after a show in Niagara Falls, and we finally had a chance to chat.

TODAY A WELL-OILED, smoothly integrated infrastructure exists to help build (and sometimes manufacture) musical careers from the ground up: agents, managers, lawyers, accountants, public relations experts, security personnel, handlers of various kinds. We had none of that in the beginning. We were essentially starting from scratch, operating not only without a safety net but also without any real knowledge of how to assemble it. Flying blind, we tended to make decisions quickly—often too quickly—because they had to be made, overwhelmed as we were by the influx of offers. We said no occasionally, but mostly we said yes, because we didn't know how long any of it would last and feared that saying no would be the wrong decision. But saying yes could be wrong as well, and sometimes it was.

Initially the "we" was just Bill Langstroth and I. But the blizzard of activity, the incessant demands for my attention, soon eclipsed our joint abilities to handle my affairs. My producer, Brian Ahern, helped me with musical choices (he would oversee the first ten albums) and lent a hand assembling the band, but in that hectic year after "Snowbird" I needed more. I found myself booking flights, reserving hotel rooms and tending to a dozen other things that were distracting me from what was always the main prize —singing. Bill did the best he could and he taught me a lot, especially about how to perform on television and how to engage an audience between songs, but it was apparent to both of us that we needed professional management. And we needed it in both Canada and the United States.

In the fall of 1970 I'd gone shopping for a manager. In California for another Campbell show taping, I had dinner with Jerry Weintraub and his wife, the pop singer Jane Morgan. Weintraub represented John Denver, and after discussions I'd been close to signing with him at MCA. But at the last minute Al Coury, vice-president of promotion at Capitol in Los Angeles, raised an objection and urged me to sign with Nick Sevano at the William Morris Agency; he was Glen Campbell's manager and had been Frank Sinatra's friend and agent for twenty-three years. By November I had agreed to go with Sevano, giving him the standard commission of 15 percent of any U.S. earnings in excess of $3,000. In Canada Bill and I muddled through on our own until the following April, when I successfully implored twenty-five-year-old Leonard Rambeau

to resign from his job as executive assistant to the director of
Canada Manpower in Halifax.

I had said repeatedly—and meant it at the time—that it
was unnecessary to move to Toronto. There I'd be just a little
frog in a big pond, I used to say, whereas in the Maritimes
I could be a slightly larger frog in a smaller pond. But with
every week it became increasingly clear that my position was
untenable. I had to stop living in denial. Virtually everything
connected to my professional life—the CBC, CTV, my record
company, my producer Brian Ahern, the recording studios,
the major media players—all of these were in Toronto.
So, while I hated the prospect of leaving Bill, my emotional
anchor, and my family and friends, I finally recognized
the inevitability.

In January 1971 Bill and I packed my things and he
drove west in my sporty turquoise Cougar convertible (white
leather interior, eight-track tape deck). I was too busy to spend
the time driving with him, so I flew. I rented a twenty-second-
floor one-bedroom apartment on Balliol Avenue for $188 a
month (including parking); for privacy purposes I listed myself
as "Alice Smith" on the tenants' roster in the lobby. When
Leonard arrived in May, he took a suite in the same building.
It was that spring that our company, Balmur Investments, was
formally formed; the name combined the first letters of our
three first names—Bill, Anne and Leonard—with Mur, my old
nickname. Balmur became the corporate umbrella under
which I would operate for almost three decades.

But even that was not enough. I needed a lawyer to parse
the accumulating contracts. George Buckley, a stockbroker
who had played banjo on *Singalong Jubilee*, put me in touch
with Anthony Grey at McCarthy's; later, when Tony went on

to launch a hugely successful mining career in Australia in 1972, I found Dave Matheson, a New Brunswicker, practising at McMillan Binch. Through Tony I also found another transplanted Maritimer in Toronto, chartered accountant Lyman MacInnis, to look after my growing accounting and taxation issues. Actually, Lyman, who also represented opera singer Jon Vickers and NHL stars Bobby Orr and Bobby Hull, among fifty-four others, did far more than that: essentially he became my business manager and a key negotiator in contracts with record companies, TV networks and band members. When he did my first tax return, I handed him a collection of shoe boxes containing my carefully accumulated but entirely disorganized receipts.

At our first meeting Lyman laid down what he called the three MacInnis Rules. First, there was no such thing as a standard boilerplate contract; absolutely everything was negotiable. Second, if anybody needed a quick answer, it was always to be no. And third, he would never trade long-term gain for short-term benefit. Could he pull this off? He said that he could—if he had my backing, because it was my status that ultimately conferred his power. If I stood resolute, then he could be more effective.

It was Lyman who suggested that I keep Leonard on salary instead of commission, which was the industry norm, arguing that it would put less pressure on him and make him more likely to make decisions based on what was best for me rather than for him. We "negotiated" his salary one night in Lyman's dining room in the following manner. He, Lyman and I each wrote down a proposed salary on a piece of paper. Then Lyman's wife, also named Anne, was instructed to pick the middle amount. As it turned out, there was no middle: one of us had written down $15,000 and the other two $15,500, which is what I paid him that first year—substantially more than he'd been making.

⁓

MY APPEARANCE on the Glen Campbell show in September 1970 was the start of a long and fruitful association with Glen. In the next few years I was a guest on eleven more *Goodtime Hours*. On one of them I was joined by the character actor Paul Lynde. I was a fan, so I approached him for an autographed photo. He saw to it that I received one but was less than cordial about the whole thing. So when the great comic Joey Bishop appeared as a guest on a subsequent show, I carefully steered clear of him, not wanting to invite a similar reaction. Years later, Joey and I happened to be guests on the same talk show.

"You know, Anne," he told me during the broadcast, "I did not form a very good first impression of you back then. You didn't even talk to me. I thought, 'Wow, what a stuck-up star we have here.'"

"Are you kidding?" I said. "That's about as far from the truth as you could get. I was just too afraid to come out and meet you."

We enjoyed a good laugh over that. Offstage, I discovered that Bishop was very warm, not at all like his comic persona, which had a harder edge. In that respect he reminded me of Don Rickles, whom I met years later in Vegas. Don was as cutting and vicious as he could be during his act, offending as many people as possible, but in person he was the soul of sweetness.

In the spring of 1971 Glen invited me to be his opening act during a two-week run at the International Hilton Hotel in Las Vegas before two thousand people a night, and a month later before five thousand at the outdoor Greek Theatre in Los Angeles. For eleven days we played to capacity audiences, most of them there to see Glen, who'd become a major star. Reviewing the show, the *Los Angeles Times* critic called me "a husky-voiced singer who has much more ability than her bland Snowbird record ever showed." On opening night guitarist Jerry Reed, who had scored two recent hits—"Amos Moses" and "When You're Hot, You're Hot"—was suffering from a bad cold and apologized to the crowd. That was another thing I learned from Bill Langstroth: never apologize; the audience has paid good money to see you perform. If you're too sick to sing, cancel the show, but otherwise go out there and do the best you can, and don't ever apologize. An apology is simply code for "You folks aren't seeing me at my best." It might be true, but it's not something they want to hear.

One night the legendary Keely Smith came backstage. With bandleader Louis Prima, also her husband for a time, she'd had several big hits in the fifties, including "That Old Black Magic" and "I've Got You Under My Skin." I loved her singing. In fact the Louis Prima–Keely Smith fan club was the only one I had ever joined. Meeting her was a major thrill.

I had played three nights at Harrah's in Lake Tahoe with Glen, but the Vegas gig was a whole different ballgame—the big time. I found this legendary town to be an alien, self-contained, completely artificial universe, one that over time would, ironically, do a lot for my bank account, but also one that I grew to despise. Because I was the opening act, I could disappear afterwards and catch the late shows of some of the other talent performing on the Strip, including a childhood idol of mine, Patti Page, as well as Wayne Newton, Peggy Lee and Liberace. Better still, I got to meet them.

For my first night at the International, in my dressing room I was not only nervous, as I often was, but nauseated, overwhelmed by fear and excitement. I came onstage in a pair of hot pants—very brief shorts that were then the fashion rage—and my customary bare feet. The hotel management was shocked and quickly informed me that such attire was not in keeping with the Vegas dress code. The next night I put on a dress, but my feet were still bare.

During my stay I couldn't help noticing a stunning $3,500 natural white cross mink coat for sale in the hotel's fur store. I'd been wearing the same fake fur with a leopard collar since Grade 10, and since Leonard assured me I could now afford it, I decided to indulge myself. Because I was appearing at the hotel, the owner gave me an $800 discount. I brought it home and didn't pay duty. I wasn't shy about advertising my great bargain: I mentioned it in several interviews and was later photographed wearing it for articles in *Maclean's* magazine and the *Toronto Star* newspaper. One night at home in Toronto, I was visited by a plainclothes emissary of the RCMP's (Royal Canadian Mounted Police's) customs and excise office.

"I understand that you have recently acquired a new mink coat," he said after we had made our introductions.

"That's right," I said, already starting to regret my stupidity.

"You bought it in Las Vegas at a cost of two thousand seven hundred American dollars and returned to Canada on May 29, is that correct?"

"How did you ever find out?" I wanted to say, because I had, after all, left them more than enough clues. I bit my sassy tongue and just nodded.

"And you neglected to declare it at Canadian Customs, correct?"

Guilty as charged. I was required to pay the entire retail cost again, plus tax, plus the duty. So that bargain mink ended up costing two and a half times its list price—a very expensive little coat indeed. Determined to derive its full value, I wore it for more than a decade at full length, then turned it into a bomber-style jacket for a few more years. Then I gave it to my sister-in-law Chris, who wore it for another seven years, and then she had it made into a mink teddy bear for sale at a charity auction. It fetched almost $2,000 on eBay.

The RCMP had taught me a lesson I would not forget.

MY SCHEDULE IN 1971 would have exhausted the most industrious travelling salesman. I felt like the pogo stick my friend Elizabeth Calder had brought from England when she moved to Springhill in 1954—the first one in town—jumping frenetically all over the place, never staying long. Another Campbell show in L.A., a day in Toronto, three days in Halifax for a *Singalong* tenth-anniversary-show taping, then a swing through western Canada—my first—with sold-out shows in Regina, Saskatoon, Edmonton, Calgary and Vancouver, each one bringing a fresh round of print, radio and TV interviews, everyone trying to figure out just how straight, clean and simple—the title of my next CBC TV special—I was. All of this before the end of March.

My week-long booking in Vancouver, at the venerable Cave nightclub on Hornby Street, was unforgettable. First, two of my band members ended up in hospital with heroin overdoses the night before we were scheduled to open. I was familiar with drug use among musicians, of course, but this was deeply troubling and threatening, not least to them. I was then and remained very particular about the quality of my work and set the bar high for myself. I expected those who worked with me, in whatever capacity, to meet equally high standards. Indiscriminate drug use clearly jeopardized the benchmarks, but I had no real control over what my band-mates got up to. Luckily the two miscreants were out of the hospital in time to play for opening night.

After that first night I made a quick exit to the airport and flew by private jet (Frank Sinatra's) to L.A. for the Grammys; I had been nominated in two categories: best contemporary female vocal (for "Snowbird") and best new artist of 1970. In the first category I was up against Dionne Warwick, Diana Ross, Bobbie Gentry and Linda Ronstadt; in the second, against the Carpenters, Elton John, Melba Moore and the Partridge Family. I felt I had no chance of winning, and my instincts proved accurate. Warwick won for "I'll Never Fall in Love Again," by Burt Bacharach and Hal David, and the Carpenters won for best new artist (and for best group). "Snowbird" wasn't entirely shut out, however; the following year Chet Atkins won a Grammy for an instrumental version.

My performance on the actual show was pre-taped. I landed, grabbed a few hours' sleep in a motel on Sunset Strip, sang my song (James Taylor's classic "Fire and Rain," which had been nominated) and went straight back to the airport for the return flight to Vancouver and the Cave. En route, I was at the door to the cockpit, chatting with the pilot, when the front windscreen suddenly cracked. He immediately pushed me into a seat and told me to buckle up. There was a pressurization problem, and he put the plane into what felt like a nosedive. We plummeted ten thousand feet in very short order and flew low the rest of the way. A nervous wreck, I didn't reach the Cave until 11:15, over two hours late—and that was for the first of two scheduled shows. That same week I also squeezed in a taping for the Irish Rovers' TV show, which added to the frenzy. To relieve my anxiety, Hal Touchie, a friend and classmate of my brother Harold, gave me a few tranquilizers. They settled me down, but maybe a bit too much. No wonder the TV critics said I looked spacey, washed out and exhausted.

I was still looking after everything in those days. Capitol president Arnold Gosewich came backstage at the Cave after one show and found me sitting cross-legged on the dressing-room floor writing out cheques to members of the band. I was scheduled to have a week off shortly after Vancouver, but Johnny Reid, who'd been so good to me in Charlottetown, called and said he needed business—could I do a week at his Prince Edward Lounge? So I flew east with the band, did the week and then collapsed.

It wasn't exactly a nervous breakdown, though I was headed in that direction. On closing night we partied until 5:00 a.m. and then I couldn't sleep. My hand and arm were literally numb and I was in a deep funk. For the first time in years, I cried—for an hour. I was booked to fly to Toronto on Sunday to start rehearsals for my next CBC special, but I simply refused to go. Nobody was terribly pleased, but I didn't care. I think I came close to packing it in right there. While

I loved performing, I'd already begun to question the restrictive strings that were attached, the impossible schedules, the loneliness, the constant travel. At that moment I simply needed to get off the treadmill, so I did—for one day. Music critic Ritchie Yorke succinctly summed up my situation at the time; he said my career was endangered by "overexposure, bad decisions and lack of shrewd planning." None of this was my fault, he wrote, but it was I who was suffering and would suffer in the end. But knowing that I needed to slow down and being able to do it were two different things.

Meanwhile, the Maritime Mafia, as our Balmur group became known, faced a critical issue: choosing the single that would follow "Snowbird." It was critical because if it bombed, it would risk making "Snowbird" and the gold record Glen had presented to me on the *Merv Griffin Show* look like a lucky fluke, the proverbial one-hit wonder, and give all sorts of people grounds for suggesting that I return promptly to the relative Maritime obscurity from whence I'd come. On the other hand, if I could chalk up another gold record, I'd be well on my way to establishing a real career, particularly in the more hit-sensitive United States. One hit might be good enough to establish yourself in Canada, but not in America.

I knew just the song I wanted, too: "Put Your Hand in the Hand," another Gene MacLellan tune, which I'd recorded on my second Capitol album, *Honey, Wheat & Laughter*, released in May 1970. For a long time the tune had had no title, so we just referred to it as "God's song," for obvious reasons. (Obvious to Gene, certainly—he'd started writing songs after he rolled his truck in a rainstorm and almost died; he was on his back for eight months and his survival helped him forge a new and deep connection to God.) Brian Ahern wanted that song too. We even had backing for our choice from Capitol Canada.

It was Capitol's U.S. office that balked. They apparently thought that Gene's song sounded too different from "Snowbird" (as if this might confuse my fans) and feared that I sounded too masculine. They insisted we go with "Sing High, Sing Low," by another talented Canadian songwriter and performer, Brent Titcomb. I liked Brent's song—I had put it on an album, after all—but there are many fine songs that aren't destined to become hit singles. They just aren't commercial enough, and this was one of them. "Put Your Hand" had *hit* written all over it, and I knew it.

I lost that battle, only to see Ocean, a new Canadian gospel-rock band, record it for my original label, ARC Records, sell several million copies and watch it climb to number two on Billboard's Hot 100 chart. "Sing High" did reasonably well in Canada, where I had my principal fan base, but bombed in the States. It did not get better after that; the third single, my cover of Kenny Rogers's and Kin Vassy's "Stranger in My Place," was no more impressive commercially. Only then did Capitol decide to release "Put Your Hand" as a single, and even then as the flip side of "It Takes Time," by the gifted Canadian singer and songwriter Shirley Eikhard. But by then Ocean's version had captured the marketplace. My disposition was not improved by the fact that the Ocean recording used the same basic arrangement as mine and that on it, virtually everyone agreed, the band was singing off-key. The whole episode made me angry, and I wasn't shy about expressing it. Thereafter I insisted on being consulted on these key decisions.

In April 1971 I made my debut at Toronto's fabled Massey Hall. It was a two-night event (four shows in all), and at the opening, for the first and last time of my life, I performed drunk. Not embarrassing, slurring-my-words, falling-down drunk; just as loose as a goose. Nerves had a lot to do with it. I had spent the afternoon in my apartment with Jack Smith, a close friend of my brother Harold and the brother of my friend Donna Smith (the one who stole my boyfriend in junior high). As teenagers Jack and Harold used to don boxing gloves and knock each other silly on our front lawn. That afternoon he and I knocked ourselves a little silly as well, courtesy of rum and Coke, and then made our way to the concert hall. The Stampeders had opened for me and the crowd was warmed up, lively and friendly. The show suffered no unfortunate consequences from the drinking, and I had sobered some by the second show that night, but the experience—that sense of not being in full control of my faculties—scared me so much that I never did it again. After that I can count on one hand the number of times I had even one drink before a show. I had been nervous before the Massey show—I was often nervous—but that was not a very good excuse.

As at the Royal York Hotel, my Massey Hall bandleader was Skip Beckwith, an extraordinary bass player whom Brian Ahern had found, and Skip assembled the other members of the band. Both he and guitarist Miles Wilkinson were relatively abstemious, but the others were pretty good drinkers. In the liberated spirit of the times, they were also ready to experiment with all sorts of pharmacological concoctions—although never in front of me. I tried to keep a lid on the problem, but I had no leverage. Besides, my agenda was so crowded with events—TV shows and the rehearsals, club dates, travel, Vegas appearances, recording sessions, press interviews—that I barely had time to look after myself. The pace that I kept up seems from this distance almost inhumane. Those early days were not fun. I hated it all. I was trying desperately to find my way, not only vocally but as a performer. It was hard work and, especially after the heroin escapade in Vancouver, I was always apprehensive about what sort of trouble the band might get themselves into.

Meanwhile, the frenzy continued. More Campbell shows. Gigs in Winnipeg and Vancouver. Recording sessions in Toronto and L.A. for a duets album with Glen—my third disc that year. It was produced jointly by Brian Ahern and Al DeLory, Glen's main man in the studio, an interesting commingling of two extraordinary talents. We were definitely the junior partners in the arrangement but were allowed to choose several songs, including "United We Stand," "Ease Your Pain" and Brent Titcomb's "Bring Back the Love." I wasn't so keen to record some of the other songs that had been chosen, among them Randy Newman's "Love Story"—not because I didn't like the song; I did. But having heard Harry Nilsson's (for me) definitive version of it, I didn't think it could be improved upon. Now that view strikes me as a little too precious; it was, as I'm sure Glen pointed out, a duet, and therefore automatically not likely to be compared with Nilsson's solo standard. In fact today, of all the songs on that album, it might be my favourite. Overall the album was a modest success and produced a solid single, a duet that combined Jimmy Webb's mournful ballad "By the Time I Get to Phoenix" and the Burt Bacharach/Hal David tune "I Say a Little Prayer"—not easy to pull off because of the conflicting time signatures the songs were written in.

In July 1971, to celebrate the success of "Snowbird," Springhill made me guest of honour at Old Home Week.

Twenty thousand people turned up, four times the town's normal population. There was a gold record presentation in the new high school gym, a two-mile-long parade along Main Street, a brief performance (by my brothers Stewart and Bruce and me) on the steps of the vocational school, a gala dinner with *Hockey Night in Canada* broadcaster Danny Gallivan as guest speaker and, inevitably, a round of press interviews. The whole thing was orchestrated by my first boyfriend, Brian Fuller, secretary of the event. But the crush of fans proved overwhelming. At one point I had to take refuge in a locked police cruiser; at another I found myself crawling on the floor of our Main Street home trying to avoid being seen by gawkers at the windows.

After a few days, seeking the peace of anonymity, I fled to Prince Edward Island, donned a friend's black wig and parked myself in a dark corner of Johnny Reid's Prince Edward Lounge. The disguise was less than effective. Nettie Blacquiere, a lounge habitué, wandered by and, without skipping a beat, said, "Anne?! How ya doin'?" It was the last time I wore a disguise, although later I occasionally deployed decoys to lure the crowd away after a show. A friend would hustle out the stage door wearing a blonde wig and climb into my waiting limousine, pursued by photographers and fans; a few minutes later I'd walk out unnoticed and casually stroll to her car and drive it back to the hotel.

One bright morning the next month, I opened an envelope from Capitol to find a cheque made out to me for $98,000, a staggering amount of money at that time. I'd known something good was coming—the first wave of royalties from the sales of "Snowbird"—but didn't know how sweet it would be. I quickly decided to buy a house and within a matter of weeks had plunked most of the proceeds into a small property on Hilltop Road in Toronto's Forest Hill neighbourhood, paying about $75,000. It had belonged to Guido Basso, the flugelhorn player and trumpeter who had played on both my albums and my CBC specials.

The day I moved in I turned on the washer, the dryer, the stereo and the air conditioner, all at the same time, like a kid in a candy store. Then I looked around and thought, *My God, why me?* There I was, twenty-six years old, staring out at my backyard with its swimming pool and award-winning garden. What had I done to deserve this, a nine-room house smack dab in one of the city's toniest neighbourhoods? I called home that night and said to Mom, "You know, I was just thinking of how lucky I am, and wondering why I should have all these things."

And Mom said, "Oh, Anne, don't brag." That was a typically Maritime piece of advice—don't brag or something bad will happen; it'll be taken away from you.

So I said, "I'm not braggin'. I'm thanking God."

"Oh, well," Mom said. "That's all right then."

In short order Bill moved in with me, and so did Leonard, allowing us to support the fiction that Bill was there operating as part of the corporate Balmur family. Various newspaper stories hinted broadly at our relationship, but for the most part it remained under wraps. Usually I deflected questions about my private life, or simply lied. On more than one occasion my remarks would prove to be uncannily prescient. A reporter would ask me what my future plans were and I'd say, "I'd like to be out of the business by the age of thirty. I want to marry and have children, and having a career at that point would be incompatible with motherhood and family life. Besides, if I were touring, then my husband would be at home, and what kind of life would that be? Who, after all, would want to be known as Mr. Anne Murray?" Which more or less is exactly what happened to Bill, with painful consequences for both of us and our children.

Apart from my second, sold-out, ten-night run at the Royal York's Imperial Room, I was seldom able to enjoy my new home that fall. I made the first of many trips to the Country Music Awards show in Nashville, sharing a dressing room with seven other ladies, including Loretta Lynn, Dolly Parton and Sarah Ophelia Colley Cannon, better known as the irrepressible Minnie Pearl, a country music legend then fifty-nine years old. You could have choked on the room's air, so thick was it with the fumes of hairspray for their bouffant-style dos. They were all fun-loving women, particularly Minnie, who at one point exclaimed in her colourful Tennessee accent, "My God, Dolly, you've got big tits!" Later I sang backstage with Mel Tillis and Merle Haggard, my all-time favourite dyed-in-the-wool country singer. He had a voice that could make me melt. Now *that* was fun.

I seemed to be flying back and forth to Los Angeles every other week. Neither the executives at Capitol nor my manager, Nick Sevano, nor the good folks at William Morris could quite get a handle on me. They couldn't understand why, with a gold record in my hip pocket and the rich cornucopia of the American dream within relatively easy reach, I wasn't leaping at the opportunity to move to the United States. It wasn't that I couldn't have an American career if I didn't, they assured me. I could and I would. It was just that by staying in the Great White North I'd be living at one remove (one too many) from where the real action was—the hot record producers, the happening songwriters, the cool talk-show hosts (with their record-buying audiences) and their bookers, the nonstop party throwers—the self-nourishing, incestuous community that determined and manufactured so much of America's pop-culture diet.

I think Nick and the others were just perplexed that an otherwise rational showbiz personality was prepared to bite the hand so willing to feed it. Canada might be a nice spot for a vacation, but live there? with its nine-month winters? They just didn't get it. What they failed to understand was just how deeply rooted was my Canadian sensibility. It wasn't an expression of political nationalism—not remotely. It was more about inherent values and lifestyle and, as always, family. I'd compromised for necessity's sake by moving to Toronto. But that's where I drew the line—at the forty-ninth parallel (iron-ically, the name of the bar at Chicago's O'Hare Airport, where, the moment our connecting flight landed, my band members would repair for the first of too many drinks). Canada was non-negotiable, and if sacrificing fortune or time or travel convenience was the cost of that decision, so it would be. Moving to the States was discussed, and discussed fre-quently, because they repeatedly brought it up—particularly when a new single was released that failed to meet our col-lective expectations—but it was never an option. Unwilling to deal with Sevano's pressure, I would have Leonard Rambeau run interference for me, effectively taking myself out of the discussion. Not the most productive way to run a business—having an assistant and manager talking without the act involved—but that's what I did to avoid the chorus demand-ing that I get a green card and live in L.A.

On one point, however, the Americans did—to my mind, at least—have a leg up. They knew nothing about me, nothing about Nova Scotia, very little about Canada. Their ignorance was astonishing, so much so that I made a point of taking promotional tourism flyers with me on trips to L.A. and handing them out. But where people in Toronto tended to deride Maritimers as second-class citizens, the poor cousins of Confederation, and to snicker a little at my association with *Singalong Jubilee*, the Americans had no preconceived ideas. They didn't care where I came from. They judged me on one thing and one thing only: could I sing? That was all they cared about. And in a sense, professionally at least, that was all I cared about too.

CHAPTER FOUR

As the new year dawned, I was moving sideways—quite literally. It was New Year's Day 1972, and I was standing on an elaborate Province of Nova Scotia *Bluenose* float, named for the famous fishing and racing schooner, in the annual Rose Bowl parade. I stood there for the next three hours or more, occasionally lip synching to "Snowbird," which blared from speakers every few minutes—a form of sonic torture, as any song played so many times would be. Waving to the crowds and cameras that lined the streets of Pasadena (and 110 million TV viewers), I thus had a continuous sensation of moving sideways. When I finally disembarked, I actually found it difficult to walk forward. I hoped it was not an omen for my career.

On that L.A. visit I squeezed in another Glen Campbell taping, an appearance on a Danny Thomas special and a visit with Johnny Carson on the *Tonight Show*. Bill was with me, and afterwards we stole away for what we hoped would be a precious week's vacation in Puerto Vallarta, Mexico. That first night we went out for dinner, and the gastrointestinal gods strenuously disapproved of Bill's choices. He spent the better part of our planned romantic interlude in bed, too weak to move. Almost no one knew we were there, of course; in Catholic terms we were still "living in sin." Unable to talk about my personal life without lying, I said nothing—a silence that had begun to puzzle my mother. She later wrote me a disturbing letter saying that she felt she hardly knew me anymore.

From Mexico I flew to New York for a David Frost show, then back to L.A. for two more Campbell *Goodtime Hours* and finally home to Toronto to record a new album, *Annie*, my sixth for Capitol. The material was at once strong and eclectic, ranging from a wonderful Robbie McNeill tune, "Robbie's Song for Jesus," to Paul Anka's powerful ballad "Everything's Been Changed" to Paul Grady's "You Can't Go Back." The album was then, and still remains, one of my favourites. I suggested in interviews that it was that spirit of eclecticism that was missing from the duets album with Glen Campbell; he was unquestionably a great singer but he liked the straight-ahead material. In retrospect I can see that my immaturity was again showing. Apart from the generosity he showed to me, Glen was then one of the hottest musical properties in show business. He'd sold millions of records—there was nothing wrong with his judgment.

Unfortunately the search for a second hit single remained elusive; "Robbie's Song for Jesus," the single chosen from the album, did no better than the five previous releases. Nor did the next one, "Cotton Jenny," a song written by Gordon Lightfoot. I'd long been an admirer of his songwriting skills and decided to let him know, going backstage after one of his appearances in Saint John. His assistant announced my presence outside his door, saying, "Anne Murray is here and would like to say hello."

And then Gordon barked, "I don't care who the fuck it is, I'm not seeing 'em."

I beat a hasty retreat. Years later I told that story to Gordon at an awards show and he laughed. "Yup, back then I probably would have said exactly that."

I could be cranky too, and must have complained loudly about my workload. In an interview with *Chatelaine* magazine that month, Leonard Rambeau predicted I'd be out of the business entirely within a year, except for recording—a clear indication of how much I hated the travel. A lovely fantasy— quitting, that is—but only that. We had no idea how much would have to go into building a real career.

But I was learning. The next month I flew to Europe for a largely promotional tour (television, radio, press, etc.) organized by Capitol/EMI. In Belgium this included a TV show on which I was joined by Julio Iglesias, then a rising star on the Continent. He was just twenty-eight years old, handsome and quite obviously interested in women. I was no exception. Proposing to start with dinner, he left me with a clear impression of his amorous aspirations for the evening. He was eventually persuaded to take no for an answer, but only reluctantly. I then forgot all about him, even his name, and when he later soared to international acclaim (selling 300 million albums in fourteen languages, making him among the ten top-selling artists of all time), I never connected him to our brief encounter in Brussels. But he remembered. Some twenty years later Julio was a guest (with Patti LaBelle and Andrea Martin) on a CBC special I hosted at Disney World, and he good-naturedly reminded me of that long-ago afternoon in Belgium and of my stinging rejection. Julio was to be the first of a few celebrities who seemed quite intent on getting to know me better, even after I was married to Bill.

Then it was on to Stockholm, where I was hosting an Anne Murray special on Swedish television. Actually I was hosting myself; there were no other performers. It was a live broadcast and I was working for the first time with a Swedish orchestra—in short, a very unnerving experience. Afterwards the show's producer and director suggested we absorb some local colour, so we repaired to Le Chat Noir, a live sex club— my first such visit but not my last. Our small group was all women, but the rest of the patrons were Japanese men, quite visibly intent on the stage performance. To reach our seats we had to briefly obscure their view as we crossed the room in front of the stage, on which, under suitably suggestive lighting, a young couple was gymnastically entangled. I knew I wasn't in Springhill anymore.

On the next stop, Paris, I did something I had never done before, or since: I deliberately missed a show. It was a television special shot in the Paris Opera House, and its production was so chaotic that I became unnerved. When it was my turn to perform, I simply failed to appear, hiding somewhere in the vast maze of corridors backstage. Later I apologized profusely and said I'd gotten lost. I'm not sure I ever told Leonard what had really happened.

The North American leg of our 1972 tour began at the Brown Shoe in Chicago, where, on successive nights, the club flooded in a rainstorm and then, a few hours before the next show, the band's instruments were stolen. No music shop was prepared to rent quality gear to travelling troubadours, so we were left to scrounge.

Our next stop was the Bitter End in New York, the basement coffee-shop-turned-celebrated-nightclub that has hosted such legends as Woody Allen, Peter, Paul and Mary, Etta James, Bill Cosby, Kris Kristofferson and Carly Simon. Considering that I was hissed at by a few cranky hippies, and considering that Pat Riccio, my new keyboard player, was enjoying his first acid trip on opening night, we did okay, eliciting a strong notice in the *New York Times*. (To be fair to Pat, that first trip, facilitated by the phenomenal jazz guitarist Lenny Breau, scared him so much that he never did acid again.) We dubbed the band Richard, which was Skip Beckwith's actual given name, and one that allowed us to make all sorts of off-colour jokes about the familiar short form of the name.

Guitarist Lenny Breau replaced Miles Wilkinson, who became our full-time sound man. Breau was a genuine prodigy. He started learning the instrument at eight; by fourteen he was lead guitar in his parents' country band and by fifteen had recorded his first album. His playing fused half a dozen musical styles—among them jazz, Indian, country and classical—and he was acknowledged a genius by no less than Chet Atkins, a pretty mean finger-picker himself, to say the least. Lenny routinely played riffs that left people in awe, both at their sheer musical conception and at their execution.

But Lenny came at a high price: a serious drug dependency, and after the heroin incident in Vancouver with the other band members, I had been nervous about taking him on. He assured us, however—and Skip Beckwith assured me—that he was clean. His subsequent conduct clearly required a new definition of *clean*. When he went through U.S. Customs, the officer asked Lenny to explain some stickers of frogs pasted onto pieces of paper in his briefcase.

"Oh, my daughter made them for me," he explained. "A going-away present."

It turned out that each sticker was a tab of acid, and he put them to extensive use during the tour. Some years later Chet Atkins quoted me in a book about Breau as saying that Lenny had been responsible for turning my band on to drugs. That's a misquote. It was only Pat that Lenny introduced to acid.

Musically, Lenny was everything he was billed to be, and then some. But his drug habit was out of control. Once, in a hotel elevator in Atlanta, he accidentally got his head stuck between the doors just as they were closing.

"Hey, cool, man," he said. "Oh, wow. Check this out." And then he stood there for what seemed like forever, letting the doors bang repeatedly against his head.

Boing . . .

"Oh, wow . . . that is so cool."

Boing . . .

He might have stayed there all night if we hadn't dragged him out.

It was a blistering day in Atlanta, so we all repaired to the hotel pool. Lenny never actually swam; he simply paced back and forth in the shallow end, his hands always up out of the water, lest it soften his string-picking fingernails. He kept his palms facing his face, staring off into space—quite an unusual sight. Later he decided to get a tan; he was out there for hours, without sunscreen, and burnt himself the colour of lobster.

On another occasion, between shows in Fort Worth, Texas, Lenny helped himself to fifty tablets of Valium that belonged to my drummer, Andy Cree, who was still recovering from his own heroin addiction. After the second show the EMI people took us all out for dinner and, not surprisingly,

Lenny could barely stay awake. When the entrée arrived, his face fell right into the food. We managed to rouse him for a time, but when they brought dessert, he collapsed again, this time putting his nose into a bowl of ice cream. The others dragged him to his room.

There was one song in the show during which Lenny had a solo, an opportunity every night to showcase his brilliance. One night, at Paul's Mall in Boston, instead of brilliance, there was silence. I turned around and, sure enough, there was Lenny playing his heart out, eyes closed and fingers flying. The difference on this night was that both his hands were an inch off the guitar, dancing in space as he played the most amazing air solo ever performed. It's not for nothing that he once said, "The sound of silence is intense."

Lenny was sweet and had a smile that could melt butter, but he was rather like a child; someone always needed to look after him. He was high all the time. I'm not sure why he came on the road with us. Perhaps he needed the money or perhaps he was just filling in a hole in his schedule; he left the band after about a year. For all the anxiety he provoked and for all the drugs he used, he was cleaner with us than he was before or for years after. A decade later his body was found floating in another swimming pool—his own, in Los Angeles. But whether he committed suicide, overdosed or, as the coroner maintained, was strangled remains unknown. A tragic loss of an enormous talent.

And it wasn't just Lenny. Other band members were casually immersed in the flourishing drug culture. According to Pat Riccio, record company reps in virtually every major city turned up to welcome the musicians with not only handshakes but ready access to weed or cocaine—just enough to keep them happy without threatening the concert. I fretted over it, worried about the possible effect of the drugs on their performance and, by implication, on mine. But, while there certainly were occasions when they were high on alcohol or drugs on stage, it seldom affected the show.

One occasion when it did involved the late Don Thompson—or, as we affectionately knew him, D.T.—my saxophonist and flutist. Don, a great musician and a gentle, amusing soul, was a serious drinker, and I often wondered what condition he would be in when he showed up. D.T. was able to play the saxophone no matter how much he'd had to drink. But the flute is a more delicate instrument, requiring real breath and mouth muscle control. I could tell from his flute playing just how much he'd had to drink.

One night in Greensboro, North Carolina, D.T. was pretty far gone. He'd spent the afternoon drinking—a full bottle of Tullamore Dew Irish whiskey (with no food)—and was staggering by the time we went onstage. During one number he was trying to play the flute but had somehow managed to get it caught up in his glasses, which were perched lopsidedly on his head. I turned to Skip Beckwith and said, "Get him offstage—now." D.T. lurched towards where the stairs had been attached to the stage for rehearsal. But they'd been taken away, so when he stepped down, there was nothing there. He fell right off, landing on Warren Baker, our new stage manager, who had come to rescue him—it was Warren's first day on the job. The audience laughed and then wildly applauded his exit, while I tried to make light of it, saying something like "Well, I guess we know what he had for dinner." Escorted backstage by Greensboro's finest, D.T. later became maudlin and contrite. I had intended to fire him, but he tearfully begged my forgiveness, and I granted it and kept him on.

D.T. didn't restrict himself to alcohol. On his farm north of Toronto he grew marijuana (illegally, of course), harvesting the crop for his own and friends' use in grades known as Uxbridge one, two, three and four. Number four, though mild, was the most potent, and he occasionally packed it in his suitcases, at least on domestic trips. Once during a night off in Winnipeg, we were all graciously invited to a party at the palatial home of the Richardsons, one of the city's most respected families. I was nervous about having "the boys" along—and with good reason. Shortly after arrival, D.T. and Andy Cree, drinks in hand, made their way to the billiards room to shoot a few rounds of snooker while someone escorted me and others on a tour of the home. When we reached Andy and D.T., I noticed a smouldering marijuana joint propped none too carefully on the lip of what must have been a very expensive pool table. I just about died. D.T. clearly sensed my alarm, because he promptly put the entire thing in his mouth and swallowed it.

D.T.'s mother lived in Winnipeg, so naturally we had invited her along. She was a little rough around the edges and, like Don, she clearly enjoyed a sip now and then. It seemed to sharpen her natural sense of humour. Among the evening's other guests were my old *Singalong* friend Catherine McKinnon and her husband, actor, writer and raconteur Don Harron.

"So," proclaimed D.T.'s mother, when she was introduced to the couple. "You're the one who finally got into Catherine McKinnon!"

Feeling somewhat responsible for my little entourage, I was mortified.

His mom might have had a few too many sips, however. On the ride back to the hotel, she sat in the back seat, moaning a little. "Don," she said at last. "Suddenly I don't think I feel so goo—" And before the sentence was finished, she proceeded to vomit all over the back seat. Alas, the ejection took with it her set of false teeth.

But she knew how to find the comedy in the moment. "Oh, damn," she said, or words to that effect. "Now I've lost my teeth." At which point she reached down into the expelled soup, fished around for a minute and came up with the dentures.

"Ah," she exclaimed. "Found 'em!" and proceeded to click them back into place.

Drunk or sober (which he was some of the time), D.T. had a terrific sense of humour. One day we arrived in Minot, North Dakota, in the middle of winter. The snow was piled two or three elephants high, the wind was howling and it was—no exaggeration—about minus 50° Celsius (–58° F). The next morning we tramped downstairs together for breakfast and the waitress said, "So, are you-all here with the sales group or something?"

And D.T. promptly shot back, "No, we're here for the golf tournament."

The irony was rich. Here I was, toasted back home as the wholesome, virginal, perpetually airbrushed girl-next-door, and I was touring America with a cadre of drug users and abusers. I complained to Bill and to Leonard, but we all knew there wasn't really anything we could do. I paid their salaries and I chose the playlist, and that was the full extent of my control.

By the summer of 1972 I was finally beginning to understand—if not come to terms with—the life that fate had dealt me. I was lonely and tired. My privacy was constantly being invaded. I was in love with a married man whom I seldom saw. I owned a beautiful home with a swimming pool but slept most nights in strange hotel rooms. I had no one close to me to confide in or hang out with. I was touring with a group of musicians who at any moment were at risk of being arrested. Again I felt like Dorothy in *The Wizard of Oz*, a young woman plucked from the anonymity of small-town Canada and thrust onto an international sound stage. I was carrying and feeling the considerable weight of my crown as Canada's de facto queen of pop culture. What I wanted most to do was just stop and go home, but it wasn't possible. I had commitments and obligations as far as the eye could see.

Later that year, the two Capitols—in Toronto and Los Angeles—would convene in a special session to discuss the Anne Murray question—was she a pop artist, a country artist, a crossover artist or all of the above? I had always resisted easy compartmentalization. I wasn't, nor did I want to be, simply a country singer or a folksinger or a pop singer. I wanted to be able to record and perform songs from all of those genres without feeling that I was somehow at risk of alienating my audience. Why assume that the audience wouldn't demonstrate the same eclectic taste in music? Why couldn't the music of Bob Dylan coexist with the music of Merle Haggard, Neil Diamond and Carole King? I think the verdict of that meeting was country/pop, and they all came away with renewed determination to find a new hit single. But it didn't happen right away.

Indeed, almost two years after "Snowbird" I was beginning to question whether I'd ever have a hit record again. I could remember all sorts of trailblazers with that dubious one-hit-wonder distinction—including the Jarmels, for a song

I'd sung in university ("A Little Bit of Soap"), Frank Ifield ("I Remember You"), Don and Juan ("What's Your Name?") and Barbara George ("I Know," a rock 'n' roll classic that became a staple on my playlist). One song and then they were all consigned to pop music history and pub night trivia contests. Would that be my destiny too?

THAT FALL I WENT OUT with the band on my first tour in the United States. I had done tours across Canada, but aside from the success of "Snowbird," I was far from a household name south of the border, and I didn't know whether anybody would show up. We were booked into smaller clubs such as Paul's Mall in Boston, the Bitter End in New York and the New World Club in Atlanta. It was during this tour that I looked around and noticed that a significant number in the audience were gay women. Of course, I wasn't the first female recording artist to attract a lesbian following; singers such as Helen Reddy, Peggy Lee, Rosemary Clooney and others had experienced the same thing.

You have to remember that it was a time of enormous social ferment. By this point the women's movement was in full flower, and across North America the gay/lesbian movement was just beginning to express its identity as it had never been able to before. A few years later I received a letter from a fan whose explanation for the phenomenon seemed credible to me. Gay women were looking for strong, independent, approachable women as role models, and I definitely fit that bill. I've always been very grateful to these women that they showed up, and a lot of them have been among my most devoted fans ever since. Without them, the clubs during that tour would not have been nearly as full as they were.

I have always enjoyed being able to meet fans when I am on the road, but that tour put me in some pretty close quarters. At the Atlanta club I shared the washroom with the club's patrons; at one point I found myself parked in a cubicle while some rather assertive women thrust pens and paper under the door, demanding my autograph. At another club, later on the tour, a few gay women aggressively followed me backstage after a show. My music director, Pat Riccio, intervened and persuaded them to leave. At another venue a large group of lesbians got roaring drunk during the opening act—the wonderful folk/country singer John Prine—and by the time I took the stage they were downright rowdy. I do like a lively audience—and for the most part these women are the ones who lift up the show because they're so enthusiastic and very vocal—but that night they were disruptive. To their credit, several of them called the club the next day to apologize.

Later, at a hotel in Baton Rouge, Louisiana, I was given a ground-floor room with a patio that connected to the parking lot. One afternoon I was stunned to see two burly women on bikes drive their motorcycles right up to the threshold of my sliding patio door. They dismounted, whipped off their helmets and demanded my autograph. "Yes indeed!" I said, and signed. There was no way I was going to argue with them.

Certainly the most brazen incident occurred one cold March night in Lacrosse, Wisconsin. On the road with the band, we'd often book a row of rooms with connecting doors, to facilitate socializing. The boys typically roomed together and I was alone. That night Pat Riccio, who was quite drunk at the time, came to me and asked if I'd mind if he crashed in my room; his roommate, he explained, had found a young woman to get close to for what remained of the evening, and Pat didn't want to be the third wheel. I said yes—we were all like brothers and sisters in any case, and there were separate beds. He fell down on the bed and passed out instantly. I watched TV for a while and then drifted off, only to wake some time later to find a body beside me in bed.

Oh, no, you don't, Pat, I thought. But when I jumped out of bed, I discovered that it was not Pat at all, but a teenage girl, no more than eighteen. She had made a connection with Stephen Lewis, the show's production manager, and after sweet-talking her way into his room, which adjoined mine, she'd managed to crawl into bed beside me—apparently her objective all along.

I said to her, "You get out of my bed right now. Get out of here. I'm going to the bathroom, and when I come out, I want you gone."

She started crying and protesting; she was drunk too. I went to the bathroom, and when I came out, she was gone. Pat had slept through all of it.

Afterwards I gave Steve Lewis a choice piece of my mind for allowing this to happen. But when you're on the road with the same people day after day, you have to put such incidents behind you, and we did.

I wasn't alone in noticing my legion of gay fans. *Rolling Stone* magazine later wrote about Anne Murray's burgeoning sub-demographic as well. In those years I no doubt encouraged my lesbian fan base by always having to be coy, if not deceitful, about my relationship with Bill. That silence inevitably fuelled speculation about my own sexual orientation. In fact,

Dusty Springfield told me once that she'd been in a bar in Vancouver where they insisted that I was gay.

"Well, I'm not," I told her.

"Gosh," she said, "they're going to be very disappointed."

⁓

"PEOPLE KEEP TELLING ME, 'You'll never be able to stop.' And I disagree. I'll never stop singing. But I don't have to sing in front of people."

I actually said those words, to a Southam news service reporter in December 1972. What was I thinking? That it was possible to have a career without having to perform in front of a live audience? I'd spent the last few months of that year doing promotional tours, award shows and a TV special for the CBC—in short, very few large live audiences. Apparently I thought I could continue doing it that way. What I was describing was my career as I would have liked it to be. Reality was something else. Somewhere inside I knew it, but I was clearly having trouble admitting it.

A few days after that interview I went back to Springhill for a traditional family Christmas. Summer or winter, going home was always a tonic. It was a restorative place where I could shed the larger persona that had enveloped me and return to being my former, more unguarded self. Christmas with the Murray family was very traditional: carols around the piano (accompanied by guitars), midnight Mass at church on Christmas Eve, followed by a meal of roasted partridge— a delicacy personally shot by Dad or one of my brothers. Mom always baked up a storm—shortbread cookies with maple frosting, chocolate strip cookies and roly-polies, a kind

of pinwheel made with biscuit dough, brown sugar and cin-
namon. As children we'd usually find thirty bottles of fresh
milk laid in to quench our thirst after the run on cookies. Dena
concocted her own brand of high-fizz root beer, properly
bottled and capped, and made molasses candies. There'd be a
tree, of course, which Dad would have cut down himself. He
usually left that chore to the last minute, venturing out at the
end of the day and, unable to see very clearly, cutting down
the tree closest to the road, often a scrawny fir soon to be the
subject of some derision.

"Carson!" Mom would bellow when he returned with
the sickly tree. "What were you thinking?"

"Pardon?"

Our tree decoration efforts weren't exactly worthy of a
Christmas catalogue either. Sometimes we had to fill the gaps
in the tree by performing branch transplants, taping or tying
them to the trunk. When we were done, it looked like everyone had stood back and just thrown the tinsel and other
baubles at it.

⁓

ALMOST AS SOON AS I HEARD IT IN 1971, I wanted to
record "Danny's Song," the ballad that Kenny Loggins had
written for his older brother Danny, who had just become a
father. Loggins had recorded it with Jim Messina and, though
it wasn't a hit for them, it had received a fair bit of airplay. I
loved the song itself, but I also recognized its potential to sell
on both the country and pop charts. It was one of four songs
that Brian Ahern and I recorded in Toronto in July 1972,
squeezing in studio time between other gigs. Capitol wanted

a new album from me, but new albums were best built around hit singles, and we hadn't had one of those for a while. So we thought we'd offer them a single and, if it took off, follow that with an album.

One of the other tunes was "Killing Me Softly," and its origins are interesting too. Norman Gimbel and Charles Fox wrote the song based on singer Lori Lieberman's experience of seeing Don ("American Pie") McLean in a club. She recorded it and released it as a single. I heard her version and recorded it myself. After I recorded it, we—Capitol Records and I—had to decide whether it or the Loggins track would be the new single. Since it was Lieberman's first single ever and we were on the same label, I decided to go with "Danny's Song."

Shortly thereafter, Roberta Flack recorded "Killing Me Softly" with a quite different arrangement, and she cleaned up. The song spent five weeks at number one on Billboard's Hot 100 and ultimately won three Grammys, including song of the year.

But I wasn't complaining; "Danny's Song" had confirmed my instincts. It reached the Top Ten on three Billboard charts in 1973, spending two weeks at number one on the adult contemporary chart and earning a Grammy award nomination for best female pop performance—which I lost to Roberta Flack. It was also my most successful single since "Snowbird" two and a half years earlier, and a big boost to my standing in the United States.

That wasn't the last time I failed to capitalize on a song that subsequently became a major hit. A few years later I decided not to record "I Honestly Love You"; somehow it didn't feel quite right for me. The song-choosing exercise is very subjective, and in the end you have to please yourself before you please others. So the song eventually went to Olivia Newton-John, who made it a number-one hit and sold two million copies.

"Danny's Song" became the title track of my next album, half of which was recorded live over a three-night concert booking at the National Arts Centre in Ottawa. For those performances, I remember wearing the same outfit I had worn in the Rose Bowl parade. It was a red and black number with very wide palazzo pants. That day in Pasadena, I had somehow managed to rip the hem with the heel of my shoe, and being the seamstress that I am, patched it up with masking tape night after night on the road. One night, leaving the theatre after a performance, my friend Nancy Webster overheard two people talking about the show.

"I wonder why she wears those big wide pants," said the first person.

"Oh," said the second, making a sweeping circle with her arms, "she has *huge* legs!"

Ripped or intact, I was beginning to develop more confidence in talking to the audience between songs. The self-deprecatory approach, so much a part of my upbringing, worked well for me. One of the lines that received a big laugh in Ottawa and elsewhere was "But I want you people to know that, under these wonderful clothes and behind this 'girl next door' façade, this body is a mass of hickeys." I had stolen the joke from Jackie Vernon, whose comedy act I'd seen on television.

I used it a few times after that, not realizing that joke theft is a capital offence among comedians. A few years later Rodney Dangerfield opened for me at the Riviera in Las Vegas. Rodney was a lovely man—one of those comics who did not feel it necessary to be "on" at every waking moment. One day he said to me, "You know, Anne, the thing I hate most in this business is when people steal your material and use it without credit." By then I had forgotten where the hickey line came from and thought I might have stolen it from Rodney. Fortunately I had not used it during those performances, and after that friendly sermon I never used it or anyone else's lines again without giving credit.

After Ottawa I returned to Toronto's Massey Hall, this time supported not only by the band Richard but also by six string members of the city's symphony orchestra and four extraordinary backup singers: Brenda Russell, Laurel Ward, Joanne Brooks and Joanne's mother, Dianne—a surprise guest. Among my theatrical props there was a camera, so I could take pictures of the audience, and a pair of opera glasses for close-up surveillance. The glasses were from Le Chat Noir, the live sex club in Stockholm.

Then it was off to the Great White North for a long-planned tour of the Canadian Arctic—ten cities in twelve days. Expecting frigid temperatures, we'd arranged through Conservative Party leader Robert Stanfield for a supply of industrial-strength underwear. In Truro, Nova Scotia, Stanfield's family owned the largest underwear-manufacturing facility in the country, and I'd seen him during my stay in Ottawa. His undies were lifesavers in Churchill, Manitoba, where it was a bone-numbing minus 40°, but redundant by the time we reached Whitehorse, Yukon, where it was an unseasonably warm 15.5° Celsius (60° F).

In Inuvik we performed in Our Lady of Victory Roman Catholic Church, a round, igloo-shaped structure. Later we went for dinner to a restaurant that had one of the most extensive menus I'd ever seen. They had everything, all frozen and flown in. One of the items was a chicken dish prepared, it said, in the cordon bleu style.

"Is that the same cordon bleu that I know?" I asked the waitress.

"Well, I don't know what it tastes like," she replied, deadpan, "but it looks like a cow-pie."

How appetizing. I laughed for days after that.

After one show in Churchill, I was chatting with a couple of teachers who were married to each other.

"Do you live here?" I asked.

"Yes, but not for long," one of them explained. "We just want to earn a little money—the isolation-pay premium—and then go back south."

"And how long have you been here?"

"Nineteen years."

What I loved most about those remote northern communities such as Inuvik, Churchill, Flin Flon and several others was exactly what was missing for me in Las Vegas—a sense of realness. Life up there reminded me in many ways of the Maritimes: daily existence was just too damned hard to get away with pretence and phoniness. Most performers seldom bothered to take their acts to these places. The audiences were small, so the money was never an incentive; the venues weren't as well equipped as the kind to which they were accustomed; and the travel logistics were challenging. Thus, when I showed up with the band and Nova Scotia folksinger John Allen Cameron, accompanied by CBC Radio and a separate documentary film crew (their footage was later turned into a TV special), the northerners gave us a royal welcome. They tended to be quite reserved during the actual performance, then exploded with applause when it was over. And their gratitude was overwhelming; at every stop I was showered with gifts—a red Inuit parka, gorgeous soapstone sculptures, a plaque with a collection of twenty gold-tipped spoons. I'd never seen anything like it and never did afterwards. By going north I'd passed up opportunities to exploit the success of "Danny's Song" in the U.S., but I was glad I had. I have seldom felt more relaxed in front of a crowd.

That northern trip was no sooner over than I had to fly to L.A. to record my first song for a Hollywood film—"Send a Little Love My Way," by Henry Mancini and Hal David. The film was *Oklahoma Crude*, starring George C. Scott and Faye Dunaway. Director Stanley Kramer had originally wanted a man to sing the song because it is the Dunaway character who hears it repeatedly. But Mancini suggested doing the unexpected, and Kramer eventually agreed. Even then he wasn't initially sold on hiring me to sing it. Again Mancini persisted, and Kramer later became one of my biggest fans.

I'd heard the song before I knew that it was the theme for a movie set at the turn of the century, and initially it didn't feel right for me. But then Capitol applied some pressure ("What do you mean you don't want to do it? It'll be good for your career!") and Mancini himself called to encourage me, so I agreed. Brian tinkered a little with Mancini's arrangement, not without some qualms, changing the chord structure here and there and adding a harmonica line. Then we took it with us to L.A. and crossed our fingers. Brian was so nervous that he buttonholed Mancini in the hotel lobby just to explain what he'd done before we played it to him. Mancini reserved judgment, but both he and David loved the results. Later that year Brian and I flew to Tulsa for the gala premiere. The song was nominated for both an Oscar and a Golden Globe, losing each time to "The Way We Were."

BACK IN TORONTO, I received a call one day from a CBC friend. Benny Goodman, the great jazz musician and band-leader, was in town and looking for a private place to swim. Could he use my pool? Of course, I said. So Benny arrived, and he had never heard of me.

"They tell me you're a singer," he said.

"That's right."

"What kind of music do you sing?"

"Well, it's hard to explain," I said. "Several kinds, I guess. Folk, pop, country, a little rock now and then."

"Where can I listen to it?"

"In the basement."

"Well, let's go."

So I took him down to the basement and put on "Killing Me Softly."

"What is that?" Goodman said. "That's music for a dentist's office."

One strike against me. So then I tried "I Know," an uptempo rock number.

"That's a *little* better," he said.

Finally I put on "Snowbird," which to my astonishment he had never heard, or even heard of.

"Now that's a good song," he said. "I like that one."

That fall I returned to Atlantic Canada for what was billed as a seven-city homecoming tour, my first appearances there since "Snowbird." Over two weeks (seventeen concerts) the shows grossed $90,000 and sold out every venue save Saint John, New Brunswick. I mention the box office only because the profit after costs would have been minimal and because our ticket prices ($4.50 to $5.50) elicited some critical comment. One local newspaper editorial suggested that success must have gone to my head for me to be "milking the public" with such exorbitant rates. In fact these prices were in keeping with what Canadians elsewhere were paying for concerts, and well below what patrons in London, Las Vegas and other cities had paid. Another critic roasted me for wearing a dress and talking to the audience, as if I should be condemned to eternally wearing blue jeans and just singing and strumming my guitar.

One day a fan in Fredericton approached me for a photograph. "Gee," he said. "I remember when I used to be able to hear you sing here for nothing."

"Well," I said, "when you could hear me sing for nothing, that's about what I was worth. Now I'm worth at least $4.50."

But going home was also an emotional high. At virtually every stop I was performing in front of family, old friends from university, teachers and students from Athena High School, colleagues from *Singalong Jubilee* and other CBC shows in Halifax. Despite those occasional critical broadsides, I felt secure about my Canadian base—and a lot less so about my stature in the U.S. For some time it had been apparent to Leonard and me that we had a management problem. I'd retained Nick Sevano largely because of the Glen Campbell/Capitol Records connection, and while I liked him personally, I never felt that he understood me very well. He seemed to be prepping me for the Vegas/Tahoe circuit, maintaining that there was no audience for my music on college campuses. I wasn't convinced. And I wasn't sure he was working hard enough to create the demand.

And money was becoming an issue. I had reached the saturation point in Canada—there was only so much Anne Murray that even largely supportive Canadians could tolerate—but my gigs abroad weren't yielding enough to cover expenses. When I'd accompanied Glen to Europe that spring—playing as his opening act in Dublin, Manchester, Newcastle, Bournemouth, Birmingham, Frankfurt (Germany) and London (the Palladium and Royal Festival Hall)—I think I earned $10,000 for the whole two-week trip, and that included the band's fees. At one point Glen suggested that we take our show on the road again that summer, playing heartland America.

"I can't, Glen," I said. "I can't afford it."

When I told him what I was being paid, he was appalled, and quickly made arrangements to substantially raise my fee for the summer concerts.

But I decided not to do those summer concerts. It was time to test my own wings and emerge from Glen's considerable shadow. Artistically I was beginning to drift away from his musical orbit. I believed that I could be a headliner and command the same kind of audiences as he did.

And so that summer Leonard and I finally decided to sever our relationship with both Sevano and William Morris, my booking agency. Leonard had been in place at Balmur for only two years and wasn't ready, he felt, to assume full managerial responsibilities. So we started to look around, and through Brian Ahern we were introduced to a tall, bearded, shaggy-haired young man named Shep Gordon.

Raised on Long Island, Gordon had moved to L.A. after university and infiltrated the burgeoning rock music scene. In no time at all he'd become the manager for Alice Cooper, then a five-member heavy metal band that provocatively shattered all the norms of traditional entertainment. On stage they wore makeup and women's clothes—no rock group had done that before—hacked up baby dolls with axes, conducted mock executions with guillotines and once threw a live chicken into a group of paraplegics at a concert in Toronto. Their offstage tactics were no less brazen: at one point Cooper (né Vincent Furnier) posed for *Rolling Stone* with a boa constrictor wrapped around his penis.

That wholesome, apple-cheeked Annie would even consort with, let along engage, a manager whose stock in trade was orchestrating sexual and other perversions must have seemed bizarre, if not scandalous. Well, welcome to show business. Shep Gordon was a modern-day P.T. Barnum with a kit bag full of conjuring tricks and a mind attuned to the ever-changing needs of the musical marketplace. We wanted more attention than we were getting, and we were convinced that Shep could make that happen.

Thus, in August 1973 we signed a five-year contract with his Alive Enterprises. Soon after I found a new booking agent as well: Fred Lawrence, then with CMA. As a Hollywood type, Fred came directly from central casting; he was flashy, but in a classic way—dapper and natty, always dressed meticulously and taking pride in it—and always ready with a facile quip or phrase. When we came offstage after a show, he'd often say to each of the band guys, "Home run, pal." He was Leonard Rambeau's polar opposite in style, but opposites attract, and they got along famously.

Fred genuinely liked my music and worked hard for me for the next twenty-two years.

Management wasn't the only thing that changed. If I was going to alter my image, the old bohemian, girl-next-door look would have to be jettisoned. Henceforth the barefoot contessa, as my friend the journalist (and later CBC executive producer) George Anthony liked to call me, would be shod and properly dressed, even occasionally gowned. Through the ever-resourceful Brian Ahern I met Patric Reeves-Aaron, a talented clothing designer then living in Toronto with her two children, including a nine-year-old son, Keanu Reeves (yes, that Keanu Reeves). Bill would often accompany me to fitting sessions in her studio, and while we nipped and tucked, he and Keanu would play chess. Patric had impressive credentials. She'd worked with Liza Minnelli and Barbra Streisand in New York and was then also designing for Dolly Parton. Soon I had a new $50,000 wardrobe, full of painted silks and satins and classy crushed velvets; among my favourites were hand-painted silk overalls. Somehow Patric found a way to dress me up in a way that would have pleased my mother without entirely erasing the Anne Murray I had been. She was expensive, but worth every dollar; she was a meticulous craftswoman and her clothes fit me better than any I had ever worn or would wear in the future.

Shep, meanwhile, demonstrated his promotional prowess soon enough. In November of that year I was booked to play the Troubadour in Los Angeles on the American Thanksgiving weekend. The whole thing was orchestrated with his signature panache: colonial foot soldiers at the door, a faux Pocahontas to welcome guests and hand out snuff and a copy of my latest single, and a lavish feast—served by Indians and Pilgrims—that included tables teeming with turkey, spareribs,

Danish cured ham, sweet potatoes, corn, nuts, fruit and two hundred gallons of wine and eggnog.

On opening night Shep's magic ensured the presence of Helen Reddy, John Lennon, Harry Nilsson (a vocal and musical genius who just might be my favourite male vocalist ever), ex-Monkee Micky Dolenz and Alice Cooper; an entourage of press and paparazzi trailed in their wake. Sans Helen, the five of us posed for a historic photograph: the chaste Canadian snowbird surrounded by some of the baddest boys in rock. (It reminded me of a gig I once played in Denver where I opened for black comedian Dick Gregory. Who dreamed up that unlikely combination?) In the photo Lennon wears dark glasses and looks, as always, inscrutable, Nilsson rests his bearded chin on my shoulder, and a smiling Dolenz gazes vacantly upwards as though he might be high. In fact they were all well lubricated by the time I arrived; I was very likely the only sober one in the group. When I got to the microphone— having just stepped out of a wooden turkey—I alluded to Shep Gordon and his fine theatrical hand, adding, "Just don't expect me to throw any live chickens from the stage."

Perhaps because of the occasion's patriotic overtones, everyone was reasonably well behaved. But you couldn't depend on that. Lennon was living in L.A. at the time, in temporary exile from Yoko Ono, and producing a Nilsson album, *Pussy Cats*. The two of them were deeply immersed in alcohol and drugs, and a few weeks after my appearance they were both ejected from the Troubadour for heckling the Smothers Brothers.

Later someone arranged for me to spend time with Nilsson. He came to the studio where I was recording in L.A. and I tried to talk to him, but he was unintelligible—too drunk and/or drugged. I wasn't sure he even knew who I was or where he was. When I was inducted into the Canadian Music Hall of Fame in 1992, we arranged for Nilsson to record a video tribute. He agreed, but the tape proved to be unusable. He clearly had no idea whom he was talking about, praising what he thought was my song about the Tallahatchie Bridge (actually from Bobbie Gentry's "Ode to Billie Joe"). Two years later he was dead of heart failure, just fifty-three years old.

It says something about the incredible power of images in modern life that that single group photograph suddenly made Anne Murray a hip and hot commodity. It was a sham, of course; my essential values and lifestyle had not changed one iota. It didn't matter. Every pop and rock music magazine on the planet ran that photograph, and the message it conveyed was that I was a player, a member in good standing of that elite and exclusive world. Overnight, cool DJs in key markets were suddenly spinning my music. *Rolling Stone*, for whom I had previously been a mere afterthought, suggested I might be the year's most talented exponent of pop. And the coverage wasn't confined to the music world: *Time*, *People* and other magazines all sent reporters to interview me. For a time we considered Shep a magician, and a godsend.

The single we handed out that night at the Troubadour was "A Love Song," another memorable Kenny Loggins tune. I'd been in L.A. earlier that year hosting NBC's late-night pop and rock music show *Midnight Special*—another Shep-conceived scheme to confer hipness on me. A writer friend of mine, Barb Wagstaff, called and said that Loggins was recording with Jim Messina in North Hollywood—did I want to meet them? So late one night after we'd finished taping, she picked me up and we drove over. Kenny was a sweet and very gentle guy, totally genuine. He complimented me on my version of "Danny's Song" and then I said, "You don't happen to have any others like that, do you?"

"Well, as a matter of fact . . ." he said. "Come with me." We found a quieter room and I took out my little tape recorder that I carried everywhere. Kenny picked up his guitar and started singing right there—first "A Love Song," which he'd written with his girlfriend of the time, Dona Lyn George, and then "Watching the River Run," written with Messina. I loved them both and, as Gene MacLellan had done four years earlier with "Snowbird," he gave them to me on the spot. I recorded both songs that summer and put them on the next album, intending to use them both as singles. Loggins and Messina soon released "River Run" as their own single, so we never followed up on that plan. But "A Love Song" was more than enough. It hit number five on Billboard's country singles chart, peaked at number twelve on the Hot 100, and was number one in the adult contemporary market. Oh, yes—and it earned me my first Grammy award, for best female country vocal performance.

In the studio that summer I suggested we cover a Lennon–McCartney tune, "You Won't See Me." It was always one of my favourites from their incredible canon, and I had sung it at virtually every singsong during my university days. But I was nervous about the idea. So soon after their glory years, it was no small matter to try to cover a Beatles song; in most such attempts the cover was no match for the original. In this case two things made the track sound truly original: a bass line devised by Skip Beckwith that operates like a pulsating subtext, and the backup vocal harmonies devised by

Dianne Brooks and sung by her, Laurel Ward and me. I think it was at the next Grammy awards in New York that Lennon came to my dressing room to tell me that of all the Beatles covers to that point—a goodly number—this was the best he'd ever heard. Now *that* made me feel good. And so did the result: the song reached number eight on the pop Billboard charts and number one on the adult contemporary roster. The flip side of that tune was "He Thinks I Still Care," (the old George Jones hit), which reached number one on the country charts—the first time, to my knowledge, that one side of a single went to the top of the country charts while the other side went up the top of the adult contemporary charts.

ON FRIDAY, APRIL 12, 1974, with the cherry blossoms in glorious bloom, we were playing the Lisner Auditorium in Washington, D.C. One night we were informed that someone from the White House was in the audience and wanted to see us after the show. It turned out to be Frank Gannon, a young aide to then-president Richard Nixon. The president, he told us, was a big fan of mine and wanted to invite me to lunch. Since we were in town for almost a week, we arranged a date, and a few days later we—a few Capitol/EMI people, Leonard's assistant, Judy Lynn, and I—were escorted into one of the most famous buildings in the world.

Apparently, however, I was less important than the strategic arms limitation talks then under way. When we arrived, Gannon apologized, saying that Nixon would regrettably not be attending the lunch; he was in a meeting with the Soviet foreign minister, Andrei Gromyko, and Secretary of State

Henry Kissinger. Not a bad excuse, I thought. But we did have a pleasant lunch, after which Gannon escorted us on a private tour of the White House. That included a brief stop in the Rose Garden, where Nixon, having finished with Gromyko, waved to us as he and his wife, Pat, made their way to the marine helicopter. They were headed, I think, for Key Biscayne.

During our conversations Gannon hinted to me—four months before Nixon was forced to resign in disgrace—that his boss was in deep trouble because of the break-in at Democratic Party headquarters in the Watergate Hotel, and would likely have to relinquish the presidency. Only a week or so later the White House released the tape with the incriminating eighteen-and-a-half-minute gap, one of the final nails in the impeachment coffin that Congress was constructing. All sorts of people, Gannon told me, were abandoning the White House like a sinking ship. But Gannon himself intended to stay on and go with Nixon to San Clemente, his California home, and help him write his memoirs; he saw it as an opportunity to be part of history. And he did exactly that. I thought occasionally about Gannon in the historic months that followed but eventually lost track of him. Then, in the winter of 2009, I went to see Ron Howard's powerful cinematic adaptation of the Peter Morgan play *Frost/Nixon*, based on 1977 interviews between the former president and British talk-show host David Frost. There was "Gannon" again (played by actor Andy Milder), part of Nixon's inner circle.

We never mentioned or sought publicity about that White House excursion. As Leonard told one reporter, we were doing everything we could at the time to appeal to the Nixon-haters. "We're just starting to get accepted and we don't want to blow it."

That 1974 concert tour was notable on a number of other counts. The first was that, perhaps for the first and only time in my career, the audiences were disappointing, often filling just over half the seats available. Thin turnouts are usually the fault of the local promoter, but it was unusual to have a consecutive string of them. My music was getting a fair bit of radio play in the U.S., but people told me they had heard very little about my forthcoming appearance. And the halls were too big for the status I then held. In New Orleans about 600 people turned up, a good-sized crowd, except that it was a 2,300-seat venue. They must have felt sorry for me, because they were very generous with their applause. I had nightmares over it afterwards, however.

In Jackson, Mississippi, I happened to be staying at the same hotel as Burl Ives, the American actor and folk legend. He got word to me that he wanted to meet me, so one night I knocked on his door. He greeted me dressed in bright red long johns—one-piece, complete with trapdoor—and told me that his ex-wife had recently died. She'd left him some land in Donkin, Nova Scotia, a coal-mining community not far from Sydney, and he wondered what I, a Maritime girl after all, could tell him about it. He showed me the map and I told him he couldn't go wrong in Nova Scotia, though he might want to avoid the winters.

Later that year, in August, I was booked as the headliner at the Schaefer Music Festival, which was held outdoors at the Wollman Ice Rink Theatre in New York's Central Park. Brewer and Shipley were the opening act, followed by Bruce Springsteen and the E Street Band. Boz Scaggs had been the original headliner but had pulled out, precipitating what I'm sure was a not-so-gentlemanly discussion between my

U.S. managers—Shep Gordon, Allan Strahl and Johnny Podell—and Springsteen's over which one of us owned commercial dominance and should thus receive star billing. At the time I clearly did; Bruce had released only two albums by that time and neither had sold very well.

So I became the headliner and Bruce became the middle act, with the stipulation that he be allowed an eighty-minute set. Bad decision. We should never have been paired in the first instance. Being a New Jersey boy, he had a huge following in the region, and of the five thousand in attendance, it's fair to say that at least 75 percent were there to see him. He put on a terrific show, of course, so much so that my managers tried to persuade him from the wings to end his gig early. I was reluctant to go on after that, with good reason. It was a horrendous pairing.

The *New York Times* later reported there were confrontations between our respective camps among the crowd. Springsteen continued, playing his full set, and I was placed in the horrific position of following him with who knows how many people, having heard the act they came for, streaming out before my eyes. I'm reported to have come onstage and said, "How do I follow that?" My first song was "What About Me"—an apt choice considering that, according to the *Times*, about a third of the audience had departed. But its review generously added that, faced with this impossible situation, I "came on stronger . . . Miss Murray is thoroughly professional." I never did meet Bruce but I certainly respected his ability, then and now. We just had totally different vibes.

The Springsteen encounter left me feeling a little deflated. Shep Gordon was doing his best to create a buzz around me as he had done at the Troubadour, on *Midnight Special* and elsewhere. That's what you did in the rock world. If you had genuine talent, so much the better, but he could create a stir, it seemed, for any artist, feeding the appetites of the hip and the cool. But I wasn't an event; I was a singer. And I wasn't remotely flamboyant. I just had a knack for finding good songs and a way of interpreting them in a direct, unembellished way that people responded to. Shep was often too busy to handle my account personally, handing it off to Allan Strahl. I don't think I knew then that my relationship with Shep would be shorter than we had planned, but the seed, perhaps, had already been planted.

THE BACK-TO-BACK SUCCESS of "Danny's Song" and "A Love Song" could not have come at a better time. In 1974 my five-year contract with Capitol Canada was nearing completion. After some discussion, Leonard and Lyman suggested that I move my recording relationship to Capitol in Los Angeles, which was housed in the famous Tower, an oval building near Hollywood and Vine. We'd gotten along well with Capitol's Arnold Gosewich and Paul White in Toronto (Paul, in fact, would later work for Balmur). But the L.A. office had more of everything—money, power, stars under contract. And since they were involved in every major decision concerning my albums anyway, it made more sense to deal with them directly. Other companies, aware that my contract was up, were also interested. We had hard offers from RCA and Columbia and feelers from a couple of other labels.

I was never directly involved in these or any other negotiations. I didn't have the stomach for it—nor, frankly, did

Leonard. In any *mano a mano* struggle over rights, royalties or advances, we both would have been eviscerated. Leonard was simply too nice a person to engage with the suits on the other side of the conference table. Make no mistake: Leonard was indispensable to me. He did have to be reined in from time to time, mostly for being too generous with Balmur money, and I fired him in jest dozens of times, but he was my essential buffer against the world. And he was impossible not to like. We were also in synch; we often said that we could finish each other's sentences, and we often did.

In dealing with lawyers, however, you don't want nice; you want tough. Stripped of all its artificial glitz and hype— the limousines, the fancy parties—the music industry is as governed by the bottom line as any other. If the label's lawyers can find a clever way to reduce the net payment owing to a recording artist, you can rest assured they will insert it into the contract. Several generations of performers can attest— and have, alas, been forced to attest in court—to just how crafty the lawyers can be.

But if they thought Lyman MacInnis and Dave Matheson were just a couple of rubes from rural Canada or that they could festoon my contract with all sorts of hidden fees and deductions from royalties owing, they were soon disabused of the notion. The negotiations dragged on for several weeks. In the face-to-face talks it was mainly Lyman and Dave and David Braun, an L.A. entertainment lawyer we retained for expert advice. Money issues aside, we had identified three principal objectives. First, the right to keep (as we had in Canada) complete creative control over the content of any album—the song list and the arrangements. Second, we wanted the right (again, as had been the case with Capitol in Toronto) to choose the record's producer. And third, given the hullabaloo over the failure to follow "Snowbird" with "Put Your Hand in the Hand," the right to pick the single. Capitol fought hard against all three demands; it ultimately surrendered on the first two but refused to yield on the third. The best we could do on that point was consultation—not entirely meaningless, but not the definitive vote. I didn't do badly on the money side, either. The four-year contract (for two albums a year) gave me an advance of $3 million against royalties, and a larger share of those royalties than I had previously had.

When all the major issues had been resolved, the final contract form was drafted and presented to Dave: a thirty-page document containing a long index of definitions at the back. By the time he had pored over it and added his amendments, the index was in the middle. His sharp eye had found repeated examples of the company's attempts to squeeze out additional advantages. When the last signatures were appended, we emerged with a contract that was then considered the gold standard for performers in the music industry.

Ironically, all of this unfolded during what was for me another period of high anxiety. I'd been recording an album in Toronto with Brian Ahern—*Highly Prized Possession*—and doing concerts on the road at the same time. I'd be up late in the recording studio; grab an early-morning flight to Dallas, then a short plane ride to whatever town I was appearing in; go through a long day of rehearsal, sound checks and performance; fly back to Toronto for another round with Brian; and then head back to Texas again. I generally accommodated stress pretty well, but my fingers were once again going numb and I found myself questioning the whole showbiz thing. In one interview, only months after signing the largest recording contract ever made by a Canadian performer, I told a reporter that my ambition in life was to be a sessions singer, doing backup vocals for Dusty Springfield and Peggy Lee—a clear indication of just how near the tether's end I was.

Meanwhile the new year loomed, and it would be a watershed for me. Whatever the state of my career, my personal dreams had been parked in limbo, languishing and unfulfilled. I was almost thirty, still unmarried, still childless. It was high time to do something about that.

CHAPTER FIVE

A NEW MANAGER, a new agent, a new wardrobe and, starting in 1975, a new hairdo—a funky afro. When my mother saw the promo picture, she called me.

"Do you really look like this?" she asked.

"Yes," I said.

"Well then, you're stupid," she said.

But I didn't stop there. That year I also changed record producers. I'd been with Brian Ahern since 1968 and we had made ten albums together. Creative, sensitive and generous, he possessed one of the finest sets of ears on the planet. If Bill Langstroth was my personal emotional rock, Brian was my musical mentor, always encouraging, always positive, always convinced that we often-beleaguered Maritimers were as good as anyone in the world and that we would prove it. But Brian's affinity for long late-night recording sessions was beginning to wear on me. It was one thing to handle when my gig dates allowed discrete blocks of time for recording, but by 1974, after Shep Gordon took the managerial reins, I was doing a hundred shows a year or more on the road and the pace and toll were punishing. Difficult as it was to break with Brian, I was ready to try something new.

The producer I chose, Tom Catalano, came with impressive credentials. He'd worked with Peggy Lee, Helen Reddy and Neil Diamond and had reportedly turned down opportunities to do albums with Sinatra and Streisand in order to do mine. He also came highly recommended by Capitol, which gave me hope that they'd throw more marketing weight behind its promotion. Watching Tom in the studio in Los Angeles in 1975, I was struck by the salient differences between his methods of recording and Brian's.

In Toronto the process tended to be looser and less scripted. Recording was done in layers. The bed tracks were laid first, with a basic rhythm section (drums, bass, piano and two guitars). The charts for the musicians were sometimes written in advance but often drafted on the spot, in the studio. Brian had a rough idea of what he wanted to hear, but he would give the musicians free rein to try things until a song came together to everyone's satisfaction. It was a very creative atmosphere, with everyone, including me, contributing. Once the basic tracks were finished, overdubs of other instruments (organ, electric guitar, strings, horns, percussion, etc.) were recorded, and finally the lead and background vocals. That process, yielding one song, took approximately five days.

Tom's method was very different. A good portion of the work was done before you set foot inside the studio. Charts and arrangements for all the musicians were drafted in advance, and an entire orchestra, including strings, horns and percussion, showed up to play in the studio. This allowed for very little experimentation. It all happened very quickly and I felt left out of the creative process, especially compared to working with Brian. At the time this system struck me as a little too well organized, as efficiency won at the expense of creativity. But in hindsight I think that view was too simplistic. It wasn't necessarily less creative; it was simply a faster, different way to go. Time was money, so expedience was the order of the day. I have to admit I was somewhat intimidated by working with some of the best studio musicians in the world, but ultimately the process was quite thrilling.

During that trip to L.A. I arranged to meet Mary Isabel Catherine Bernadette O'Brien, better known to the world as Dusty Springfield. I have admired so many great women singers over the years, from those whose songs filled my childhood home in Springhill—Patti Page, Doris Day, Rosemary Clooney, Sarah Vaughan, Keely Smith and Mahalia Jackson—to my contemporaries Bonnie Raitt, Barbra Streisand, Aretha Franklin, Olivia Newton-John and Patti LaBelle. But if I had to pick one artist who, song after song, always touched something deep inside me, it would be Dusty.

I loved her work from the moment I heard "I Only Want to Be with You" in 1963, her first major hit. The sound was different from anything I had heard before—it made a visceral connection. Clearly I wasn't alone. In the next seven years she put seven songs on Billboard's Top 25. Her voice was at once unique—songwriter Burt Bacharach, who worked extensively with her, said you could recognize it in three notes—sensual, powerful and soulful. It was that element of soul that I think Elton John was acknowledging when he called her the greatest white singer in history.

Dusty and I had met once before, in London in January 1973. I was returning home from Cannes, and one night Bill, Brian Ahern and I caught the second of her two shows at the London Palladium. Brian disappeared afterwards, but Bill and I waited with what seemed like hundreds of people backstage. Finally we were ushered into her dressing room—a complete mob scene—and talked to her for a while. Suddenly she grabbed one of Bill's hands and one of mine and yelled, "Everybody get the fuck out of here—now!" Then she turned to us and said that we were the only real people there. Her security detail emptied the room in minutes. The three of us sat quietly and talked for a short time—Dusty, it was obvious, was pretty spaced out—and then we said our goodbyes.

The next time I saw her was in L.A. in 1975. I had called her up to see if she would sing backup vocals on *Together*, that first Tom Catalano album, and invited her to our room at the Continental Hyatt House, where Bill and I were staying, for drinks. I'm not sure what Dusty was expecting, but she was clearly unhappy to see Bill with me in L.A. Perhaps she'd had a few drinks before she arrived; she had a couple more with us and was soon quite drunk. At one point she excused herself to use the washroom and then, on the pretext of a snag in her zipper, summoned me to join her. There she came on to me verbally and wanted to know "what was up" with Bill. I spurned her advances, telling her that Bill was the man I planned to marry. When Dusty returned to the room, she physically attacked Bill, scratching his face with her fingernails. It was quite a scene, but she calmed down after that and Bill ended up driving her home.

Dusty did agree to sing backups and later that year came to Toronto to record them. We got along just fine, and there was no mention of the scene in L.A. We had a few parties at the house and sang together a lot, impromptu. She'd been battling drug and alcohol abuse for some time, but she was clean then and drinking only Fresca, as far as I knew. Although she never really became a confidante, she did tell me that she could only dimly remember seven years of her life. That was no exaggeration. One night after a day in the studio, a group of us trooped back to my home for a delivery of Chinese food. Over spareribs and chow mein my brother Bruce told Dusty how much he'd enjoyed a performance of hers in the Bahamas in the early 1970s; he'd been there during a vacation. She said, "I've never been to the Bahamas in my life."

At some point during those recording sessions, she had a heart-to-heart with Bruce and me and talked about her addictions. She told us that before her performance at the London Palladium that Bill and I had attended, she'd taken a few Quaaludes. No wonder she seemed out of it. A few years earlier I'd taken half of one pill—my first and last—and I fell asleep sitting up in a chair.

Dusty and I kept in sporadic touch after that. In 1984, when I went to Britain to tape "Sounds of London," my CBS TV special, I asked her to be a guest. Our time together there was spent mostly on the set. She arrived three hours late for rehearsal. An entire crew from Canada and the United States was left irately cooling its heels while we waited for Dusty. When she arrived, her first excuse was that she was having her nails done. But when I buttonholed her later and asked, "What the hell was that all about?" she explained that she was nervous about working with me and wasn't sure she could "cut it." She had said the same kind of thing when she sang backup vocals in Toronto.

I asked, "Dusty, what are you talking about?"

"It's too high for me there," she said. "I can't sing the part."

"Dusty, don't be ridiculous. Of course you can sing there. You sounded fabulous in rehearsal!"

So she sang it—and of course it was magical.

On other occasions she'd say, "You're so good," and I'd say, "What are you talking about? You're the greatest." I *was* singing well at that time, as well as I had ever sung, but there was nothing wrong with her pipes. As part of that London special we staged a concert at the Royal Albert Hall, and more than half the people were there to see her. We sang a medley together and it was terrific. But Dusty had to be told repeatedly how good she was; she would otherwise quickly lose confidence. Her insecurities flummoxed me—of all the people who needn't have felt insecure about their talent, she'd have been at the top of the list. She simply had no idea how good she was.

Dusty had a reputation for being difficult to work with, in part because she was meticulous and in part because her ears were so good that she could hear if one of a dozen string players was out of tune and then identify which one. In the recording studio she'd insist on take after take, a standard of perfectionism that sorely tested the patience of her producers. But there was none of that when she worked with me.

I saw her again at her house in L.A.—there were walls of gold records and the writer Fran Lebowitz was there—but in 1981, when Dusty lived in Toronto with Carole Pope (formerly with Rough Trade), she never called me. Then in 1999, not long before her death, I received a call from a friend of hers; Dusty had drawn up a shortlist of people to say goodbye to, and I was on it. First I sent her a tape we'd made of our rehearsals from the 1975 album, and then I called her. She was tired and failing, but we spoke for about twenty minutes, reminiscing about some of the good old days. It was very hard to say goodbye. She seemed a tortured soul, but for all the excesses and all the demons she fought within, I will always remember a sweet and vulnerable woman and my favourite singer of all time.

The other backup singer on that album was the amazing Dianne Gwendolyn Brooks. She'd sung with me before, both on tour and in the studio, and I'd dedicated the album *Danny's Song* to her. I had never met anyone who was so innovative vocally. She had started singing and composing as a teenager in New Jersey and she could sing everything—jazz, rock, blues, soul, country, it didn't matter—and always make it her own. On the *Annie* album I had her coach me, teach me how to let go, allowing the voice and the emotion to release as one. Dianne could do that—just open her mouth and let that gorgeous instrument of hers run free. She also taught me back-phrasing—how to hit the note just after the beat, for dramatic effect—a bluesy musical trick that did not come naturally to me. On the road it wasn't uncommon for reviewers to single out her vocal gifts for special citation, and deservedly so. In 1976 Brian Ahern produced her second album, *Back Stairs of My Life*, on which I finally got my wish to sing backup vocals for her.

During those L.A. recording sessions I made another guest appearance on the *Merv Griffin Show*. He had been a strong supporter of my work but, like many in the industry, was a little puzzled by my eclectic tastes.

"I think the music biz is confused by who you are," he said to me on this show. "You don't live here . . . and last year you were nominated for a Grammy for best country singer and this year for best pop singer . . . Who are you?"

I was just formulating my answer when he jumped in: "Do you care about show business at all?"

"Well, I like to separate and retreat," I conceded. "But I think they're as confused as I am, 'cause I just sing the songs I like as they come along. It all depends on the songs."

Merv had put his finger on the pulse of the lingering Anne Murray mystery—how to define me and, thus, how to sell me. Because we used a steel guitar from time to time on songs, there were those who labelled me country. This was more than a little ironic since, of all my musical influences, country was the weakest. Other country artists had occasionally crossed over into the pop arena, but fewer seemed to slide into folk or even rock, as I did. I saw that eclecticism as a potential strength, something that could broaden my appeal. Even if I was wrong, it was how I wanted to operate. Artistically, one has to be true to one's instinct. And mine is simply to find songs I like, whatever their genre. In my formative years I was hearing everything from the Mills Brothers to Andy Williams, from the Womenfolk to Louis Prima and Keely Smith, and from Buddy Holly to the Beatles; all those disparate styles helped shape my musical sensibility.

I did the talk-show circuit a lot. I liked Merv, Mike Douglas and Dinah Shore but had a little trouble with Johnny Carson. His format seemed tailored more to guests who were loud, glib and fast-talking, and I was none of the above. Someone who was naturally reserved, who chose words with care or thought before responding, was deemed of low value. I did his show only twice when he was hosting, and made it once to the hallowed couch for a chat. As a general rule he didn't talk to singers because, as he told one interviewer, they had nothing to say. Not surprisingly, perhaps, my other appearances on the *Tonight Show* were all with guest hosts, including Freddie Prinze, David Brenner, David Letterman and Burt Reynolds. On those occasions I felt very comfortable and did just fine.

Repartee wasn't particularly my forte, but occasionally I managed to fire off a zinger. Once while taping a guest appearance on the *Dean Martin Show*, I went next door to Merv's talk show for a quick chat.

"Oh, that Dino," he said. "He's such a pro, isn't he?"

"Well, he should be," I said. "He's been doing it for fifty years."

The audience laughed, but Merv looked a little horrified.

⌒

IT HAD TAKEN A LONG TIME, but Bill's divorce papers finally came through. As soon thereafter as we could obtain the marriage licence, William Maynard Langstroth and Morna Anne Murray were officially married. It was June 20, 1975, my thirtieth birthday. The ceremony took place in the living room of my home on Hilltop Road on a beautiful summer evening. For my mother's sake we arranged a Catholic ceremony. Since Church doctrine prohibits divorce in most circumstances, it was no simple matter to find a renegade priest willing to marry us, but eventually we did. It was a small, informal affair, attended by my parents; Bill's dad, Cecil; his brother Dave (the best man) and sister-in-law Dawn; my brother Bruce and his wife, Corinne; Leonard Rambeau; and Joanne Taylor, my roommate from college, who was maid of honour. I'd spent the day recording in a studio downtown and came home for the function.

"What are you going to wear?" Mom asked me.

"Oh, I don't even know," I said. "Let's just go through the closet and pick something."

We picked a green muumuu, hard as that is to believe now. Bill wore a casual off-white suit. To set the mood, Bruce had artistically arranged a few dozen candles around the room. The only hitch was that during the ceremony our photographer, Ed Harris, caught fire, his jacket set ablaze when he backed into one of the candles. We had to interrupt the proceedings to put him out, but managed to do so without injury. Afterwards we all enjoyed lobsters in the beautiful back garden. Our chocolate wedding cake was from a box, courtesy of the fine bakers at Sara Lee, and adorned with a Raggedy Anne and Andy motif.

The next day Bill and I flew to Prince Edward Island for a two-week honeymoon. A year or so earlier Lyman had gone there on a reconnaissance mission to find an investment property for me. The result was a ten-unit motel, the Heather Dunes, on a beautiful beach at Savage Harbour, on the north shore, and that's where we went. My old friends from *Singalong Jubilee* Karen Oxley and her husband, Jack Lilly, were there (they managed the place for me in the summers) and my brothers and parents came to visit from Nova Scotia. We feasted on lobster dinners, took boat rides, went jigging for mackerel and took long walks on the beach. But that was the last summer we spent there. After Will was born I wanted to be closer to my family on the other side of the strait, so we started taking our vacations at Northport. A few years later I sold the P.E.I. property.

A few months before the wedding, one of my all-time singing heroes, Perry Como, had invited me to join him on a CBS TV special shot at Lake Tahoe. Given our often tenuous grasp of musical history, many people may have forgotten what an extraordinary career he had. Fourteen of his songs went to number one, and most of them during an era when he was competing with the likes of people named Crosby, Clooney, Sinatra, Torme, Page, Brewer and Martin. Starting with "Till the End of Time," Perry had forty-two Top Ten hits on the Billboard charts between 1945 and 1958; only Bing Crosby had more. He even had a number-one hit posthumously—when his old rendition of "Jingle Bells" made it to the top of Billboard's Hot Ringtones chart.

I had loved Perry Como's effortless style of singing since I was a child watching him on black-and-white television on cold winter nights with my father. His approach was usually so relaxed that, listening to him, you might get the impression that his voice lacked power—but you would have been dead wrong. When I arrived at Harrah's showroom, where we were scheduled to meet, Perry was already on stage rehearsing. I took a seat at a table in the back with a few others listening to him, and his power was incredible, operatic, without the amplification of a microphone. That lung power and breath control were what enabled him to make it look so easy. And he was then sixty-three years old.

A group of us were just sitting and talking when I suddenly felt a pair of warm and gentle hands on my shoulders. It was Perry. He leaned over and said, in that calm and benevolent tone that was so much a part of him, "And this must be Anne." It was precisely what I thought Perry Como would say. I can't properly describe the thrill it gave me.

We had a great week. On the special I was joined by Billie Jean King, Bob Hope and Suzy Chaffee, the Olympic down-hill and later freestyle skier. The pro golfer Sandra Palmer was there as well, and she took Billie Jean and me to a driving range. Billie and I duelled with each other to see who could hit the ball farther. I strained so hard to hit the damned ball that I pulled a muscle in my back, and it took months to heal. Neither of us, needless to say, came close to out-driving Sandra, who seemed to be barely trying. On the TV special I sang "Danny's Song" and did a medley with Perry (a child-hood dream come true) and a full-blown dance routine to "Everything Old Is New Again," a bouncy old-fashioned tune written by Peter Allen. This would later become a fixture in my act, complete with top hat, cane, a little magic trick and some choreography taught to me by the indispensable Warren Baker. With me from 1973 until 1979, Warren was at various times my road manager, lighting director and stage manager, and sometimes all at once.

A few years later Perry was responsible for my meeting another idol from my childhood, Greer Garson. Along with Joyce DeWitt and Buffy Sainte-Marie, she and I were guests on a Como Christmas special taped in Santa Fe, New Mexico. Greer lived in the area. Several of her films—*Mrs. Miniver, Random Harvest* and *Goodbye, Mr. Chips*—are among my all-time favourites. I was delighted to have the opportunity to tell her how wonderful an actress she was and what a pro-found impact her work had had on me. Stars are accustomed to hearing such things and some may regard the compliments as mere politeness, but I was effusive and totally sincere, and she could see that. She'd been out of the Hollywood limelight for many years and was touched, I think, that someone still remembered her work. Indeed, when I told her what she had meant to me growing up, she started to cry. This occasionally happens to me now too—a fan telling me, in person or by letter or via email, how deeply affecting they have found my music—and it's at once gratifying and deeply moving.

I don't think I consciously copied Perry's style, but I'm sure he was a subliminal influence. Later, when I was making another appearance on Merv Griffin's talk show, he flattered me by comparing me to Perry.

"You never seem tense," Merv said. "You have exactly the same attitude as Perry Como has. You're never uptight."

"It's because both of us are half asleep," I quipped. "No, seriously, inside I'm not really that—"

"Do audiences frighten you?" Merv asked.

"Oh yes."

"Well, what form does it take?"

"I get diarrhea."

That degree of candour drew a big laugh from the studio audience.

"You're not upset now, are you?" said Merv, pretending to look a little concerned. "Gee, you learn such wonderful things on talk shows."

"Aren't you glad you asked?" I said.

"Well, I know that certain stars—Helen Hayes, for example—she upchucks before her stage entrance . . . Wouldn't the two of you be thrilling to work with."

"I find that vomiting is not a very pleasant experience, so I—"

"Right," he cut in, before I could finish. "Well, I hate to say this phrase, but moving right along . . ."

EVERYTHING IS CLEARER when we look back at our lives. In hindsight I can see that asking Bill, a man of forty-five, to become a father of young children for the second time was asking a lot. It would have been one thing if I had been a traditional stay-at-home mom, or even a mom who worked regularly but was home in the evenings. But I led a different life. And that left Bill to struggle through a difficult transition, from productive writer, performer and TV producer to part-time Balmur creative consultant, photographer and full-time dad. To his credit, he willingly signed on for the role. In fact, not long after I became pregnant, we had an evening with Leonard and Lyman at our home and Bill said, "When this baby comes, one of us is going to have to stay home. And given your earning power, Anne, it doesn't make any sense that it should be you." Despite the sacrifices he made, he never complained, not once.

I loved being pregnant. Finally I had a compelling reason to get off the dizzying showbiz roller coaster, and I did. I gave my last concert in Pembroke, Ontario, in May 1976, flew to L.A. to record my second album with Tom Catalano, *Keeping in Touch*, and then came home to bask in pure, complete, unadulterated idleness.

During that trip to L.A., Shep Gordon arranged for me to stay at Alice Cooper's house in Laurel Canyon; Alice was out of town but had kindly left me his Rolls-Royce Silver Cloud to tool around in. Later I moved into Shep's own place in Bel-Air. Shep was also travelling; he thoughtfully had his assistant leave a welcome note on the kitchen counter and a surprise in a kitchen drawer—a vial of cocaine. My bandleader, Pat Riccio (he had taken over when Skip Beckwith stepped down in 1975), was staying there as well. One night after dinner we decided to play backgammon. Pat was a serious drinker in those days, and by the time we sat down to the board, he'd already made a decent start on a twenty-six-ounce bottle of rum, which he subsequently finished. Intermittently he'd sample the contents of the vial of nose candy until it was gone too; somewhere along the way he managed to smoke a joint as well. We played late into the night and, needless to say, Pat's mind was largely missing in action—I had no trouble winning. The next morning he staggered downstairs for breakfast and said, "Is your stomach upset this morning?"

"No," I said.

"Well, mine is. I thought it might be something we ate."

That summer I swam thirty lengths in the pool each day, read books, relaxed around the house and watched TV. My sole obligation was going to the doctor. When he asked me if I needed a reminder card for my next appointment, I refused it. "This is the only time I leave the house each week," I told him. "If I can't remember this, I'm in big trouble."

The pregnancy itself was largely uneventful. I had no nausea but did suffer from severe heartburn, and I gained thirty-two pounds. Bill and I went together to prenatal classes. One night they screened a film showing actual child-birth; *that* made me nauseated. It was a bad copy and the colours were all off. I found it unwatchable and had to leave the room and sit in the hall until it ended, my head tucked between my knees—no easy feat at eight months pregnant.

My friend Karen Oxley was staying with us as my due date drew close. There was a wonderful Chinese restaurant nearby—China House, a Toronto institution—and one night we ordered takeout for dinner. I forget the dish details, but I know there was plenty of garlic. Someone had told me that if a pregnant woman eats Chinese food, it brings on labour. An old wives' tale, of course—or maybe not, as it turned out.

In the wee hours of the morning I was awakened by rushing water—my own. My amniotic sac had broken. I think Karen was more anxious than I was, but I was a bundle of nerves as well. After a couple of hours the contractions were getting closer together, so we decided it was time to go to the hospital. I donned a special outfit I'd selected just for the occasion, all neatly ironed. But just as Bill and I were climbing the steps of the hospital, at about 7:00 a.m., out gushed more water, completely ruining the outfit—and my carefully planned entrance. Orderlies brought me a wheelchair and whisked me into the labour room.

I was in intense pain. On examination, the doctors discovered that the baby was pressing on my spine. When Bill briefly replaced the wonderful nurse, Aurora, who'd been doing such a professional job of rubbing my back, I barked at him, "You're not doing it properly!"

Eventually they administered an epidural and wheeled me into the delivery room. The epidural nicely relieved the pain and relaxed me, but now the garlic-laced Chinese food came back to haunt me—I threw up.

"I think I'm losing my sense of humour," I complained, drawing a big laugh from everyone present.

When I finally turned the corner into the last delivery lap and it was time to push, I said to the attending nurse, "I have something to tell you."

"What's that?" she asked with some concern, afraid that some vital piece of medical knowledge had been missed.

"We had Chinese food for dinner."

"Yes?"

"I'm awfully sorry about the garlic."

Bill held my hand through the labour and was in the delivery room when William Stewart Langstroth, weighing 7 pounds, 4 ounces, was born on August 31, 1976. Thanks to the anesthetic, my brain was more than a little foggy. I remember noticing a strange man wearing a surgical mask and wondering what he was doing in the room. That was Bill. Only minutes after I gave birth, he asked if I was game to try for a second—the best time, he reckoned, to get an honest answer from me. And I immediately said yes.

I had loved pregnancy, but I loved motherhood even more. Long deferred, it proved to be a hugely empowering experience, richer and more fulfilling than I had anticipated. For the first time in seven years I was liberated from the constant pressure (as much psychological as actual) of the business. It was such a relief not to be the focus of incessant attention—the endless discussions about my career, my albums, my singles, my band, my tours, my TV specials, where I stood in the pecking order, etc. Now the star of the show was the baby. I had taken a few months off before Will's arrival, and I took four more afterwards, luxuriating in the everyday demands of breastfeeding, bathing, dressing and playing with the marvellous creature that was young Will. Interviews I gave at the time reported that I hadn't seemed so relaxed in years.

But I wasn't always so relaxed. Because of the pregnancy I'd been forced to cancel or postpone a few performances, including what would have been my first appearance at the Stratford Festival Theatre. They graciously rescheduled it for a fall date, but it was only five weeks after Will's birth. When

I turned up for the event, I was still nursing and, quite frankly, a basket of frayed nerves. In part that was because I hadn't performed, sung a note or even thought about it since June, and was concerned about how well I'd be able to sing. It doesn't take long to lose your performing chops.

In addition, I was exhibiting the customary anxieties of first-time mothers, for whom the child's needs are the top, if not the only, priority. I was all the more rattled because the schedules—for my rehearsal and for Will's feeding time—were in conflict. When he needed to be fed, I was unavailable, so Bill had to give him a bottle of milk that I had expressed. Then when I was at his disposal, his appetite was sated. Unable to feed him, my breasts became engorged, which added severe discomfort to my growing emotional stress. I tried to pump the milk manually to relieve the pressure, but show time was rapidly approaching. Leaking profusely, I sent Bill to find some wide adhesive tape. Just before the concert he swaddled my chest in bandages so that I would not spray the first few rows of the audience with new mother's milk.

Afterwards, I was relieved—in every sense. The voice, it turned out, was still there. Will soon returned to his regular feeding schedule. And no one from the audience sent me a laundry bill.

THIS CAREER TIME OUT also gave Balmur time to reassess our direction. Lyman had early on identified a gap in the Canadian marketplace when it came to management of musical artists. He suggested that we find and develop new talent. In some cases, as with Maritime folksinger John Allen Cameron, we could promote the artist by having him or her serve as my opening act or appear on my TV specials, helping them build a following of their own, much as Glen Campbell had done for me in the U.S. Later we added several others, including my brother Bruce (whose first, self-titled album I helped produce in 1976), Rita MacNeil, Michael Burgess, George Fox and Frank Mills.

I had some decisions to make about my own path as well. The time had come, we concluded, to sever our connection with Shep Gordon. He'd done what we had hoped and expected—created a buzz about me that had not been there before, opening performing doors that had been previously closed. Shep understood that voice and talent were not always enough, that to reach the top you had to market yourself relentlessly, create events, court the media. And he was right; I shuddered at some of the circus-act gimmicks, but his instincts were always correct. I had to learn the same lessons about wardrobe, initially arguing that it didn't really matter what you wore on stage, and only later realizing that the best performances are made of many parts, and that clothes are definitely one of them.

Leonard now had five years under his Canadian management belt and he felt ready for prime time. Our relationship formed a perfect circle. I trusted him because he understood me as well as anyone, and he understood me as well as anyone because I trusted him. I knew exactly how lucky I was. I'd heard the horror stories about artist–manager relationships going sour and the bitter litigation that often followed. At any rate, we amicably terminated Shep's contract a year before it was due to end.

In an ideal world I would have taken a full year off, not five months, and just savoured the abundant joys of motherhood.

With Lyman's sound tax-planning advice, I had been fortunate to accumulate some sizable savings and investments. But I couldn't afford to live off them. Singing was still my livelihood and, as Bill had wisely noted, I was the family's logical breadwinner. What I needed was to take more control, to find a better balance between the competing demands of career and family. I wanted to sing again and I needed to, but I wanted to do it on my terms.

IN 1976 I'D BEEN INVITED to give a series of concerts in Japan; we scheduled the trip for the following year. Will was still an infant, so Bill's daughter, Margot, then eighteen, came along to help out. It was a multi-city tour, with dates in Tokyo, Osaka, Kyoto, Nagasaki, Nagoya and Fukuoka. As far as I knew I was a virtual unknown in Japan and my expectations were low. I certainly wasn't prepared for the welcome I received. After the marathon plane ride from Vancouver, I got off the plane in Tokyo looking exhausted, wearing just jeans and a T-shirt and cradling Will in my arms. There to greet me were not only a phalanx of cameramen and reporters but literally hundreds of cheering fans—young teenage boys, seeking autographs and offering flowers—rather a different demographic than I was accustomed to in North America or Europe. I said to Bill, "Gee, I guess it's a good thing I washed my face." Later the boys also thronged to my concerts.

Everywhere the attention to courtesy impressed me. Once one of our crew members lit a cigarette and dropped his match on the sidewalk; a Japanese man walking behind him immediately picked it up and handed it back, bowing. In each city the same Japanese stagehands would set the stage for us every night, and their precision was extraordinary; they did it exactly the same way every night—to the inch.

Musically, the Japanese tour was an enormous success. The act had always been more about unpretentious, straight-ahead delivery than splashy pyrotechnics, and that appealed, I think, to the natural Japanese sense of refinement and simplicity. Reviewers there compared me favourably to Olivia Newton-John, Doris Day and Helen Reddy and likened my subtle style, oddly enough, to that of Canadian jazz pianist Oscar Peterson, a huge star in Japan who was also visiting at the same time.

Pat Riccio was known as *bandoreeda* because there is no Japanese word for bandleader. He led a quartet supplemented by saxophonist Genji Sawai and trombone player Michio Kagiwada. I memorized a number of Japanese phrases, including *Minasan, konbanwa*, which means "Good evening, everyone."

Offstage I was usually busy with Bill and the baby (although we did manage to take in a sumo wrestling match), so the band saw a somewhat different side of Japan. One night they went to a bar in Nagoya that was part strip club, part circus: horses and a tiger shared the circular stage with the strippers. Another night they were invited to Genji's apartment for dinner. The walls of the apartment were grey concrete—a status symbol, Genji said, since most homes were made of light wood and paper. His wife did all the cooking, which was absolutely delicious, but she was not allowed to sit at the table.

In stores the women would gather around Will in his stroller, marvelling at his bright baby-blue eyes. One day I went shopping for shoes in Tokyo and saw a pair in a store

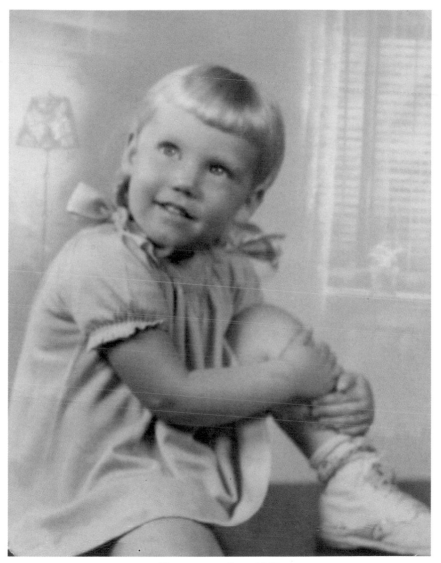

First promo shot, 1948

Mom and Dad, 1937

(left to right) Daniel, David, Stewart, (back) Harold

Dad

Mom, Christmas 1952

Preparing for life with five brothers

David (left) and Daniel

Daniel (left) and Harold

16th Birthday Party

The Freshettes, 1961

Singalong Jubilee Gang, 1968

Manager Leonard Rambeau, 1971

Brothers Stewart (left) and Bruce on a CBC television special, 1971

Songwriter Gene MacLellan, 1972

Mom and Dad seeing me off to do the first Glen Campbell show, Halifax Airport, 1971

Glen Campbell, 1971

Bill, 1972

Producer Brian Ahern, and songwriters Roger Nicols
and Paul Williams, 1971

Gordie Howe, CBC TV special, 1971

(left to right) Eddy Arnold, Lynn Anderson, Loretta Lynn and Tennessee Ernie Ford at the Grand Ole Opry in Nashville, early '70s

(left to right) John Lennon, Harry Nilsson, Alice Cooper and Micky Dolenz
at the Troubadour in Los Angeles, 1973

Steve Martin on the *Midnight Special*, 1973

My first Grammy ("A Love Song"), 1974

John Denver at the 1975 Canadian National Exhibition

Leonard and his wife, Caron Rambeau, at Carnegie Hall, 1979

Producer Jim Ed Norman and songwriter Randy Goodrum, 1978

Will with his first drum set, Christmas 1980

Dawn at the keyboard, 1980

William, Dawn and Bill, 1982

William and Dawn, 1983

Perry Como, 1979

Billie Jean King, 1980

Rodney Dangerfield, 1980

Rosemary Clooney, 1986

Hollywood Walk of Fame, 1980

Jane Curtin, Burt Reynolds, Gilda Radner and Garret Morris on *Saturday Night Live*, 1980

Co-hosting the CMA Awards with
Willie Nelson, 1983

Wayne Gretzky backstage at the Riviera,
Las Vegas, 1982

Johnny Cash and June Carter Cash,
late 1980s

Alan Thicke, 1988 CBC TV
Christmas special

Kris Kristofferson in Monte Carlo, 1980

Anthony Hopkins and Burt Reynolds, 1981

Harrah's postcard, 1981

Bertha at the Nugget in Reno, 1984

Brother Bruce, 1983

Patti Page, 1998

Kenny Rogers, 1989

Julio Iglesias, Paul Janz and Patti LaBelle
My 1991 CBC/Disney TV special

Diane Sawyer, *Good Morning America*, 1999

Producer Tommy West, 1992

The Right Honourable Jeanne Sauvé, Governor
General of Canada pinning on the insignia of the
Companion of the Order of Canada, 1984

Calgary Olympics Gala, 1988

Dusty Springfield,
Royal Albert Hall in
London, England, 1984

Prime Minister Pierre Trudeau, Mrs. Reagan and President Reagan in Ottawa, Ontario, 1981

Silver Springs, Florida, 2002

Toronto skyline, 2002

Canadian postage stamp, 2007

Celine Dion and Shania Twain at the 1997 Juno Awards

Manager, Bruce Allen, 2004

President George H.W. Bush backstage at
my Kennedy Center concert, 1992

P'tricia Wyse and Cynthia McReynolds in
Las Vegas, 1999

Her Majesty the Queen and Rita MacNeil
on Canada's 125th birthday, Ottawa, July 1, 1992

k.d. lang, *Country Gold* TV special, 1992

Olivia Newton-John in the studio recording DUETS, 2007

Doris Day in Carmel, 1995

The "Chicks" in Scotland, 1995

Sarah Brightman and Jann Arden at the 2008 Juno Awards

Platinum and gold album awards presentation with my band: (left to right), Steve Sexton, Peter Bleakney, Gary Craig, Georges Hébert, Aidan Mason and Debbie Ankeny

Mom and Michael Bublé backstage at the
Hummingbird Centre in Toronto, 2005

Bobby Orr after a golf game in Florida, 2005

Bryan Adams, 2009

(back row) David, Bruce, Daniel
(front row) Harold, Mom and Stewart, 1994

My band, crew, bus drivers and Dawn on the 2008 Canadian tour

In the studio with Will and Dawn recording DUETS, 2007

On stage on my Canadian tour, 2008

window that I just had to have. Then I noticed some of the salesgirls tittering behind a post, apparently amazed by the size of my feet. The store didn't carry size 8½—in any style.

There was one thing about the culture that really bothered me. When a Japanese man wanted to discuss something with me, he would always address his remarks to the man standing closest to me, never directly to me, as if I were part of the wallpaper. This began to rankle after a while, and more than once I put up my hand and turned the man's face so that he was forced to look me directly in the eye, and said, "Don't talk to him. Talk to me." Then he would giggle and bow and say "Ah, so" and comply, however reluctantly.

I'd been given this kind of treatment before and always resented it. In 1970 the Canadian government flew me to Frankfurt for an Air Canada promotion event. I was alone and dealing with a group of German musicians, all male, who were disinclined to listen to my suggestions about how they might approach a song. It wasn't a language issue—they understood English, but they simply chose to ignore me. On the flight over I'd been invited into the cockpit to meet the pilot, Eric Cartmell. Frustrated by the Germans, I called Cartmell and asked him if he might have a word with the bandleader on my behalf. He promptly came down and lectured them sharply, telling them he was going to stand there until they did it my way. And they did.

The most dramatic incident of the Japanese trip was one we all shared. Early one morning in Tokyo, where we were staying on the twenty-eighth floor of a hotel, we were hit by an earthquake—my first. Mild by Japanese standards, it shook the bed and bedside lamps and rattled the hangers in the closet. My heart rate didn't slow down for a long time.

MY PREGNANCY AND THE TIME I TOOK OFF following Will's birth caused a certain strain in my relationship with Capitol. It wasn't simply that I had temporarily stopped working and, thus, helping them to sell records. It was that, under the terms of my 1974 contract, I owed them another album, one that required them to pay an advance of $250,000. But I was in no condition to go back into the studio. I was enjoying motherhood too much.

The level of tension continued to rise until finally Bhaskar Menon flew into Toronto to read us the riot act. Bhaskar, former president of all Capitol-related companies in North America, had just been made the first chairman and CEO of the parent company, EMI Music Worldwide. He was, in short, among the top five most powerful music executives on the planet, and without ever raising his voice, he came to deliver a simple message: give us an album, as per the contract.

Following this high-level meeting, the Balmur brain trust called a meeting of our own. Leonard and Lyman both felt that Bhaskar didn't have a good grasp of what the contract actually said or how much it favoured me. As Lyman noted, I retained complete creative control of the album's content. I could, therefore, he said—only half in jest—legally honour the contract by recording anything I liked, even songs composed of numbers from the telephone directory or words from the dictionary. Asked for his legal opinion, Dave Matheson allowed that technically Lyman was right, although he wasn't going to recommend that approach.

I had a better idea: since I had babies on the brain, why not record an album of children's songs? But instead of recording only the traditional silly stuff, I'd assemble songs that even adults would like, many of them songs I knew from my childhood, such as Frank Loesser's "Inch Worm" and Jimmy Kennedy's "Teddy Bears' Picnic." This album became *There's a Hippo in My Tub*. The song that gave the album its name was written by a children's dentist from Alberta, Dr. Bob Ruzicka, and Pat Riccio did all the arrangements.

When it was done, we took the finished master tape to Capitol in Los Angeles, presented it and asked for payment of the $250,000. They were not at all amused. I wasn't in the room at the time—that's what I paid Leonard and Lyman for—but the meeting and conversation, I'm told, went something like this:

A Capitol executive turned on the tape and heard the opening strains and lyrics of the hippo song, "Hey Daddy." The executive turned off the tape. "Excuse me, but what the hell is this?"

"It's Anne's latest album."

"What?"

"*There's a Hippo in My Tub.*"

"Please tell me this is just some sort of weird Canadian practical joke."

"No joke. It's a children's album."

"I can see that. *There's a Hippo in My Tub* would definitely be a children's album. But Anne Murray is a pop and country singer."

"She's branching out."

"You can't do that."

"Actually, we can. The contract gives Anne complete creative control over content. You can choose the single, however."

"Don't be ridiculous. The contract says she has to deliver material in keeping with the kinds of material previously provided."

"That clause is no longer there."

"Who's going to buy it? Her country fans? Pop fans? No. Do children know who she is?"

"Oh, c'mon. It's Anne Murray, for goodness sake. We'll sell a few copies, don't you think?"

"You might, but not under the Capitol label."

"You mean you won't release it?"

"That's correct. We won't release it."

"Well, then, we'll take it elsewhere."

"Be our guest. But she won't be getting the $250,000."

"Wait a minute. The contract expressly stipulates that we can give you any album we like. Here it is."

"I repeat: she will not be getting $250,000."

"But we have fulfilled the contract to the letter. If you won't pay the advance, you should at least cover the costs of its production, since it was made on your behalf and in good faith."

"All right. We'll pay the recording costs, how's that?"

"That's fine."

"And Anne will give us an album more to our liking within eighteen months."

"She will, with the customary advance applying."

End of discussion. We subsequently took the *Hippo* album to the people at Sesame Street Records. They loved it and released it successfully in the United States. Capitol's Canadian arm was more than happy to distribute it north of the 49th parallel. Its sales performance in both countries did not escape the attention of Capitol's parent company, EMI, which soon repurchased rights from Sesame Street. As of March 2009 it had sold 783,000 copies worldwide.

I RECALL VERY CLEARLY the circumstances of how I discovered Randy Goodrum's song "You Needed Me." Music publishers were constantly sending me tapes of their material. So were writers. I had them by the hundreds, stored in a box the size of a refrigerator. Typically I'd spend the better part of a morning or afternoon listening to them. Most were rejected because, quite frankly, they were bad songs, and others because they simply weren't right for me. But after a few hours of listening, your ear tends to become a little thick; you're not hearing the song as freshly as you should. So I kept a separate, smaller box into which I put tapes that I wanted to hear again.

I don't remember playing "You Needed Me" for the first time. But I had definitely played it, because one day in 1976, not long after Will was born, I went down to the basement on Hilltop Road and found my box labelled "Listen to Again" and it was there. I was looking for new material because, after the great *Hippo* kafuffle, I owed Capitol an album and needed songs. I put Randy's tape in the machine, and after only a few bars, I had to sit down. *My God*, I thought. *Listen to this song.* It was Randy Goodrum himself playing the piano and singing— he sings quite well—and it had more or less the same pacing and cadence as the version I later recorded. I was dumbfounded at how good it was and wondered how I could have so casually set it aside the first time I played it. It was utterly amazing.

I had enjoyed working with Tom Catalano and I liked the albums he produced, but they hadn't done as well as

Capitol or I—or Tom, for that matter—had hoped. It's often hard to know why something doesn't work and why it sometimes does. At any rate, Leonard began looking around for a new producer. In London for meetings in 1976, he was introduced to Jim Ed Norman by Jennie Halsall, a mutual friend. Jim Ed was a young Floridian who had played keyboards and arranged strings for several songs of the Eagles (including "Desperado") and had also done arrangements for Kim Carnes, Linda Ronstadt and Bob Seeger. At the time he'd produced only one album—*Right Time of the Night*, by Jennifer Warnes—but he was eager to do more.

After Leonard told me about meeting Jim Ed, I listened to the Warnes album and I was impressed. So we flew to L.A. to meet him. Jim Ed had done his homework. He'd studied all my records and, while he did not say expressly what he felt—that the Catalano albums were too eclectic and thus off the mark—he did say he wanted to take me back to my roots, to a country base that could be used as a platform to do the odd pop or even adult contemporary song. He wanted careful attention to detail, with a firm emphasis on the voice. I liked him immediately.

A few months later, Jim Ed came to Toronto and we started picking songs. One of the first tunes I played for him was "You Needed Me." He liked it but had no idea whether it might already have been spoken for or recorded. So Jim Ed dialled Nashville information, found Randy Goodrum's number and called him up.

"Has that 'You Needed Me' song been recorded yet?"

"Nope."

"Spoken for?"

"Nope."

"How would you feel if Anne Murray recorded it?"

"Anne Murray? Yeah, that would work for me," Randy said. (Today you can still find Randy's number in the Nashville phonebook, just in case another piece of serendipity comes his way.)

Randy, incidentally, grew up in Hot Springs, Arkansas, and went to high school with a young man named William Jefferson Clinton. In fact, they played in a jazz combo together, the Three Kings. The future U.S. president was then considered the hottest young tenor saxhorn in the state, but Bill ultimately put aside music in favour of politics. Some years later I went to hear him speak at a business networking event near my summer home in Pugwash, and we chatted briefly about Randy and their connection. In his speech later, he told us that he was still seeking his first electoral victory when "You Needed Me" became a hit record. His mother had said to him, "Perhaps one day you'll be as successful and well-known as Randy Goodrum."

But the truth is the song very nearly ended up in Randy's wastebasket. When he played it for the first time for his wife, Gail, she said she liked it, but her response apparently wasn't as unqualified as he had hoped. He started to tear it up, as he had many others.

"No, no, don't do that," she said. "I really do like it."

So he kept it—a good thing for all of us. With the royalties earned from "You Needed Me" he bought himself one of the world's most expensive pianos, an Austrian-made Bösendorfer.

After I recorded it, I was in Reno with young Will, lying on the hotel room floor listening to a rough mix. My agent, Fred Lawrence, was with me. I played the tape for Fred and he just went, "Wow." I had known immediately when I recorded it that it would be a hit. Everyone in that studio knew it too. It was one of those magical moments when everybody looks at each other and no words are necessary. It was the same feeling, in many ways, that I'd had with "Snowbird," except that then my excitement and confidence were tempered by lack of experience.

When Capitol's artists and repertoire (A&R) guys flew to Toronto to hear the album, their first response was, "Gee, wouldn't it be nice if there were a few more uptempo songs on the disc." Radio stations liked "up" tunes and were a little more eager to play them than the ballads. "You Needed Me," as beautiful a song as it was, wasn't exactly uptempo and didn't even have a chorus. So their first choice for the single was "Walk Right Back," the snappy Sonny Curtis tune that the Everly Brothers had made a hit in the fifties.

Soon after, Bruce Wendell, a senior promotion executive at Capitol, took a briefcase full of new single releases home to sample. He was playing "You Needed Me" in his den when his wife stepped into the room and said, "What's that? That's beautiful." He was instantly sold. But even with Wendell as an ally, Capitol again wanted a different song for the second single: the title track, "Let's Keep It That Way," by two other Nashville writers, Curly Putman ("Green, Green Grass of Home") and Rafe Van Hoy. Capitol had only planned to put "You Needed Me" on the B-side.

The second single was already being pressed when I decided to intervene. In the past, whenever there had been an issue, I'd always let Lyman or Leonard handle the discussion. But on this occasion I was determined to make my own voice heard. I went to see Capitol CEO Don Zimmerman at his office in the Tower; as calmly and collectedly as I could, I explained why I thought he was making a mistake. Every musical instinct in my body told me that "You Needed Me" would be a hit, but if it were released as a B-side, it would be ignored. When I finished speaking, he immediately picked up the phone and ordered them to stop the presses and make Randy's song the A-side. I was in shock for some time after, and Don instantly became my hero.

My vindication did not come quickly, however. The song's climb up the charts was long and slow. "You Needed Me" had some early success on the country charts, but it wasn't until a woman program director in Georgia started playing the song on pop stations that it started to move. Even then it took nine months to reach number one on the Hot 100, a long time by Billboard standards. But its crossover appeal remained: in 1978 "You Needed Me" was also a Top Five country single. That first Jim Ed Norman album went platinum and earned three Grammy nominations, winning for best pop vocal.

I ended up doing my next nine albums with Jim Ed, a pairing that represented another stage of my musical maturation. I'd begun to see that making records wasn't only about satisfying your own artistic aspirations—it was also about entertaining people. That's why you were in the business, and the more people you entertained, the more records you sold.

The timing of "You Needed Me" could hardly have been better. My five-year contract with Capitol was ending and we were due to start negotiating a new one. Let's just say we went into those talks with substantial leverage. Lyman put out feelers and later met with RCA, Warner Music and CBS. The latter evinced the most interest and made an offer that actually topped

Capitol's. The prospect of losing me unnerved Capitol, which quickly sweetened its offer, raising the royalty rate to within pennies of the CBS bid. At that point it made sense to stay with Capitol, because we'd more than make up the difference on sales from the backlist. Thus a greatest-hits release would be calculated at the new rate, whereas, had we signed with CBS, Capitol could have issued such an album while paying the old, lower royalty. In the end I was rewarded with a five-year contract and a $1-million advance. I quickly deposited the cheque, but I kept a photocopy as a souvenir. Later I showed that copy to my dad, who stared at it with a mixture of pride, awe and disbelief—feelings that matched my own.

ONE DAY IN 1977, Lyman took a call from a friend who worked at the Bank of Commerce, as the CIBC was then known. Would I be interested in becoming its celebrity spokeswoman? Lyman later presented the proposal at one of our regular Balmur meetings. I would have full creative control over the ads and a veto over the images used. I had never been keen about these overtures. In fact I had turned down almost every such offer that came my way and had publicly criticized other celebrities who attached their name to products of one sort or another.

But there were obvious cracks in my position. As early as April 1971 I had agreed to sing in a short film to be shown to General Motors dealers. They paid me $6,500 and gave me something I considered just as valuable at the time: the use of a sporty new Corvette convertible for a year. In 1975 I had recorded vocals for four commercials for Eastman Kodak.

And after my tour of Japan in 1977, I'd been invited to sing on a Japanese-language ad for Trident sugarless gum, which they apparently played thirty times a day.

With the Commerce, Lyman and Leonard argued that I'd be endorsing an institution, not a product per se, and one whose services I had personally used since I opened my first bank account in Springhill at fifteen. And the fee, for the number of days required, was hard to ignore. And so from 1978 to 1984 I shot commercials in locations across the country, a commitment of about two weeks each year. I took some heat for this decision; the accusations flew that I had somehow sold out and was acting hypocritically. In retrospect, perhaps that's true. Looking back on them now, those ads do leave me with a certain unease. The contract also contributed to my overexposure in Canada, so it might not have been the smartest career move. At the time, however, I didn't view it as selling out. Virtually every adult Canadian had a bank account, so I wasn't pitching something people didn't need or use. And the extra income dramatically reduced the number of days I'd have to spend on the concert circuit, giving me more time for priority number one, my family. That, for me, was the compelling argument. And the campaign worked for the bank, significantly increasing its recognition factor among Canadians.

At the initial signing ceremony the bank presented the document for me to sign. "Just a minute," said Lyman. "I haven't yet had a chance to read it." The bankers weren't very happy at having their integrity implicitly impugned, but I signed only after Lyman had verified that all the provisions were exactly as had been agreed.

I did the commercials for six years. Every few years, bank chairman and CEO Russell Harrison would invite Lyman,

Leonard and me to lunch with him and other senior bank executives in their fifty-sixth floor aerie high above Toronto's Bay Street. These sessions were always pleasant, but one year the chairman surprised me with a point-blank question: why did I think bankers had such a bad reputation? I suppose the polite response would have been to say that their reputation wasn't really all that bad, but, candid to a fault, I said, "Well, it's because you're so boring. You have no individuality." A pall of silence fell over the group.

The chairman wasn't fazed, however, and followed up with, "Well, Anne, why do you think that is?"

"Well, just look at you," I said. "You're all wearing exactly the same colour suit—blue, the same colour shirt—white, the same dark tie and the same style of wingtip shoes. I rest my case."

At our luncheon a year or so later, Harrison said he was very pleased with how our relationship was working, but he wondered whether there might be a way to get me more involved in the bank. I wasn't sure what he had in mind, but before I could respond, Lyman jumped in and said, "Why not put her on the board of directors?"

"Well," the chairman said, "we already have our token woman on the board."

Again a leaden curtain descended on the room, only this time it marked a turning point—the beginning of the end of our relationship. Soon after, we resolved to terminate the agreement. In fact, Leonard and Lyman went off to a meeting to do just that, but CIBC beat us to the draw. Before they could open their mouths, the bank's marketing man announced, with regret, that it had decided to buy out my contract and go in another direction. It was time.

And then there was my film career, which ended even before it began. The director Dino De Laurentiis had seen my picture in *Variety* and asked for a meeting. He was casting his new film, *Hurricane*, a torrid romance set in Hawaii. My agent, Fred Lawrence, arranged for us to meet in L.A. It was simply an exploratory chat and nothing came of it, which was probably a blessing. I was uncomfortable even seeing De Laurentiis, because I couldn't justify taking on anything else, particularly something I knew nothing about—acting. I was already scrambling to juggle the conflicting demands of family and career, but at least music was something I understood. Mia Farrow ended up with the part. When it was released, the *New York Times* reviewer called the disaster movie a real disaster: "wet and windy, the sort of expensively foolish enterprise that suggests that everyone connected with it needs either a new agent or a legal guardian. It enhances the reputation of no one."

Later I also turned down a chance to appear with Buddy Ebsen in his TV series, *Barnaby Jones*, for the same reasons. A few years after that I was sent the script for *The Best Little Whorehouse in Texas*. Burt Reynolds, who was promoting the film and would later star in it, encouraged me to audition for the part of the hooker Mona Stangley, the female lead. I loved the idea of playing a hooker, so far removed was it from my own persona, but I had to decline—not because I feared offending my audience or tarnishing my pristine image, but for precisely the same reasons as before: I didn't know the first thing about acting. I might have taken training, but that would have required a huge commitment of time, and I didn't need another distraction from my family and music career. Dolly Parton eventually co-starred with Burt, and she was terrific in the role.

Instead, I finally returned to a city about which I had serious misgivings—Las Vegas. In November 1977, for the first time in six years, I opened for comedian Gabe (*Welcome Back, Kotter*) Kaplan at the Aladdin Hotel. I had spent only two and a half weeks at the Hilton in 1971, and the whole scene was as foreign to me as anything could possibly be. On the stage you never knew what percentage of the audience—the hotel's Baghdad Theatre boasted seven thousand seats—was there expressly to see you and what percentage was just working its way up and down the Strip, consuming shows at random. But on the strength of the Grammy for "A Love Song," I was suddenly in demand and commanding a healthy stipend. In fact, the Aladdin had doubled my salary to open for Kaplan. It also agreed to eliminate dinner service during the shows, which had made me feel that I was being served up like baked Alaska for dessert. Instead, for a cover charge of $17.50, ticket buyers received three cocktails or a bottle of champagne. And I didn't complain when they offered Bill, fourteen-month-old William and me (and our nanny, Wendy) a sprawling eight-room suite and chauffeur-driven car.

Even so, making my peace with Vegas was not easy. Two shows a night with a three-hour break in between was a deadly recipe. Not really enough time to unwind but too long to hang around the dressing room. And the boys in the band would inevitably be drinking, which did not please me. But at least I wasn't taking three flights a day town-hopping across America and sleeping in a strange bed every night. The Vegas bookings ran for only two weeks at a stretch, and, most important, I'd be able to take young Will, his nanny and Bill with me.

I think it may have been during that first gig in Vegas that I had an epiphany, a kind of mental wake-up call. You'd have thought this idea would have occurred to me much sooner, and that it didn't is telling. I looked out the window from my hotel suite one night and saw my name emblazoned in lights on the billboard. Across the street at Caesar's Palace, I saw the name of Frank Sinatra, roughly the same size. *Face it, Anne*, I said to myself, *you're in show business*.

———

A FEW MONTHS LATER I competed in what was the first—and mercifully the last—NBC Rock 'n' Roll Sports Classic. The premise of this misguided concept was that selected stars of the entertainment world would compete against each other in a variety of sporting events while members of the Dallas Cowboys cheerleader squad flounced their pompoms and flaunted portions of their anatomy. For me it was a good excuse to regain my pre-pregnancy fitness level, and I dutifully found a gym in Toronto and, weeks in advance of the event, started to work out. I thought I had emerged in decent shape, but I was seriously mistaken. All kinds of stars were there: Kenny Loggins, Sha Na Na, Tanya Tucker, Gladys Knight (without the Pips), Rod Stewart, Joan Jett and the Jackson brothers, who won all the races. I competed in the hundred-yard and sixty-yard dashes, and the best I managed was a second place. Of course, I was thirty-two years old and Joan Jett was nineteen—or so I rationalized to myself. After one swimming heat, I thought my heart was going to explode.

That was a busy winter for me. Getting back into high gear, I did a week at the Bottom Line in New York; another week at the Aladdin (with Jim Stafford, a singer and comedian best known for the novelty song "Spiders and Snakes," as

my opening act); appearances on *Fernwood Tonight* with
Martin Mull and the Jim Nabors TV show; a weekend gig in
San Francisco; and a week at L.A.'s famous Sunset Strip rock
nightclub the Roxy. Even without Shep Gordon's conjuring
hand, we managed a pretty fair gathering of stars for
the opening, among them Dusty Springfield, BJ Thomas,
Bernadette Peters, Kim Carnes, music mogul Lou Adler and
Donald Sutherland's wife, Francine Racette. Unfortunately
I was plagued by faulty sound equipment on opening night,
forcing me to stop the show twice, once just as I set romantic sail on "You Needed Me."

"This can't be happening," I said to the audience. "I mean,
this is Hollywood. This is the big time."

Later that year, while "You Needed Me" continued to
climb on charts, I was given an honorary degree by my alma
mater, the University of New Brunswick—at thirty-three,
probably its youngest honouree ever. I played a six-night sold-
out run at Toronto's Royal Alexandra Theatre (I was only the
second singer, after Tony Bennett, to be invited to perform
there) and then returned home to Springhill to sing at a high
school reunion in the town's hockey arena. I renewed old
acquaintances and had a few dances with Herbie McLeod, an
old boyfriend who had taken me to the graduation prom. And
I had a chance to properly thank Catherine Ward, my Grade
10 geometry and history teacher, and to tell her she'd been the
best I'd ever had.

Early in January 1979, the four of us—Bill, Will, the
nanny and I—moved house. My friend Nancy Webster had
become a real estate agent and she found us a nice, good-sized
home with an outdoor swimming pool in Thornhill, away
from the hurly-burly of midtown Toronto. It was also three

minutes by car from the Thornhill Golf and Country Club, and I was interested in developing my golf game. The house needed a lot of work and we renovated it extensively over the years. Bill's brother, Dave, designed an addition that included a large family room and a few extra bedrooms. He also gutted the kitchen and redid it. And later Ken McReynolds, an architect, neighbour and friend, drafted plans that enclosed the pool, created a skylit atrium and added a squash court. A year or two later, Lyman suggested that I buy the properties on either side of us, for extra privacy. We managed to buy one house and that was sufficient. We razed it, creating a huge yard where the kids could play, not unlike the one my brothers and I had enjoyed in Springhill.

Soon after, newspapers started to report that Anne Murray had been stricken with a mysterious illness. She had gone underground and was declining big money to perform. What grave malady could be afflicting Canada's Snowbird? Actually there was no mystery at all. My iron was low, I had developed a terrible case of chronic sinusitis and I was pregnant again—and deliriously happy to be so.

Leonard, Lyman and the Capitol cadres weren't exactly thrilled by the news. Months earlier, they had anticipated the possibility and had, with future bookings in mind, discreetly asked me when Bill and I might be planning an addition. At that point I said I wasn't sure. They suggested waiting until the fall, allowing me enough time to capitalize on our momentum. That annoyed me, but I humoured them by saying that I'd wait. As they were leaving the house I said, "I just hope you're not too late." It turned out they were. The next week I went to the doctor and learned that I was pregnant. I was hoping for a girl.

CHAPTER SIX

THE CAREER OF A PROFESSIONAL ARTIST traces an inevitable
arc. The precise path is governed by the show business
equivalents of the laws of physics: a rise and an eventual fall
determined by an arcane calculus of speed attained, distance
travelled and the always variable atmospheric conditions—
the social and cultural environment in which one works. The
arc of writers, it is said, generally reaches its apogee early,
before they turn thirty—though of course there are many
exceptions to this—while actors, painters and symphony
conductors seem able to cruise at high altitudes almost indef-
initely, sustaining powers of creativity well into their twilight
years. Some singers too are blessed with longevity—think of
Tony Bennett, Patti Page, Perry Como, or Ella Fitzgerald—
although in that category the final calculations must include
an additional factor: the quality of the voice, which is hostage
to the ravages of time.

Luckily, in my case the career and the vocal instrument

ran on almost parallel lines; that is, I was singing at my best during precisely those years when my career was firing on all cylinders: the late 1970s and 1980s. No doubt some feedback mechanism was involved—my success as an artist gave me more confidence in my voice, and that confidence in my voice translated into better performances on stage and on disc.

I suspect that starting a family also played a critical role. It had been so fervent a desire of mine for so long that some part of me was always looking for an avenue of escape from the business—and, it seems to me now, unconsciously holding something back. However glamorous it might have looked from the outside, for a time I actually had the worst of both worlds. Single and without children, I was unsatisfied on the personal level and I was cruising along in middle gear as a singer, wearing myself out on the road, not certain where the career was headed. Abilene, Wichita, Great Falls—the parade of cities went by, and some days I wasn't even completely certain where I was.

Paradoxically, perhaps, having a baby—though it took me offstage and out of the limelight for several months—was at once both grounding and liberating. Liberating because, with the family unit established, I was free to give the career a clearer and stronger commitment when I returned. And grounding because, when I did, I could enjoy my professional success for what it was, without surrendering my values or losing sight of what was truly important. Success in turn gave me the ability to take more control over the career, to say no more often than I had, or when I said yes, to do so only on my terms. Nevertheless, feeding the ever-hungry maw of show business did take me away from my family for long periods of time, with deferred costs that ultimately had to be paid.

There's one additional variable that must be assessed in drawing a performer's arc: dumb luck. What if someone else had been given Gene MacLellan's magnificent song "Snowbird" to record? What if I had not had the good fortune to meet the people I did just when I did—Bill Langstroth, Brian Ahern and Leonard Rambeau—who encouraged me to keep going when I was ready to quit? What if I hadn't had the hard-headed counsel and negotiating flair of Lyman MacInnis? What if, when I was looking for songs for my first Jim Ed Norman album, Randy Goodrum's "You Needed Me" had never been sent to me, or had been recorded by another artist? You might say of that song that "I Needed It," because it took me professionally to a whole new level. But what were the odds of my being the beneficiary of all of this? These questions are, of course, unanswerable. Again, I am not being modest—I had talent. But for all the talent I had, I doubt that the arc of my career would have been the same without the unpredictable blessings of enormous good fortune.

AS WITH EVERYTHING—playing guitar, hitting golf balls, knitting scarves or entertaining forty thousand people in the Astrodome—the more you do it, the better you are likely to become. But confidence is a fickle partner. Take nine months off and your bravado can disappear entirely. You begin to question not only whether you still can hit the note "smack dab in the middle" (as Rosemary Clooney, bless her memory, once said of my singing), but whether you can hit it at all, and whether you can sustain an audience's interest for ninety minutes or more.

Five months pregnant with my second child, I gave what would be my last performance for many months at the Aladdin Hotel in Las Vegas on December 16, 1978. During that run I was delighted to "stand" at the marriage ceremony of actress Ruth Buzzi and businessman Kent Perkins. We'd become friends when Ruth (along with Valerie Harper and calypso singer Lord Laro) had appeared on a CBC TV special I'd hosted in Jamaica earlier that year; the telecast actually outdrew *Hockey Night in Canada* by a million viewers. Ruth's wedding was, like my own, an almost impromptu affair, performed in one of those classic drive-in Vegas wedding chapels. We were in and out in half an hour. More than thirty years later, Ruth and Kent are still together.

But with the exception of two weeks' rehearsal in a Toronto high school auditorium, I did not sing another professional note until the following September, before a sold-out audience of nineteen thousand at the Civic Center in Allentown, Pennsylvania. In my dressing room before that gig, my stage fright was acute—to the point of nausea. My agent, Fred Lawrence, later told me we'd "lost" about a million dollars in bookings during the layoff, but I didn't care.

The intervening period had not been uneventful. There was, most notably, my second Grammy (best pop vocal for "You Needed Me," nominated with Carly Simon, Donna Summer, Olivia Newton-John and Barbra Streisand). I watched the event from home, seven months pregnant and fighting a bad case of flu. The award soon had Leonard's phone ringing off the hook with new offers for concerts, TV shows and, later, a Broadway musical. In my expectant condition I couldn't possibly have committed to it, and the thought of taking up residence in Manhattan for a year or more filled me with dread. But for those gigs to which I did commit, my fee jumped 20 percent overnight.

We followed "You Needed Me" with "I Just Fall in Love Again"—from my second album with Jim Ed Norman, *New Kind of Feeling*—and it too was a certified hit. Bearing several authorial fingerprints (Stephen Dorff, Larry Herbstritt, Gloria Sklerov and Harry Lloyd), the song had been recorded two years earlier by the Carpenters but never released as a single— another lucky break for me. Dusty Springfield told me that she had recorded it too, but her album didn't get much attention; I would recall that conversation almost thirty years later when I started preparing for my *DUETS* album with some of the great ladies of song. My version of "I Just Fall in Love Again" topped Billboard's country and adult contemporary charts—the first of three straight number-one country and four straight number-one AC hits in the next two years— and reached number twelve on the Hot 100.

Among the many things I liked about Jim Ed Norman was that he was willing to record in Toronto, even though it meant weeks away from his own family. But with one child at home and another on the way, I wasn't looking to spend more time in Los Angeles, a city I was able to enjoy only in small doses. After a few days there I was always itching to get out, and in almost every case, as soon as our work was done, Leonard and I were on the first plane home.

And there was work to be done at home. During my maternity hiatus, Leonard and I had resolved to take aim at the brass ring. How far could I go? Neither of us knew, but we would never find out if we didn't try. And again there was that sense of empowerment that motherhood confers. I felt that if I could bear a child, there wasn't anything I couldn't do.

It wasn't really a quest for supremacy in record sales or earnings; rather, it was more about maximizing my own potential, seeing just how far my talent and resources could take me. If I were carefully managed and continued to find and record hit songs, we were optimistic that the top rung was within reach. To that end, knowing that Leonard would have to spend more time in Los Angeles schmoozing with the music industry, Balmur bought a one-bedroom condominium in Westwood that could be his home away from home.

Our confidence was soon validated. In March 1979 I signed my first contract with the Riviera Hotel in Las Vegas, guaranteeing me a fee of $125,000 a week for four weeks a year. The gig would begin in February 1980, with two shows nightly. The demand for tickets was so strong that the contract would later be renegotiated so that I earned $150,000 a week in 1981 and $250,000 a week in each of the following three years. The deal included the standard Vegas fringe benefits: a sprawling ranch-style house for the family, with pool, tennis court, staff and wall-to-wall security. The ceiling of our grand house, it turned out, leaked when it rained; in Vegas, fortunately, that was not too often.

This arrangement seemed the best possible compromise. If I had to be on the road (and I did), then at least I'd be parked in one place and surrounded by my family—or so I thought. It was far from a perfect arrangement. My time with the kids was limited. If I came home between shows at the Riviera, they were already asleep. And I was seldom in bed before 3:00 a.m., and thus rarely saw them in the morning. On one of those mornings the nanny took Will to the rides at Circus Circus and proceeded to lose him. Security guards eventually found him wandering around and asked where his mother was. "Sleeping," he said, thus portraying me as the sort of mother who sends her three-year-old off to enjoy Las Vegas on his own. Fortunately Will knew our street address in Toronto, so they made an intercom announcement: "Would the mother of William Langstroth, 11 Hilltop Road, Toronto, please come to . . ." The nanny heard it and quickly responded.

On April 16 I signed an even more important contract, giving birth (after a relatively brief four-hour labour) to Dawn Joanne Langstroth. Born at precisely 3:33 a.m., she weighed 8 pounds. She'd been so physically active in the womb that the doctor was sure it would be another boy, and so, therefore, was I. I was utterly delighted to have my powers of intuition proven wrong.

One day about a month after her birth, I was taking a 1.5-litre bottle of Coca-Cola from the fridge when it exploded in my hand. The glass flew everywhere, some of it ending up in my foot, opening a lovely gash. My dad, who was visiting at the time, said it was serious enough to require stitches. Bill ran up the street and got our surgeon neighbour, Dr. Robson, out of his garden on a day off, and we all went to Branson Hospital, where he stitched me up. While I was waiting in Emergency, an older woman was rolled in on a gurney. She was hysterical, wailing and crying and complaining. Then she happened to catch sight of me. "Oy vey," she yelled, sitting bolt upright. "Da singaa!" Her transformation was miraculous. The life-threatening ailments she appeared to be suffering from disappeared instantly; she settled right down and we had a lovely chat. But I was hobbling on crutches for a few weeks after that, a handicap for a nursing mother trying to scramble up the stairs to her hungry newborn.

One of the post-Grammy calls to Leonard was from Bob Hope's managers: would I accompany Bob to China for a TV special (with Mikhail Baryshnikov, Crystal Gayle and others)? The answer was no. I was still breastfeeding and not about to take an infant on such a long trip. That was the second time I'd rejected Bob; in the early 1970s he'd invited me to join one of his many expeditions to Southeast Asia to entertain U.S. troops, but it would have meant Christmas without my family in Springhill, and I was already lonely enough. I doubt that Bob took it personally.

Instead of Beijing and Shanghai, I went to Calgary with Dawn to shoot a commercial for CIBC. I spent my thirty-fourth birthday there, contentedly watching "Shadows in the Moonlight," another single from that second Jim Ed Norman album, climb to number one on both the country and adult contemporary charts.

Jim Ed and I made our third album that year—*I'll Always Love You*. It contained another beautiful Randy Goodrum song, "Broken-Hearted Me." Released as a single, it topped both the country and the adult contemporary charts and went to number twelve on the Hot 100. I loved the tune, but I didn't end up singing it much in live performance; the lyrics were so sad that I often felt it took the audience too long to come back from the dark place it had taken them. That album also contained my cover of the old Monkees hit "Daydream Believer" (written by Kingston Trio member John Stewart), which again did well on all three Billboard indexes.

When he wasn't producing albums for me, Jim Ed Norman had other projects on the go. One of them involved arranging tracks for a Hollywood film, *Urban Cowboy*, which starred John Travolta, Debra Winger and Scott Glenn. Jim Ed was already working with Mickey Gilley on a new arrangement of "Stand By Me" when he discovered a song that he thought might be suitable for me to sing as a duet: "Could I Have This Dance," by Wayland Holyfield and Bob House. I loved the tune—I'd always been a sucker for a waltz in three-quarter time. It had actually been written a decade earlier and had been nominated for a Grammy, but it never had much of a commercial life.

I cut a demo of the song, singing both parts—my own and the part that we hoped would be sung by Kenny Rogers. I included the latter just as a rough guide to what the harmony would sound like. I sent it to Jim Ed, who gave it to Becky Shargo, the film's music producer, who said she liked it just the way it was—she saw no need for a second voice. I remember Jim Ed saying when we had finished the master recording, "This song will be played at weddings from now until the end of eternity." I can't vouch for eternity, but I do know that it has been very popular. The *Urban Cowboy* soundtrack that Shargo assembled, incidentally, included several other great songs, including Johnny Lee's "Lookin' for Love," Boz Scaggs's "Look What You've Done to Me" and Kenny Rogers's Top Five hit "Love the World Away." Like those tunes, "Could I Have This Dance" was released as a single and went to number thirty-three on Billboard's Hot 100. I was subsequently offered a number of other songs for movies, including a Marvin Hamlisch tune for *Chapter Two*, one for a Superman sequel and another for *Roadie*. I turned them all down; none felt right for me.

I had booked several more U.S. gigs after my Allentown comeback, but these were warm-up climbs for one of the Everests of show business: New York's Carnegie Hall. I'd been scheduled to play there earlier in the year and had been forced to cancel because of illness. Now, on a warm September evening, the crowds were thronging to this justly revered temple of song. The inspired Leonard Rambeau arranged for every woman who entered the hall—about 1,800—to be given a red rose. You can imagine the wonderful scent that greeted me when I came onstage. In addition to the band I was backed by a thirteen-piece string section, snappily dressed in tuxedos. My dad was ailing, so my parents could not make it, but other family and friends flew down for the event, including Bill, who'd been working on a film set in Toronto and surprised me by turning up at the last minute.

"So this is Carnegie Hall," I said, when the cheers of welcome subsided. "So friggin' what? Does that mean I've made it? Do you think I should stay in the business?"

Despite the faux irreverence, I was even more anxious than usual, both because of the grand scale of the occasion and because we'd spent a long afternoon being sniped at by the stagehands' union. The union ran the hall with an iron fist. We were not permitted to touch our instruments except to play them, and any moving of them or microphones or stools had to be done by stagehands. My nerves were so frayed it took me five or six songs to settle down.

At the end I sang what some people considered my signature song, Robbie MacNeill's "A Million More," and dedicated it to "those who saw me last year in New York at the Bottom Line or even earlier, at the Bitter End—which it was." They were standing and cheering at the end and I wept, for the first time on stage since my homecoming tour of the Maritimes two years earlier. Afterwards there was a gala reception at the Stork Club.

I was appearing at Harrah's in Reno a few weeks later when my brave, bulletproof scheme for portable motherhood hit a sudden and inescapable roadblock. I had both Will and Dawn with me, and they both developed ear infections, a problem that had plagued my own childhood. Dawn had to be briefly hospitalized and then sent home, accompanied by Will and the nanny. Soon after, the doctors in Toronto informed me that Dawn would need tube implants to help facilitate fluid drainage. It was a common and low-risk procedure, but she was too young to have it done, so it was advisable that she avoid flying for a few years.

The implications were obvious: the nanny would have to remain with Dawn in Toronto, and so, therefore, would Will. I'd be gone and my children would be without me—and I without them—for weeks at a time. This constituted a major setback, and the consequences—for both my mounting parental guilt and Dawn and Will's emotional development— were profound.

Back in Toronto I co-hosted a luncheon to commemorate the United Nations Year of the Child. I'd been honorary chairwoman of the Save the Children Fund for some years, and Bill and I had sponsored three children in Jamaica, Turkey and Senegal. I was seated at the head table with Queen Elizabeth's daughter, Princess Anne. Though our respective upbringings could not have been more dissimilar, we felt an immediate rapport and laughed ourselves through the lunch. She recounted amusing stories of her days in British boarding schools, while I told her the story of how Catholic nuns in Canada instructed young girls not to wear patent leather shoes, lest prurient boys use them as mirrors to look up their dresses. She got quite a kick out of that.

Later a reporter approached the princess and asked, "So how's your mother?" She replied, "Well, she's still the queen." And she would still be the queen when, a decade later, I made one of the biggest gaffes of my life.

$$\smile\!\!\!\curvearrowright$$

I HAVE NEVER PAID MUCH ATTENTION to astrological forecasts. I was always more interested in another kind of chart—Billboard's. But if there's any substance to astrology's claims, then my planetary conjunctions at the dawn of 1980 must have been extremely favourable. Every single that Capitol released seemed to be a hit; every album flirted with or surpassed the gold-record benchmark. By the end of that year, including *There's a Hippo in My Tub*, two discs of collected hits and four with Jim Ed Norman, I had sold 5.3 million albums in North America over a twenty-three-month period. On my behalf, Leonard and Fred were turning down more requests than they were accepting, some of them quite lucrative. Even the deceased seemed to be in my corner. About that time, Linda Thompson, girlfriend of the late Elvis Presley, said in an interview with a radio station in Los Angeles that my version of "Snowbird" had been the King's favourite record, that he played it all the time and that he loved "my depth of feeling and vocal range." I'd never had a chance to meet him—we were never playing Vegas at the same time—but that endorsement meant a lot to me. It still does.

I began the new year in London, where I taped an episode of *The Muppet Show* with Miss Piggy—as much fun, I think, as I'd ever had in television. And because of all the repeats of that show over the years, it's also the most viewed

TV show that I've ever done. The trip also gave me a chance to have dinner with the Muppets' creator, the delightful Jim Henson, and his wife, Jane, and to meet his extraordinary team of puppeteers. Henson and I were actually rivals that year: both of us were later nominated for Grammys for children's records, mine for the *Hippo* album and his for the music to *The Muppet Movie.* Jim ended up with the trophy.

What was puzzling and disappointing to Leonard and me was that, despite three number-one country songs and three top-selling country albums, I was not nominated in that Grammy category. Ostensibly sales were not factored into the voting process, but the jury let it be known that I was not even to be considered a country artist. This edict was a little bewildering, since that's precisely the category to which everyone else wanted to consign me, and also since they did grant "country" admission to Kenny Rogers, another huge crossover artist. Fred Lawrence, my agent, made some inquiries and was told that, despite my success on the country charts, my songs projected "too much of a pop consciousness." In other words, I was guilty of reaching too broad an audience. On the one hand, I was annoyed; on the other, I was laughing all the way to the bank. And the following year the jury made amends: I won the Grammy for best country vocal performer, for "Could I Have This Dance."

When I returned from London, I was booked to appear at the Sunrise Theatre in Fort Lauderdale. The concert took place just days after six American diplomats had been spirited out of Tehran on false passports with the help of the Canadian embassy—one of the most dramatic news stories of the year. The six had fled the American embassy after Iranian militants seized it the previous November, taking fifty-two other hostages. The Canadian ambassador to Iran, Ken Taylor, had given them safe harbour for more than two months while preparations were made to get them out of the country. When they finally came home, they were welcomed as heroes, and Canadians visiting or living in the U.S. suddenly found themselves basking in that same heroic light.

I was about to start my third song when someone in the audience shouted out, "Thank you, Canada!" Everyone immediately stood up and applauded for the next four minutes. The ovation had nothing to do with me or my music; it was based entirely on my nationality—a demonstrative thank you from appreciative Americans. It happened again the next night as well. The remaining fifty-two hostages were not released until the following January, the day of Ronald Reagan's inauguration as president.

It was during that same Florida trip that I met Burt Reynolds. He had said publicly that he was a big fan of mine, and he had, I suspect, orchestrated an invitation for me to appear with him as a guest on Dinah Shore's daytime talk show. Dinah had once been his girlfriend and they had remained good friends. That was the start of what I would call an extended flirtation with Burt. I liked him a lot. In many ways he reminded me of my brothers, blessed as he was with the same very sharp, self-deprecating sense of humour. But it never went beyond flirting. I was married, and there was another woman in his life at the time, actress Sally Field. In my company Burt was never less than a complete gentleman.

I may be flattering myself, but I sensed that his interest transcended his oft-expressed appreciation for my music. He sent flowers on several occasions, called me while I was on tour and turned up once in Atlanta when I was performing there and he was shooting a film. None of this was kept hidden. In fact, I used to tell audiences about our friendship and joke about "taking him home with me" to Toronto, to which Bill, in his droll fashion, said, "Well, I certainly hope he's good with young kids."

The Shore show was taped at the Burt Reynolds Theatre in Burt's hometown of Jupiter, Florida. During the show he invited me to see a performance of *Same Time Next Year*, in which he was starring with Carol Burnett in the same theatre at night. After the show Leonard and I went backstage to say hello and Burt said, "If I make a telephone call, will you sing 'You Needed Me' for a friend of mine?"

"Sure," I said. And then he made the call and put me on the line. I didn't know for sure, but I had a pretty good idea who it was. I sang a few bars and Sally Field said, "Oh, my God! Is it really you, Anne Murray?" And I said, "Is it really you, Sally Field?" Sally told me that she had listened to the song every day on the set of the film *Norma Rae*, which she had just finished shooting, using it as inspiration for her role.

Two months later Burt arranged for me to be his musical guest on *Saturday Night Live*, which he was hosting in New York City. I'd been on the show five years earlier, during its first season. Then in June Burt was sitting in for Johnny Carson as host of the *Tonight Show* in L.A. and again invited me to be a guest. On that occasion we compared our knee-surgery scars, mine from my childhood brush with chondro-malacia patella and his from college football injuries that effectively ended his dream of a pro career.

We had one more encounter that I recall, at the end of that year. I was invited to attend a Variety Club testimonial dinner in his honour, hosted by Carson. I again sang "You

Needed Me"—this time the complete version—and afterwards planted a big fat kiss on his lips. After that we lost contact, although he did arrange for me to sing "I Don't Think I'm Ready for You," the theme song for his 1985 movie *Stick*. It may have been in thanks for that recording that he sent me flowers for the last time. When I called to thank him, a woman answered—it might have been Loni Anderson, whom he was then seeing and whom he subsequently married—and she put him on. That conversation, more than a little awkward, was very brief. I thanked him for the flowers and that was that. It was the last time we spoke.

But it was Burt who suggested, at our first meeting in Florida, that I consider buying a vacation home in Jupiter. It's a small town with all the well-known amenities of south Florida but removed from the noise and bustle that affects towns a little farther south, such as Fort Lauderdale and Boca Raton. Not long afterwards I learned that a partner of Lyman's was building a condominium project on Jupiter Island. I bought a three-bedroom unit and used it extensively for more than twenty years. It was hard to improve on the view: one side of the apartment looked out on the vast Atlantic, and the other on the inter-coastal waterway.

There were other celebrities who appeared to be drawn to me by more than my singing ability. A less subtle suitor was country singer Jimmy Dean. Best known for his 1961 novelty hit song "Big Bad John," he later became a very successful entrepreneur, co-founding Jimmy Dean Sausage, a purveyor of food products, which he ultimately sold to Sara Lee. Although eighteen years my senior, Jim was a lot of fun and I certainly liked him. We went out for dinner one night in Nashville; afterwards, in my hotel room, he made it clear what he wanted for dessert—me. I made several overt attempts to discourage him, but he was quite persistent. I then excused myself, went to the washroom and used the phone there to call my bandleader, Pat Riccio, asking him to drop by the room immediately, if not sooner. A few minutes later Pat turned up with a few other band members and Jimmy's ardour was quickly cooled.

And then there was Larry Gatlin, another man with a roving eye. He and his brothers were a popular Nashville act that opened for me several times on the road as well as in Vegas. At one of those early tour stops, Lincoln, Nebraska, Larry seemed to take a distinct shine to me, and once again I ended up in my hotel room with trouble on my hands. In a virtual replay of the Jimmy Dean scenario, I used a lifeline and called Pat Riccio. He gathered up a few guys from the band and crew and joined Larry and me in my room for drinks. Pat confirmed my instinct that Larry was transparently on the prowl. We all talked for a while; then, as the conversation ended, Larry was left holding a dish of peanuts. He turned to me and said, "What do you want me to do with my nuts, Annie?" We had a laugh, he got the message and we enjoyed each other's company after that.

When I began my first two-week run at the Riviera in Las Vegas in February 1980, Rodney Dangerfield was my opening act. I still remember some of his great one-liners ("I asked the cabbie to find me some action and he took me to my house. . . . Take my wife. I went to a bachelor party before my wedding and she was starring in the movie . . ."). Eleven billboards trumpeted my presence in town, my face was plastered over every newspaper box and all twenty-eight shows were complete sellouts. In addition to my own ten-piece band there was an eighteen-piece house orchestra. The act I followed was the great Kenny Rogers. I went to his final show, and afterwards Wayne Newton and Pia Zadora (then the wife of the Riviera's owner, Meshulam Riklis) turned up to present him with a token of the hotel's appreciation: a gleaming white Italian-made Stutz Bearcat, driven right out onto the stage. I hoped I could look forward to exactly the same expression of gratitude, but alas, it didn't happen.

In Vegas it was not uncommon for visiting celebrities to come backstage after the show and say hello. They didn't always come back—Frank Sinatra dropped in one night and apparently instructed handlers not to mention that he had been there. But usually they did, just as a courtesy. These visits typically involved little more than brief pleasantries, but occasionally one caught glimpses of the essential character. For example, Colonel Tom Parker, the Svengali who managed the career of Elvis Presley, generously brought me teddy bears for my kids and, though I hadn't asked for it, an autographed photograph of himself.

Another time a group of us were standing around in my dressing room after the show when the irrepressible actress Cloris Leachman and Ernest Borgnine and his wife, Tova, came in. I'd met Cloris before, on Mike Douglas's talk show in Miami Beach. She had a thing about healthy eating and the evils of cigarettes—I remember her whacking Pat Riccio on the rear end and chastising him for smoking. In Vegas she went after my bassist, Peter Cardinali. She detected the scent of tobacco on him and asked if he was a smoker. Knowing that she was what he called a "smoke Nazi," Peter hesitated. Before he could answer, Cloris wrapped her arms around him, gave him a big kiss and stuck her tongue into his mouth.

"That's what I thought," she said. "You *are* a smoker."

Peter was a little stunned, to say the least. Then she went after him for his considerable girth. "Peter, you don't really want to be that fat, do you? You're a good-looking man. Just think how gorgeous you would be if you lost weight." Cloris repeated that sermon a few times.

In Tahoe, Sammy Davis Jr. came to see my show one night—he was scheduled to follow me in the same venue—and stayed afterwards for an hour. He said to me, "Anne, I just wanted to thank you. I have never in all my years in show business felt so much warmth in a room as I did tonight. Thank you for warming it up for me, because I'm sure I will still feel it when I open tomorrow night." It was vintage Sammy, at once completely over the top but entirely genuine. And it was one of the nicest things anyone has ever said to me.

But from the highs induced by the standing ovations at Carnegie Hall and the Riviera Hotel, I was quickly brought down to earth. My dad was visibly failing—I had seen it when I'd been home in Springhill the previous Christmas. Seventy-two years old, he had been suffering from lymphoma for a few years, the result, I suspect, of years of exposure to X-ray radiation at the hospital. His liver had also been damaged, the lingering effects of an old case of hepatitis C, probably contracted in the operating room. One night in late March, he realized something was happening to him, and he told my mother that he needed to see a neurologist. He asked her to call an ambulance, then to call my brother Harold to meet him at the Infirmary, a hospital in Halifax. Dad had suffered a cerebral hemorrhage, and he went into a coma shortly after arriving at the hospital. He was put on life support, but

Harold soon made the decision to let him go—it's what Dad would have wanted. Bill, Dawn and I flew down the next day. I was in shock and emotionally a complete wreck. My bond with my father had been as strong as anything I had ever felt. Nothing had ever hit me so hard.

James Carson Murray left a family who loved and respected him and a forty-year record of exemplary medical achievement, service and sacrifice, one that would be hard to equal. To let the citizens of Springhill pay their respects, Mom decided to leave the casket open at the funeral home for two days. After the funeral we all gathered that night in the old bedroom upstairs and watched television, just as we had in the late fifties and sixties. In fact we watched the Juno Awards show, Canada's version of the Grammys. I know Dad would have been proud: I won four Junos that night.

THROUGHOUT THAT FIRST DECADE in the business I'd been fortunate to meet and work with some of the biggest names in country music, from Glen Campbell to Johnny Cash, from Mac Davis to Kenny Rogers, and from Willie Nelson to Kris Kristofferson. I found myself working with Kris for the first time in June 1980, on a TV variety show in Monte Carlo. He was not only a great performer, he was a great person— humble (despite his many accomplishments), sweet and as easy to work with as anyone I have met. His songwriting talent was extraordinary, and I ended up putting three of his tunes on a later album, *Country Croonin'*.

Monaco being the attraction it is, a large group of us went over. We were all gathered in the dining room of the Hôtel de

Paris one night when Liberace made a grand entrance with a small entourage. He and his much younger principal companion were dressed in matching white ship captain's outfits, laced with diamonds and fur wrist stoles and complete with shiny white sailor shoes. They apparently went everywhere dressed like twins. Some band members saw them one morning in the hotel elevator, wearing matching red sequined jackets with tuxedo pants, frilly shirts and patent leather shoes.

I'd met Liberace before, in Las Vegas, and like almost everyone I met, he'd been very kind to me. In Monaco he made a special point of coming over to my table to chat. He ended up sitting at another table right across from me, and I couldn't take my eyes off him. You could see that he'd had a ton of cosmetic facial surgery. He looked, in fact, like a heavily embalmed cadaver. The effect, on me at least, was so mesmerizing that I had trouble finishing my dinner.

During that trip I found an absolutely stunning Piaget watch, its face covered with small, understated, discreetly placed diamonds. Apart from my infamous Vegas mink coat, I had never been particularly self-indulgent when it came to baubles and other jewel-encrusted extravagances, but I was sorely tempted by the watch. In the end I resisted the temptation to buy it; breakfast in Monte Carlo seemed to cost hundreds of dollars, so I could only imagine what the watch would be priced at. Then, a few months later, shopping on Toronto's Bloor Street with Mom and my brother Bruce, we found the same watch in the window of European Jewellers—a providential sign, clearly indicating that it should be mine. They actually had two models on display that were very similar to each other, and I asked Mom which one she thought I should buy.

"It doesn't matter to me," she said, "but anybody who pays $1,100 for a watch is silly."

I bought it, and it was a bargain compared with its Monte Carlo price. But Mom had misread the price tag, and I didn't have the heart—at least not at that moment—to tell her that it actually cost $11,000.

———

THE WEEK OF MY THIRTY-FIFTH BIRTHDAY and fifth wedding anniversary was a Californian whirlwind: a sold-out theatre in San Francisco serenaded me with the strains of "Happy Birthday" and impresario Bill Graham rolled out a huge birthday cake on wheels. I heard it again the next night in San Diego, then it was on to L.A. and a four-night run at the five-thousand-seat Greek Theatre, also sold out. One day— Anne Murray Day, in fact—the mayor of L.A., Tom Bradley, personally turned up with three hundred fans and Capitol executives to unveil my star on the Hollywood Walk of Fame, near the Capitol building. I had read about this ritual as a child, never thinking that I would one day be its honouree. A bagpiper from Nova Scotia musically escorted me to the dais and two uniformed RCMP officers stood as an honour guard. You can still find the five-pointed version of me there, parked between stars belonging to radio-tube inventor Lee de Forest and broadcaster Lowell Thomas, and just down the block from some pretty fair musical company: John Lennon, Tina Turner, Beverley Sills, Garth Brooks, Bonnie Raitt and Natalie Cole. After the ceremony Capitol hosted a celebratory luncheon at the Brown Derby. When it was over, Leonard and I went back to the Westwood condo only to find ourselves locked out. He had left his keys with his wife, Caron, and the nanny had taken Will and Dawn to the zoo. I sat in the lobby, very un-star-like, for a long hour.

⸺

IF YOU ASK ANYONE CLOSE TO ME, they will tell you that meeting Cynthia McReynolds was one of the best things that ever happened to Anne Murray. I still find it amazing that this extraordinary woman—cherished friend, golf and tennis buddy, shrewd business adviser, road manager, bartender extraordinaire, comedienne and perpetual life of the party—lived only a few doors away from me in Thornhill, north of Toronto. Cynthia seldom met a table she didn't want to stand on after a few drinks. A stay-at-home mom, she became a great role model for me. Among other things, she taught me a lot about parenting. But it took a while for us to meet.

It was Bill who made the first connection with the McReynoldses. He met her son, Shane, one of the many kids on our street in the late 1970s, and Shane immediately went home and told the family that Ann-Margret had moved into the neighbourhood. Later Bill also met Cynthia's husband, Ken, a successful architect, and their fourteen-year-old daughter, Sloan. She was doing a school project and asked if she might interview me; since I was then pregnant with Dawn and had time on my hands, I naturally agreed. We did the interview and Sloan got an A-plus on it; Cynthia then wrote me a nice thank-you note and invited us to play tennis on their backyard court.

I wasn't much of a tennis player and I didn't immediately take her up on the offer. In fact, a few years passed before

I was formally introduced to Cynthia. It happened when the four of us got together for drinks at our house. They came over at about 8:00 p.m. and didn't leave until after 1:00 a.m., a very promising start. Not long after, Cynthia and I played golf at the Thornhill Golf and Country Club—on the short, par-three course, since neither of us was then a very good player. The relationship evolved from there: we'd have dinners at each other's homes, light fireworks together with our families on the Victoria Day weekend, and trek out to tree farms in search of suitable firs for Christmas. Ken, who'd been a ranked junior player, taught me how to play tennis; later he designed an addition to our home.

After that, Cynthia invited some of her many women friends to play doubles on their court and encouraged me— *cajoled* may be more apt—to join a club with indoor courts so that we could play during the long Canadian winter. Typically, I was reluctant, but I did join and played regularly. For the first time I had met a group of women whom I could befriend. Until then I tended to live inside a comfortable but isolating self-created cocoon. Most of my close friends from university lived elsewhere, and my professional life was so public that I wanted my private life to be very private. When Bill and I socialized, it tended to be either with other music industry types or with family. I barely knew anyone outside those small circles.

Cynthia insisted, forcefully, that this was unhealthy and that it had to change, that just because I enjoyed a certain celebrity status didn't mean I wasn't allowed to engage socially with ordinary people. And she was right—I was much too secluded. In retrospect I'm glad she pushed me; I never would have done it on my own. Over time I became quite close with

several members of this group, friendships that have enormously enriched my later life.

Eventually our golf games improved and Cynthia and
I became full-fledged members at the Thornhill club. Once or
twice a year, with ten or twelve other women golfers, we'd go
north to someone's cottage or chalet for a couple of nights. We
cross-country skied, cooked, drank wine, watched movies and
always had a great time. This group of women became known
as "Chicks with Sticks"—"the Chicks" for short. In later years
we planned and executed a series of three unforgettable travel
adventures—to Scotland in 1995 (we played the "new" course
at St. Andrews and several other legendary layouts), the
Maritimes in 1997 (playing courses in Nova Scotia and P.E.I.,
including the Highland Links at Keltic Lodge on Cape Breton
Island, easily one of the most spectacular courses in the world)
and Spain in 2000—a dozen women leaving behind our work-
aday cares and setting off for ten days of pure fun, following the
lead of the consummate laugh-maker and fun-lover, Cynthia.

I WENT TO EUROPE AGAIN IN 1981, first in Holland and
then England, where I played the Palladium. The shows were
popular, but I was torn up inside. This was a two-week trip,
the longest I had been away from the kids, and I was finding
it stressful. Then Pat Riccio, my bandleader, fell ill. He had
been drinking far too much and eating not nearly enough,
and he was already sick by the time we reached London.
Eventually his body just shut down and we had to put him
on a plane back to Toronto; he was hospitalized and diagnosed with an acute case of pancreatitis. The doctors told

him later that he was a lucky man—he had almost died. He gave up drinking immediately and today consumes only the occasional glass of wine.

By that time Pat and all the other members of the band were on a retainer from Balmur. This wasn't entirely unheard of in the industry but it was extremely rare, because it meant paying salary and health-care benefits even when the musicians were idle. I kept them on retainer for the next eighteen years. The cost was huge—a factor often overlooked when simply adding up performance fees—but so were the benefits: they were always on call, available to me when I needed them. This applied not only to concert tours but also to private corporate shows (I played a number of these for IBM) and TV appearances. When I didn't need them, the band members were free to take on other gigs or work as session players, which they often did. But if they had a conflict, I always took precedence. I derived no small comfort from this arrangement and doubtless spared myself some grief. For them, working in a field where you often never know where your next paycheque is coming from (or when), it offered a degree of security that was the envy of other musicians. I also think it helped the group feel more cohesive, more like a team, an important consideration when you're away from home for weeks or months at a time.

Back from Europe, I was watching the *Tonight Show* one night and discovered a new talent: a young comedian named Jerry Seinfeld. In those days he was still largely unknown and playing the comedy-club circuit. His act had me in stitches, so much so that the very next day I called my agent, Fred Lawrence, and said, "Find me that guy. I gotta have him." So that fall Jerry opened for me at Harrah's in

Lake Tahoe—his first stand-up gig outside of a comedy club and the only one that resulted from his *Tonight Show* appearance. Over the next four years he opened for me once more in Tahoe, at least three times in Vegas and at several one-nighters on the road.

Jerry was a class act, as real offstage as he was on. Pat Riccio said that Jerry was so normal he was almost too good to be true. His material, like mine, was clean, and you never had to worry about him turning off an audience or establishing a sour mood in the room. Quite the contrary. Having laughed until their sides ached, most audiences were content to settle down and listen to some good music. And he and I were temperamentally alike as well: always calm and in control, even when disasters struck.

Except for the fact that he didn't play an instrument, Jerry might well have been another member of my band. He hung out with all the guys. My bassist, Peter Cardinali, recalls doing his laundry with Jerry at a local laundromat; he maintains that it was one of those laundry trips that inspired what may be Jerry's most famous bit: the missing-sock routine.

With Peter, Pat, my brother Bruce, guitarist Aidan Mason and keyboard player Steve Sexton, Jerry also shopped at the mall, went skiing and played tennis and racquetball. He was naturally athletic but liked to play around on the court, trying to throw the other guys off their game by making them laugh. One of his tactics was to sing—very loudly and very badly—"From Now On," a tune Bruce sang in our show. He maintained to the guys that Tim Gallwey's book *The Inner Game of Tennis* was the reason for his winning ways. I'm not sure anyone believed that—my guys were novices, and easy prey.

Every night the band would play Jerry onto the stage with a David Sanborn song, "Port of Call." And every night he would say, "Thank you, thank you—and thank you, band!" and then mention that they were all "naked back there" getting ready for my portion of the show. Downstairs in my dressing room, his show would be piped in through the intercom; in time we had all memorized his entire act—I can still recite parts of it to this day. Even my kids knew his material after I brought home a tape of it. He in turn watched our show every night, either from the wings or somewhere in the room.

My dressing room tended to be Grand Central Station; everyone hung out there, including Jerry, though he was always very respectful, a little nervous and careful, he later told me, never to overstay his welcome. For me it's been fun to watch the phenomenal arc of his career and to see millions of other people discover what I saw that first time on the *Tonight Show*: the kernel of pure comic genius. A decade or so later, when I was inducted into the Canadian Music Hall of Fame, Jerry contributed a very generous video tribute.

That year I celebrated two Christmases. The first was in October at Keltic Lodge on Cape Breton Island. There, surrounded by friends and twenty members of my extended family (including Bill and the kids, my mom, brothers, sisters-in-law, etc.), we shot a CBS TV show for broadcast in December, "A Special Anne Murray Christmas." I had not been back to the lodge since the summer of 1963, when I'd been part of the low-waged summer staff. Needless to say, my accommodations were rather better this time around. My principal guests included Kris Kristofferson, the Men of the Deeps (a Nova Scotia coalminers' choir) and a group of Halifax schoolchildren playing the ukulele. The show drew 37 million viewers in the

U.S. and another 3.1 million on CTV, the Canadian carrier—
the largest audience it had recorded up to that time.

It was while we were shooting that special that my old
friend from *Singalong Jubilee* Karen Oxley felt the first symptoms of the illness that would eventually take her life. She was
then working with Chalmers Doane, who was in charge of
music for the Halifax school system, and she'd come to Keltic
to help out with the performance of their ukulele students.
The day before production began, we were sitting in the bar
downstairs having drinks. Karen had two beers, and when she
got up, her legs wouldn't hold her. At first some people
thought she might be drunk, but I knew better.

"Karen, what's wrong?" I asked.

"I don't know," she said, with some alarm.

A couple of guys helped her to her room. My brother
David, a doctor, who was with us at the time, later said he
didn't like the look of her symptoms. Not long after, she was
diagnosed with multiple sclerosis. But Karen was a fighter,
and she fought the disease for another eleven years. At one
point she had to learn to walk again—and did. For therapy
she took up horseback riding and loved it. Every summer
she'd come to my cottage at Pugwash and we'd spend a glorious week catching up. She loved that place, so much so that
she requested that, when she died, her ashes be distributed
over the property. When she passed away in 1992, her
husband, Grant Kennedy, flew his private plane over the site
and honoured her wishes. Karen Oxley—a great broad and
a wonderful friend, deeply missed.

FOR SOME TIME Bill and I had been looking for a cottage property in Northport, to be closer to my parents and brothers in the summer. But when we were looking, no one was selling. My brother Harold was always on the lookout for prime cottage land as well. He found the site near Pugwash and called me right away. He was, uncharacteristically, very enthusiastic, saying that he wouldn't hesitate to buy it himself but couldn't afford it on his own. So, sight unseen, I went in on it with him. Together we paid $98,000 for 32 acres—twenty of them on the water. We then subdivided, selling 5 acres to my brother David, 1.2 acres to Stewart and 1.4 acres to Daniel. Harold sold his remaining portion to me in about 2000, so I now own 12 acres on the water and 12 more across the road, in a deeply wooded lot.

Bill and I renovated the main house immediately, adding a beautiful and spacious sunroom, and spent our first summer there in 1982. The following year we put in a tennis court. For years the wider Murray clan convened for as many weeks each summer as time permitted, allowing the next generation an opportunity to bond as tightly as my brothers and I had. Will, Dawn and their cousins were busy from morning till night. They played tennis, go-karted, swam, water-skied, picked mussels, dug clams and hunted for crabs, starfish and sand dollars. At night, swatting mosquitoes, they played manhunt, a kind of tag game, until they were called home for bed. On rainy days they retreated to a huge loft in "the barn," a utility building we had filled with toys and costumes for dress-up. They performed skits for family get-togethers—Bill taught them to mime to Spike Jones tapes—and used our Betamax video camera to make home movies, complete with disappearing acts and puppet shows. It was often hard to drag the kids away from their fun; to summon them to meals, I installed a bell on the side of the cottage.

As the kids got older, the loft became music central for a Murray/Langstroth orchestra made up of guitars, a bass, drums and an electric keyboard (we shipped Will's drums down every year). Will and his cousins Dale and Brian Murray even attended a rock music camp in Halifax for two consecutive summers. Dale and Brian were also blessed with the talent and performing genes; they are now professional musicians.

EARLY ON, Leonard had established an Anne Murray fan club. One of its principal activities was to send out photographs of yours truly along with an autograph. In 1971 we received a piece of fan mail (and a few seeds of wheat) from a young farmer in rural Saskatchewan named Robert Charles Kieling. We sent back the usual thank-you note and a photograph. Unfortunately Kieling took the message "Love, Anne" seriously. He was in love with me, and he was convinced that it was reciprocal. The clinical term for this disorder is erotomania—the delusional belief, often associated with schizophrenia, that the object of your affections is in love with you.

Thus began a torturous stalking affair that would last almost two decades. The full Kieling dossier would eventually fill several cabinet drawers. It includes records of the hundreds of telephone calls he made to Balmur offices and of his repeated visits to my parents' home in Springhill, even when I wasn't there—Mom later had to have an alarm system installed. He even turned up at my father's funeral and at my high school reunion.

Apparently affluent, Kieling managed an 800-acre farm near Blumenhof, southeast of Swift Current. He sent money orders, airplane tickets and letters asking me to meet him. Once he put a letter under my door that said: "For God's sake, stop this insanity and fly with me to Saskatchewan." He even claimed to have sent me a diamond ring—if he did, I never saw it—and took my failure to return it as further evidence that I secretly loved him.

He travelled across the country attending several of my concerts, and he approached me more than once. In Vancouver, at the Queen Elizabeth Theatre, he brought flowers to the stage and, when I bent to accept them, he grabbed my arm and would not let go; I had to struggle to get free. In Toronto in 1978, I was about to do my encore at the Royal Alexandra Theatre when Kieling, who had somehow managed to get backstage, came towards me from the wings. A member of my band intervened to block him. Another time, when I was leaving a venue, he came out of the shadows as I was getting into a car and grabbed my arm. Most of the time, however, he would simply come up to the stage and stare longingly at me. Even after being ordered back to his seat and warned of eviction if he approached the stage again, Kieling would just stand there staring.

The more he was rejected, the more certain he became of his conviction that I loved him. The fact that I was happily married with children was, for Kieling, simply a public relations front. "It's a matter of her using poetic allegorical expressions of her career," he told one journalist.

I was never frightened of him and I didn't believe he was dangerous. He seemed to have a gentle soul, and he was certainly intelligent. He read widely, had taught himself French and German, and could converse on a broad range of subjects. But you never really know in these situations, and that was disconcerting.

It wasn't until 1980, four years after he had turned up at our front door in Springhill at Christmas, that we secured a peace bond ordering Kieling not to communicate with me or visit Balmur's Toronto offices. The very next day, he came to the offices with roses and a letter for me. For violation of restraining orders he later served jail sentences in Regina; Toronto; Penetanguishene, Ontario; and Amherst, Nova Scotia.

Both Mom and I were called to testify at one of Kieling's trials. There he stated that when the famous Canadian Armed Forces aerial squadron the Snowbirds flew over his Saskatchewan farm, he understood their formation to be spelling out a message to him from me, the original singing Snowbird. Similarly he thought that the longing expressed in the love songs I sang was my attempt to encrypt my feelings for him in musical code.

This pattern continued for years—court orders issued and repeatedly breached. When Canada's Charter of Rights and Freedoms was enacted, Kieling studied the legislation in jail and argued in court that the restraining orders infringed his freedoms of speech and association, which were guaranteed under the Charter. On more than one occasion he was released after trumping the courts on points of law.

Perhaps inevitably, the notion of a literally lovesick farmer and his quixotic pursuit stirred the imagination of dramatists. Playwrights Paul Ledoux and David Young wrote a musical about my stalker and his obsession, *I Love You, Anne Murray*. It was first mounted in 1984 and later, under a different title—*Strange Love*—played in theatres across Canada. Two decades later Ledoux gave *Strange Love* yet another title, *Still Desire You*, and staged it again, using the same basic storyline and twelve songs written and performed by the talented Haligonian Melanie Doane.

Kieling eventually disappeared from the headlines, but the questions raised by his fixation did not. If newspaper editors had grown weary of the Kieling story, the man himself failed to tire of me. The saga dragged on endlessly. By 1987 he'd been arrested thirty-seven times and fined thousands of dollars. In the first six months of 1988 he phoned me 263 times. As late as 1993 he was still serving time for restraining-order violations. There seemed to be no permanent solution. The offence was never deemed serious enough to warrant a long-term sentence, and no quantity of warnings, citations or fines seemed to deter him. However, it's been more than a decade since he made an effort to contact me. I think Balmur spent more than half a million dollars on security and legal costs.

Kieling, of course, was an extremely determined and single-minded stalker. At the same time, however, I think he was part of a phenomenon that our celebrity-obsessed culture bears some responsibility for creating. In music, movies, fashion modelling and sports, stars are manufactured and profiles inflated to such an extent that some people—deranged stalkers such as Mark David Chapman (John Lennon's killer) and John Hinckley Jr. (the man who was obsessed with actress Jodie Foster and tried to assassinate Ronald Reagan)—are no longer able to separate the fantasy of celebrity hype from the real world. In that illusory state, anything is theoretically possible, such as Kieling's belief that we were destined to be lovers or Chapman's mad conviction that Lennon had to be murdered.

I have no answers to offer here—the system is deeply entrenched, and not only in North America—simply the observation that there is a darker side to our cultural excesses.

⌒

BY 1983 I HAD CLEARLY TURNED A CORNER, at least professionally. Leonard's strategy was working. In Canada and the U.S. he was able to associate my name with significant cultural events or institutions—a week-long gig at the O'Keefe Centre in Toronto, the opening of the same city's Roy Thomson Hall, two or three appearances at New York's Radio City Music Hall, the Grand Ole Opry in Nashville and other prestigious venues. That year also saw my first tour of Australia and New Zealand, and two nights at Edmonton's Devil's Lake Corral nightclub, for which I earned $220,000. When a radio reporter there asked me if I was embarrassed to be making that amount of money, I replied, "Not at all. Last time I played here I went $5,000 in the red, so I'm just catching up."

The highly-rated CBS special at Keltic Lodge, which was produced by Dwight Hemion and Gary Smith, two of the top names in American television, would be followed in the early 1980s by three more. The themes were a Caribbean cruise, with guests Eddie Rabbit, Richard Simmons and José Luis Rodriguez; Quebec City's winter carnival, with Glen Campbell, Dionne Warwick and Claude Léveillée; and Merry Olde London, with Frank (Miss Piggy) Oz, Dusty Springfield, Bananarama and my brother Bruce. TV exposure was the engine that helped power record sales: by May 1983, based on nineteen albums and thirty singles, I had sold about 20 million records, twenty of them platinum (sales of a million or more).

But although my recording and television careers were solid, problems were brewing on the domestic front, problems that I was blind to or refused to see. I was trying desperately to strike a reasonable balance between the obligations of motherhood and career. I made a point of being home for every school break and spent five or six weeks every summer with the family at our Pugwash summer home. Still, I was usually away about a hundred days a year. Having to leave my children crying at the door as I flew off to L.A., Las Vegas or anywhere else made me miserable. The guilt gnawed at me.

It wasn't just that I was away too much. Even when I was there, my celebrity status fundamentally changed the childhood my kids enjoyed. I fought hard to keep them out of the limelight and preserve their privacy, but when Bill and I took the kids to Disney World for the first time in the early 1980s, we could barely move without being thronged by people milling around, snapping pictures and asking for autographs. Will, who was about seven at the time, was so unhappy that he asked me if, the next time we planned such a trip, I could stay at home. And in fact, I did; twice thereafter Bill took them back without me. Later Will instructed me to drop him off a block from his school so that no one would see me. He was a boy struggling to find normalcy while growing up in a family that was anything but normal. In time, despite his own remarkable gifts—singing and playing drums—he would renounce any aspirations to a life in music, maintaining that he could never pursue a career, never find happiness, in a business that had robbed him of his mother. Dawn would have her own, quite separate issues; while these were suppressed for many years, they eventually surfaced with a vengeance.

But all of that lay ahead. Back then I kept telling the press that I had found the almost perfect formula, and that the only serious question we faced was how to keep the winning streak going. I desperately wanted to believe it too, and only wish that I could have.

CHAPTER SEVEN

BOB DYLAN ONCE SAID, "He not busy being born is busy dying." You can apply that cryptic aphorism to all sorts of situations, but it applied best to my own as I approached the mid-1980s. While in many ways things could scarcely have been better, I had reached a professional plateau and was no longer busy being reborn creatively. At some level I knew it, too.

But it was easy to be distracted. In 1985, in a moving ceremony at Rideau Hall, the Governor General's residence in Ottawa, I was inducted into the Order of Canada along with jazz legend Oscar Peterson. We were both made companions of the order, the highest civilian honour the nation can bestow.

The next year, in cooperation with the provincial and federal governments, Balmur announced plans to build the $1.5-million Anne Murray Centre on Main Street in Springhill, Nova Scotia. For years the local residents had noticed an annual caravan of tour buses rolling off the main highway into town, giving visitors a chance to take photos of my old family home. Eventually someone in the tourist agency wondered aloud whether a formal centre—I refused to call it a museum, insisting, "I'm not dead yet, thank you"—might not be an even bigger draw. And thus the wheels were put in motion.

The Town of Springhill donated an acre of land and the 4,000-square-foot facility opened in July 1989. In its first twenty years it has drawn 300,000 visitors and generated roughly $4.1 million in revenue, plus a healthy multiple of that for the town and for provincial tourism generally. Leonard Rambeau was key in making this happen. He envisioned the idea early on and logged many long hours helping it achieve liftoff. I remember his telling me after my Rose Bowl Parade appearance in 1971 to save the outfit I was wearing because it would one day be in a museum—a statement that perfectly reflected his unshakeable belief in me. That outfit is encased there today, complete with masking tape.

The centre could never have been built, however, without Mom and our housekeeper, Dena, who for years faithfully kept and preserved an attic full of childhood memorabilia: my cherished stuffed monkey, my first ice skates, my baptism dress, a high school prom dress and all my school report cards, as well as dozens of scrapbooks that documented every stage of my career, plus many other things that became part of permanent exhibits at the centre. Its creation also helped me empty my basement of accumulated trophy hardware, plaques and gold and platinum records.

Despite the strains caused by my performance schedule, I was happily married, and Bill and I enjoyed watching our offspring transform themselves from toddlers into children and develop their own unique identities. Will had his first drum set at four and never looked back. By the time he was a teenager he was taking drum lessons and practising as much as five hours a day. He also took piano lessons, eventually earning his Grade 5 conservatory citation. At fourteen he received his high school's drama award, even though he was still only in Grade 9. He played drums in various bands and sang in jazz choirs and an a cappella quartet that once performed at a Globetrotters' game at the SkyDome in Toronto.

Will was an extraordinary mimic with a natural sense of comic timing. Once when he was about four years old, kneeling for prayers before bedtime, he said, "God bless Mommy and Daddy and Nanna and all my aunts and uncles and cousins. And God bless Anne Murray"—after which he looked at me out of the corner of his eye with a mischievous twinkle. That humour is still there, and Will often leaves me convulsing with laughter.

Dawn also had a keen sense of humour. When Will turned seven, I decided to take him along on one of my tours as a birthday present, leaving Dawn at home alone with Bill. One day she was bugging him and he asked her to stop. "Who'll I bug?" said she.

Dawn was blessed with the soul of an artist. By seven— taught by Bill, no mean sketcher himself—she was demonstrating a level of originality and technical skill in drawing that was well beyond her years. She took years of art lessons and, painting in acrylics, has developed a style all her own.

As we had with Will, we started Dawn on piano, but it wasn't her natural métier and she resisted learning. She took lessons for about three years, hiding when her teacher came to the house; we typically spent the first ten minutes of her lesson trying to find her. When she was eight, she spent hour after hour singing along to K.T. Oslin's *80's Ladies* and the Trio (Dolly Parton, Emmylou Harris and Linda Ronstadt) albums, developing her skills in harmony. When she discovered the guitar at age thirteen, that was it. She played it day and night and sang non-stop. In Grade 5 her teacher once paused in the middle of a lesson and said, "Dawn!" When Dawn replied, "What?" he said, "Stop singing!" She had no idea she was doing it. But most of the singing she did for herself rather than for public or even familial consumption. It was much later that we discovered she had the voice of an angel—how fitting that she should have been born on Dusty Springfield's fortieth birthday.

The three main pillars of my professional life—albums, concerts and TV—were humming along in high gear. My CBS TV specials, simulcast in Canada, were drawing millions of viewers. The new albums, *Where Do You Go When You Dream* (1981), *The Hottest Night of the Year* (1982), *A Little Good News* (1983) and *Heart Over Mind* (1984), continued to sell robustly, each achieving gold or platinum status. It was a struggle to limit my concerts to a hundred dates a year. And there was no shortage of ticket buyers. When I again played the cavernous O'Keefe Centre in Toronto in May 1985, the week-long gig grossed $529,000 and filled the three-thousand-seat venue to 97 percent capacity.

In front of audiences I found that I was increasingly more confident and comfortable—a function of experience and my track record. I no longer felt that I had to prove my mettle every time out; the hit records did it for me, and I could relax and just deliver them. I used to say that I would always sing my hits through in their entirety—no medleys—because that's what concert audiences had come to hear. But after a while I broke that rule; it almost couldn't be helped. It was an enviable problem to have—so many hits that it would have taken up the whole program to sing them all. And that would have meant not being able to introduce material from whatever new album I was promoting.

Some of my stage script was canned and eminently portable; it consisted of a lot of self-deprecating banter. "Gee, it's great to be here tonight in . . . North Podunk," I would say. "Haven't played here in eighteen years. Back by popular demand, clearly." Or I'd spot someone with binoculars and say, "I see you have binoculars, sir. But you're sitting in the third row. What the hell are you looking at? Trying to see how the old broad is holding up?" Later, in my fifties, if I momentarily blanked on a song lyric or miscued in some way, I'd apologize and explain, "It's this damn menopause, you know." Most women in the crowd could relate to that. And I invariably introduced my high-stepping top-hat-and-cane number, "Everything Old Is New Again," by ridiculing my own footwork: "I find wherever I go people are just crazy to see me dance . . ." Cyd Charisse I wasn't.

But I also liked to engage the audience spontaneously; there were always moments that could be exploited for a good laugh. In Vegas once I saw a young couple sitting near the stage, and as soon as we started to chat, they volunteered that it was their wedding day. "Your wedding day?" I said. "Then what the hell are you doing here?" To which another patron responded, "They're on their break!"

Years later I was appearing at the Warwick Music Theatre in Rhode Island, not long after Canada's Toronto Blue Jays won their second consecutive World Series. When I teased the audience about that, one man yelled out, "Yeah, but they're all Americans!" To which I quickly responded, "Yeah, well, all the New York Rangers are Canadians!" (the Rangers had recently won hockey's Stanley Cup).

My confidence allowed me to do things like that. I worked hard at it, though, particularly in Vegas, where you could assume that some portion of the audience wasn't familiar with your work. And I liked the off-the-cuff exchanges for another reason: people pay good money for live performances because they want to catch a glimpse, however limited, of the human being hidden beneath the hype and the makeup. Often— perhaps most of the time—they don't get that; too many shows are flying on automatic pilot. But within the constraints of the format, I wanted to give audiences a better sense of who I was, and I think I did.

I still got nervous on occasion. In March 1983 I co-hosted the Country Music Awards, broadcast live from Nashville's Grand Ole Opry House, with Willie Nelson—the first non-American to be accorded that honour. (I would later do it again twice—once with Kenny Rogers and once with Kris Kristofferson.) When the show cut away to an early commercial, I turned to Willie, who always seemed the epitome of relaxation, and said, "Are you nervous?"

"No. Are you?"

"Yeah," I said. "A little."

Willie paused. "Well, maybe I am too."

I'm still not sure if he meant it or if he was just trying to make me feel better.

One week in the following month I was the top-grossing performer in North America, with revenues of $466,844, ahead of Kenny Rogers, Duran Duran, Culture

Club, the Grateful Dead and the Scorpions. I couldn't have known it then, but commercially these would be my peak years. I was earning about $4 million annually (offset by significant overheads). While I could have earned triple that figure or more by adding a few dozen play dates, I refused to do it. Time with my family was too limited as it was. Money, in any event, had never been a prime motive; it was simply a fringe benefit.

The revenue engines in the early 1980s were fuelled by a string of hit singles—"Another Sleepless Night," "Somebody's Always Saying Goodbye," "Blessed Are the Believers" and "A Little Good News." These songs had their best reception on the country charts, but they performed respectably on the pop and adult contemporary lists as well, reaffirming my crossover profile.

Every year, it seemed, I'd be nominated for a new Juno, Country Music Association or American Music award, and almost every year I'd attend the trophy ceremonies. At the Grammys one year, I was looking for the washroom just after the show ended and found myself trailing behind Olivia Newton-John. Tugging on her dress, I said, "It's time you and I met." Just at that moment we were interrupted by Gene Simmons, the lead singer of KISS. "Oh, my God," he said, "it's Ann-Margret." The name was no sooner out of his mouth than he realized his mistake. "Oh, I'm so sorry," he said. "I didn't mean to say that."

Olivia and I made our way to the washroom, which was located in a dismal, dimly lit sub-basement of the theatre. My stall, as it happened, lacked toilet paper.

"Excuse me," I called out to Olivia. "Do you happen to have any extra toilet paper in there?"

Afterwards, as we powdered our noses in the grungy mirror, I said, "This is disgusting. I'm not coming to this show ever again."

Olivia laughed. "Oh, we say that every year."

"I know," I said. "And then we do it again just to prove we're not dead."

Several of my hit singles were the work of Nashville writers Charlie Black and Rory Bourke. My producer, Jim Ed Norman, had a strong connection with that writing team, having recorded songs of theirs with other artists. As a result, we sometimes heard their new material even before their publishers did. That's exactly what happened with "A Little Good News," a song (co-written with Tommy Rocco) clearly in synch with the prevailing cultural ethos. I sang it for the first time at the Ohio State Fair in Columbus in August 1983. The temperature was 39° Celsius (103° F), the hottest day there since 1955, and the stage felt like the inside of a blast furnace. When we played the song, the whole audience—17,500 people—suddenly went crazy. The moment was almost electric. They stood up and wouldn't stop applauding. The same thing happened when we played it again at the evening show, to 18,000 people, although by then the temperature had fallen to a frosty 35° Celsius (95° F).

I liked the song, but I had clearly underestimated the power of its message for heartland America. The lyrics constitute an indictment of the pandemic of violence, not just in America but around the world, and articulate fervent hope for a change in focus and direction.

Just once how I'd like to see the headline say
"Not much to print today, can't find nothin' bad to
      say," because . . .
Nobody robbed a liquor store on the lower part of
      town
Nobody OD'ed, nobody burned a single buildin'
      down
Nobody fired a shot in anger, nobody had to die in
      vain
We sure could use a little good news today.

Later, President George Bush (the elder), who was a fan and for whom I performed on two occasions, even quoted the lyric. "We sure could use a little good news," he'd say, apropos of whatever new military or economic setback had occurred.

"A Little Good News" didn't do much in the pop spectrum, but it went to number one on the country charts and was voted both album and single of the year at the Country Music Awards in Nashville. I was not only the first woman to win that double honour but also the first female solo artist to win the coveted Album of the Year award. It earned me my fourth and final Grammy as well.

Although most of my songs were recorded in Toronto, this one had been produced in Nashville and thus failed to qualify as Canadian content under CRTC regulations. As a result, most Canadian radio stations refused to play it, even though it was a certified hit in the U.S.—one of the few occasions on which I failed to win broad domestic support. Leonard was infuriated and complained mightily, but to no avail.

I followed that hit with another one, "Nobody Loves Me Like You Do," a duet with Dave Loggins. Jim Ed Norman was always getting calls from publishers saying, "Boy, have I got the perfect song for Anne." One persistent fellow in L.A. had sent him dozens of tunes, none of which he'd ever recorded. This time, however, he was pleasantly surprised. It's what Jim Ed calls a testament to the tenacity on both sides: the song plugger, continually rejected but refusing to quit, and the producer, continually disappointed but willing to try again, just in case. Hit songs always retain an element of serendipity: you just never know where the next one might come from, so you keep your doors, your ears and your heart open.

Jim Ed played the song, written by James Dunne and Pamela Phillips, at our next meeting and I liked it. Dave Loggins was an obvious candidate for duet partner. I had loved his 1974 pop hit "Please Come to Boston" (probably my favourite record of all time), and I loved his voice, so there was already an affinity of sound and style. At Capitol's behest Jim Ed had assembled a list of other prospects, some of whom had expressed interest in singing a duet with me. But all of that—discussions with agents, managers, other record companies—would have taken time. So Jim Ed proposed that we cut to the chase: "Look, we've always loved Dave's voice. He's an amazing singer and a perfect fit for this song." Less than a week later, Dave was in our Toronto recording studio.

The duet with Loggins was from *Heart Over Mind*, the last of the one-a-year albums I contractually owed Capitol. That disc also included "Time Don't Run Out on Me," written by one of the most prolific songwriting teams of the 1960s, Carole King and Gerry Goffin. Married and later divorced, they had each been working with other writers; this song, the result of their first professional collaboration in many years, made it to number two on the country charts. With my contract about to expire, Lyman and Dave resumed negotiations with Capitol and fielded overtures from several of its rivals. But with eight number-one country hits in five years, the company wasn't about to lose me to the competition, and they certainly made it worth my while to stay. It was the richest contract ever signed to that date by a Canadian performer.

Everything considered, then, I had nothing to complain about, not even the rigours of the road. Although travelling was always difficult—I could probably fill a chapter on air turbulence and the many nausea-inducing flights I've taken—Leonard insisted that a certain level of luxury was required. To play in the big leagues, you had to behave as though you belonged in the big leagues. Thus for a number of years we always flew first class, stayed in five-star hotels, ate in the best restaurants and ordered expensive wines with dinner. The riders attached to my performance contracts—specifying (among other things) food, drinks and snacks for the band and entourage backstage—got longer and longer, all at my cost. The promoters supplied it all, but as is the custom in the business, the artist pays the bill.

Although my business manager, Lyman, fought hard to rein Leonard in, the truth is that, in those years, we could afford it. And I don't want to lay the blame entirely on Leonard; I was complicit, as caught up in it as he was. I also thought that's how things were supposed to be done. It was only later, after his death, that I realized how many of these costs had been unnecessary, that I was seldom in the posh hotel room long enough to enjoy it. Then I started cutting back. For the past several years on tour I've bunked in a wide variety of hotels, from five-star to no-star, always insisting that the room have windows I can open. (An ear, nose and throat specialist had once told me that the worst thing one can do to a singing voice is to expose it to the drying effects of air conditioning.) Occasionally the hotel management would decide to grace me with a suite on the house—an offer that it would have been discourteous to refuse.

The single greatest asset I enjoyed in those years was the companionship of my brother Bruce. In addition to his own solo career, he'd been singing backup vocals on my albums since 1975 and had appeared on television specials with me on many occasions. In 1980 he effectively put his career on hold to join me on the road, and he stayed for six years. He sang backups and duets with me and had his own spotlighted segment in the show where he delivered a solo or two. Audiences loved him.

Bruce was equally indispensable offstage. During my years at the Riviera in Vegas, as well as in Tahoe and Reno, he lived with me. On the road, from Sydney to London, from the Grand Ole Opry to the not-so-grand state fairs, he was the perfect antidote to my hermetic tendencies. Just as my friend Cynthia had done in Toronto, he forced me to leave the security blanket of my hotel room, to which I was inclined to retreat, and to explore whatever city we happened to be in, checking out the art galleries, museums and other cultural or historical sites. Endlessly curious, Bruce soaked up knowledge like a sponge and shared it generously. He was the best thing that ever happened to me on the road. In fact, with Bill and my children so far away, I don't know if I could have gotten through that period without him.

My act in those days featured a duet with Bruce of the great Everly Brothers hit "Let It Be Me." We'd face each other onstage with the spotlight on our heads and shoulders only; the rest of the stage was black. Once, performing in Lake Tahoe, we were about a quarter of the way into the song when Bruce accidentally spit in my face. Lit the way we were, people saw the spray immediately, and we both started laughing and couldn't stop. Every time we tried to start into the song again, one of us would break up. I don't know whether we ever finished it.

Eventually, however, Bruce faced some difficult choices: whether to release a new album and tour it extensively, answer the call of Broadway (he was under consideration for a couple of leading roles) or, with a second child on the way, find something meaningful to do that would keep him closer to his family. He was blessed with a remarkable singing voice, but you have to live this life to comprehend fully just how hard it can be and the gut-wrenching sacrifices it requires. Eventually Bruce decided that he wanted and needed to be closer to home. He became a teacher of music, English, history and science—a selection of subjects reflecting his catholic range of interests—and director (over the past twenty-two years) of school productions of eighteen Broadway musicals. He has absolutely no regrets.

NOTHING REMAINS STATIC. Like everything else in the mid-1980s, the zeitgeist of popular taste—and with it, the climate of popular music—was changing. "A Little Good News" and "Nobody Loves Me Like You Do" were major hits only on the country charts; the lovely ballads that had once commanded airplay across the spectrum of the AM and FM dials no longer had much pop cachet. The Billboard Hot 100 was now dominated by new musical fashions, populated by the likes of Boy George, Pat Benatar, Genesis and Duran Duran, sounds often infused with whiz-bang electronic effects and sequenced instrument simulators. I was still being heard on country and adult contemporary stations, but it had been five years since a single of mine had penetrated the Top 30, and I wanted to do something to change that. Or at least try—*he not busy being born is busy dying.*

One obvious option was to ignore the fashion and record an album of old standards, the songs from the forties and fifties with which I'd grown up. The concept had a lot of appeal, and not just for me. The incomparable Harry Nilsson had recorded *A Little Touch of Schmilsson in the Night* in 1973, a collection taken from the great American songbook. Willie Nelson and Linda Ronstadt had later done the same. Leonard and I decided not to crowd the marketplace with yet another homage to Gershwin, Berlin, Arlen et al., so we put that idea on hold.

The other alternative was to join the pop explosion. I'd been musing about moving in that direction too, anxious to break out of the mould, if not the straitjacket, of crossover ballads. Indeed, I said at one point that if I had to record another album of ballads, I'd scream. An exaggeration, perhaps, but it made the point—I needed something new. Pop critics suggested later that this deliberate shift into the realm of rock-shaded pop posed a risk for me, the possibility that I'd alienate the strong and loyal country following I'd spent more than a decade building. I saw no great risk. If the album didn't sell, then no one would hear it. I could certainly go back to making the music I had made before or even try something else. It was, after all, just show business. "I'm sorry if people are mad at the change," I said in a number of interviews. "But this isn't just something I want to do. It's something I have to do."

Going the pop route, however, was going to require a new producer. Jim Ed Norman had been given a management opportunity with Warner Music in Nashville. While he'd been able to continue making albums with me for a few years, he was now being offered the top job, one that required him to work exclusively with Warner artists. He later said that the separation was painful for him but the opportunity too good to pass up.

So in the spring of 1985 I started talking to prospective producers. Since the new album was going to be, by definition, something of an experiment, we decided to try a different approach. Instead of working with a single producer, I'd do tracks with several and see what the results were. We finally settled on three, all of whom came with impressive pedigrees: Germany's Jack White (né Horst Nussbaum), who'd worked with Laura Branigan and was among the leading exponents of the Euro disco sound; Trinidadian-turned-New-Yorker Keith Diamond (né Keith Vincent Constantine Alexander), who had written and produced Billy Ocean's great song "Suddenly"; and Canada's David Foster (né David Foster), who was then accumulating a long list of writing and producing credits with big-name performers.

David proved to be the most reluctant to get on board, perhaps because he didn't then have what he considered good material available. "So write me a hit song," I told him, "and then we'll both be happy." Which is exactly what he did, getting together with Randy Goodrum to write "Now and Forever."

There was another song I was keen to record for that album and release as a single: Shirley Eikhard's "Something to Talk About." I'd known Shirley since she was a fourteen-year-old prodigy on *Singalong Jubilee*, a hugely talented singer and songwriter with an enormous musical gift. She had music oozing from every pore. She'd sent me that song and I loved it, playing it in my car for more than a year. I knew it would be a hit, but all the producers I sampled it on—Foster, White, Diamond—somehow couldn't hear it. I should have insisted, but I didn't, so I never recorded the song (although I borrowed the title and used it for the album).

You can guess the rest. Five years later I was walking through the Bay department store when I heard Bonnie Raitt's note-perfect rendition of the song. It was a huge hit, just as I had predicted, peaking at number five on the Billboard Hot 100. It took Bonnie's career up more than a few flights. Had it been almost anyone else I would have been more upset, but I was thrilled for Bonnie because I was a fan. I wrote her a note telling her so, adding my own back story of frustration with the song. I was also thrilled for Shirley, who reaped some sizeable royalties as a result.

I had worked with David Foster once before that same year. Together with a large group of other Canadian performers, I participated in the recording of "Tears Are Not Enough." That song, co-written by David, Bryan Adams and Jim Vallance, was Canada's contribution to the famine relief effort in Ethiopia and had been the brainchild of Vancouver-based manager Bruce Allen. Similar singles were also made in the U.K. ("Do They Know It's Christmas?") and in the United States ("We Are the World"). By 1990 the project had raised $3.2 million for famine relief projects in Africa.

David, who produced the record, was in the control room when I recorded my part of the song. When I'd finished my first take, he said it was very good but asked if I could do it one more time.

"Why?" I asked. "I don't think I can do it better than that."

"Well," he said, "just to give us some choices."

In the end I did it three times.

"Okay," I said. "Now tell me, which one are you going to use?"

"The first one," he said—an "I told you so" moment, and one that gave us all a good laugh.

Later, producing songs for the new album, David was the same way. He worked me much harder than any other producer, asking for take after take. From his vantage point it was just insurance, but in my judgment at least, a lot of it was unnecessary. Still, I humoured him and complied; it just wasn't my style to play diva in the studio. As a general rule I was easy to work with and gave different producers the benefit of the doubt, always thinking that perhaps their way could be the better way or that I might learn something.

Ironically, considering that the objective had been to reach a pop audience, the finished album performed much better on the country charts (reaching number two) than it did on the Hot 100 (number sixty-eight). Although some people considered it a failure, I certainly didn't. It still went gold and sold about 800,000 copies—the kind of miss I'd be happy to take any day. (It was also the first album that my kids, then aged seven and nine, actually said they enjoyed.) Similarly, "Now and Forever" became a number-one country single while making it to only ninety-two on the Hot 100. So the country backlash never materialized. By this point I was so ensconced in the country music milieu and the radio stations were so supportive that they played "Now and Forever" even though it wasn't remotely country.

It was that same year that I again became embroiled in a long-simmering Juno Awards controversy. I had physically boycotted the event since 1975—the first year that the show was broadcast live on national television. Compared to the flair and polish that Americans brought to these annual award ceremonies, the Juno telecasts were slipshod and amateurish. People ate and drank liberally throughout the evening, even while major stars were performing. Apart from the TV crew, nobody seemed to care about what was happening onstage. Such a situation did nothing to burnish the reputations of those artists who took part or of the domestic music industry generally. Although I had assembled a small roomful of Juno statuary, I stayed away after that. But I continued to watch the show on TV, appalled by the bush-league manner in which it was conducted. Actually I did more than boycott the ceremonies; I took out paid ads in music publications outlining my criticism. I was embarrassed for people such as Gordon Lightfoot and pianist Glenn Gould—true stars who did not deserve the treatment they were getting.

My position eventually led to a very public war of words with Bruce Allen, who was then managing Bryan Adams and other major acts. He insisted that I had an obligation, even a patriotic duty, to support the event. My attitude remained: if you want to honour professionals, make it a professional event. I finally said that to Bruce: "Come up with something that isn't an insult to the very people you claim to be honour-ing, and I'll do it." He said, "All right then, let's make it happen." And he did. The Juno format was changed dramatically, and the following year I returned. My apprehension about the reception I would receive after an eleven-year hiatus disappeared quickly when I walked out onstage to a standing ovation. When the applause subsided, I said, "So this is where you hold this thing?" The room erupted in laughter. Some years later I even hosted the show.

I was still making preparations for the pop-rock album when I celebrated my fortieth birthday and our tenth wedding anniversary. Answering press inquiries about my plans, Leonard said that he knew of only two events on my agenda— a meeting with producers at Balmur's offices, to be followed by a not-so-happy-birthday root canal procedure at the dentist. At the offices, however, I was pleasantly surprised when my band members strolled in with a Baskin-Robbins ice cream mud pie and a case of beer.

A bigger surprise awaited me. That night I came home to find the house filled with familiar faces, including my mom, three of my brothers and their wives, a niece and lots of friends. Bill had secretly arranged it all, complete with what seemed like enough lobster to fill a Nova Scotia trawler.

PEOPLE SOMETIMES ASK ME if I've had any particularly memorable or embarrassing moments as a performer. The answer, of course, is yes—too many. Once I made the mistake of eating a fajita, loaded to the gills, just before show time. Its spicy ingredients stewed actively, but more or less silently, inside me for a while, finally making their presence felt on the final note of "Snowbird." Except that what emerged from my mouth was more belch than note. I immediately apologized and then explained that I was the victim of fajita reflux syndrome. The sympathetic audience thoughtfully started throwing half-finished rolls of Tums and Rolaids onto the stage. We redid the last chorus of "Snowbird," this time without additional sound effects.

My act included a dance routine during which I ripped off a pair of tearaway trousers, attached with Velcro, to reveal a pair of sequined hot pants. Once, before a huge crowd in Michigan, the poorly secured pants fell to my ankles fifteen minutes before the dance number, right in the middle of a romantic ballad. It was like having a pair of pantyhose clumped around your ankles. The band, needless to say, was roaring with laughter. I had to stop the song and enlist my giggling backup singer, Debbie Ankeny, to help me get untangled while I tried to explain to the audience what had happened. They thought it was all part of the show.

But two of my most embarrassing moments actually occurred offstage. The first occurred in 1985. I'd been invited to sing "Time Don't Run Out on Me" at the Night of a Hundred Stars at New York's Radio City Music Hall, a celebration for the Actors' Fund of America. It was, as billed, a star-studded evening, featuring Elizabeth Taylor, George Burns, Lucille Ball, Yul Brynner, Danny Kaye, Donald O'Connor and many more. Normally I generally kept a low profile at such events, but this time, with so many legends and larger-than-life stars present, I decided to make a conscious effort to introduce myself. Among those I met were Ann-Margret and Julie Harris (I walked back to the hotel with them on successive days), Robert Preston, Christopher Reeve and, in a particularly thrilling encounter, swimmer and movie star Esther Williams, who had made all those great films in the forties—movies I adored. I even shared a dressing room with the McGuire Sisters, who wore matching white bugle-beaded dresses and ate oranges, which they said were good for the throat. I met Rock Hudson there too—shrunken, grey and dying of AIDS, a very sad sight to behold.

The embarrassing moment occurred as I was riding the elevator in our hotel with Leonard Rambeau and a few of the performers. Leonard whispered to me, "I think that's Sarah Vaughan," nodding at the person standing in front of me. Sarah Vaughan! I was overwhelmed. I couldn't actually see her face, but I wasn't going to pass up a chance to meet one of the true giants of jazz. So as we were leaving the elevator, I said, "Miss Vaughan?"

Then she turned towards me, and in that terrible, humiliating moment I realized that Leonard had set me up. It wasn't Sarah Vaughan at all.

"I'm afraid you've got the wrong person," she responded, and walked out of the elevator.

I apologized, but I was mortified. As she walked away, I realized that my elevator companion was Marla Gibbs, from the TV sitcom *The Jeffersons*. I still shudder to remember it. I should have expected something like that from Leonard. He loved orchestrating those little pranks.

At that New York gala evening I wore a dress made for me by Lee Kinoshita-Bevington, the third and last of my designers. When Patric Reeves-Aaron and I parted company in the late seventies, I turned first to Juul Haalmeyer, whom I had met on the set of the *Bobby Vinton Show*. I associate Juul with my glitz period. He had a penchant for the flamboyant and worked outside the rules of fashion. He said that his approach was to bring a new elegance and sportiness, which involved lots of sequins and beads. His wardrobe included a number of beaded jogging suits, very sporty and comfortable ensembles that I loved wearing. Lee continued the glitz theme, particularly for the stage, but simplified the look, using cleaner and more classic lines. Lee wasn't simply dressing me for concerts; he was both designing and buying my clothes for media interviews and photo shoots as well.

Lee's dress for the New York event was beautiful, except for one problem: I couldn't move in it. It was a black and silver panne velvet sheath with a V-shaped neck and back and short cap sleeves. The vees, front and back, were hand beaded with glass bugle beads in an art deco style, as was the hip-level belt. But the belt kept catching on the nap of the velvet and slid up with every step I took. Lee tried pinning it to the dress, but that only made the whole dress ride up. The best we could do was control how it came up.

"You friggin' male dress designers," I barked at Lee as we made our way towards the stage. "This is what I'd call a serious design flaw. You should put me on a dolly and just wheel me out there." This playful head-butting with Lee was not uncommon. Unlike Juul, he was very fashion conscious, and he tried his best to make me *au courant*, with tight skirts and really high shoes. But in the ongoing conflict between looking hip and being comfortable, comfort usually won—fashion be damned. Somehow I managed to get to the stage and sing my song without the belt sliding up to my waist and making me look like a fool.

The second embarrassing incident involved genuine royalty—Queen Elizabeth II—and it was much worse, although it wasn't really my fault. The occasion was Canada's

125th birthday, July 1, 1992, and despite a chilly evening, a jubilant crowd of 100,000 packed Parliament Hill in Ottawa. A host of Canadian dignitaries were in attendance, including Prime Minister Brian Mulroney and his wife, Mila. A stellar list of performers was on the bill, among them Gordon Lightfoot, Roch Voisine, Rita MacNeil, Jeff Healey, George Fox and David Foster.

I'd been asked to close the show with two songs—"Now and Forever" and "Could I Have This Dance?" When I asked what I should do when I finished the songs, I was told to "go down and meet the Queen."

I was deeply moved by the whole experience, seeing that vast sea of faces and hearing them sing along with me during the final song. The Queen, sitting in the front bundled in a blanket, looked as though she wished she were anywhere but in Ottawa. I was so caught up in the moment that when the song ended, I did as I'd been told. I went down the stairs and first greeted Brian Mulroney, who then presented me to the Queen. I continued down the row, shaking various important people's hands. It wasn't until I reached the end that I noticed all the other performers were assembled in a receiving line, waiting to meet Her Majesty. No one had told me about it, and because of that rather serious oversight I had breached royal protocol: commoners never approach the Queen but always let the Queen come to them.

At that moment I wanted to royal-flush myself down the nearest commoner's toilet. I joined the receiving line, but when the Queen reached me, she passed me by without a glance or a word. Anyone watching on TV might have thought I had been granted my own private audience with Her Majesty, but that was no consolation. I pride myself on always being in control and aware of the situation, of knowing exactly what I need to do. It did not matter that I was a victim of someone else's incompetence. Embarrassing myself in front of the Queen and the entire nation is not something I will ever forget. It still rankles.

⌒

I CONSIDER *Something to Talk About,* my foray into electro-pop, as simply an experiment I needed to try. And while it did not yield any crossover hits, it did generate three Top Ten country tunes. Most of the criticism I garnered was focused less on the music and more on the new look that went with it, a spiky streaked hairdo and a new wardrobe heavy on the padded and the layered. We took that album on the road for almost two years, complete with some pretty elaborate choreography, courtesy of Marla Blakey, that even had the boys in the band dancing. We were a little out of our element, but it was a challenge and eventually we had fun with it. The music from that album was more uptempo than our usual and definitely helped re-energize the act.

I had enjoyed working with Jack White, so in 1987 we decided to do a second album with him, which was called *Harmony.* Jack put down most of the bed-tracks of drum machines and synthesizers in Germany and the rest were done in Los Angeles by his associate producer and arranger, Mark Spiro. Apart from choosing the songs, I had little or no cre-ative input. I recorded the vocals in Toronto, but the whole process felt "phoned in." The songs were good and the album sounded great, but people just weren't buying my voice with that synthesized sound. The warmth had been lost.

The bitter truth was that—with or without synthesizers, with or without spiked hair—by the late 1980s I was no longer getting the same amount of radio play, which promotes record sales. When I recorded Rita MacNeil's "Flying on Your Own" on the next album, I would have been willing to wager money that it had Top Ten potential. And I would have lost. Number fifty-two on the country charts was as high as it went.

After *Harmony* was released we mounted a cross-Canada tour, a major endeavour financially and otherwise. We were twenty-three people in total, including seven musicians, two backup singers, a hairdresser-cum-wardrobe-assistant, a road manager, a crew of eleven and me. The gear for the show travelled in two 48-foot tractor-trailers accompanied by a 40-foot bus for the tech crew. The overhead was huge, one of the main reasons I hadn't previously undertaken such a tour. I was able to this time because a portion of the costs was, for the first and last time, underwritten by Ford Canada. I took some heat for that alliance, but by then sponsorship had been a fact of life in the concert tour business for some time. Elton John, Michael Jackson, the Rolling Stones, Tina Turner and others had gone that route before me. It eased the fiscal burden but imposed an exhausting physical one—after every concert there was a large meet-and-greet reception for Ford dealers and their clients from across the country. We had a film crew with us who seemed to shoot our every move, for putting together a television special at a later date. That never materialized, but the tour itself was a resounding success.

As I Am, the album that included Rita's song, was produced by Kyle Lehning in Nashville. Kyle has produced most, if not all, of Randy Travis's albums as well as several other big country acts. In 1988 Capitol had moved its country music division to its natural home, and it unilaterally decided that I was a country singer after all, and that was where I belonged. I had no vote in the matter, and it was hard to argue with their bottom-line logic. The country domain was where the bulk of my sales were. Although we had reservations about the move, Leonard, as always, saw a brighter side: a chance to work with a new group of writers and producers in one of the most musically creative cities in America, and perhaps to be a bigger fish in the smaller pond. I was seldom physically there, but in 1990 Balmur bought a townhouse not far from the city's fabled Music Row, and Leonard, George Fox, Rita MacNeil and others under our management were able to use it.

One woman I made a point of meeting in Nashville was K.T. Oslin. I'd heard her song "80's Ladies," from her album of the same name, on the car radio one day and I was so struck by it that I pulled off the road to listen. When I reached home, I called the radio station to find out who was singing. Later, when I'd heard the entire album, I called her just to tell her how impressed I was by it. It is still one of my favourites, right up there with *Nilsson Sings Newman* and *Dusty in Memphis*. K.T.'s music had a country feel and her lyrics had a certain cleverness that I admired. Whereas most romantic ballads can be sung by either men or women with a simple pronoun change, her songs clearly expressed a woman's point of view.

A couple of years later, when I was performing there, K.T. and I spent two or three convivial hours together over lunch in Nashville. I wanted to ask her to write a song for me but would never have been so presumptuous. Evidently she read my mind. The next day, unsolicited, she turned up on my doorstep with a song—and a good one—"Who But You." I promptly put it on that first Nashville album.

Over the years I was able to get to know another classy Nashville woman, Loretta Lynn. From my earliest days there she made a point of looking out for me, offering advice about show business and about life itself that was always practical or just plain smart. "Whatever you do, make sure you spend as much time as you can with your children. I didn't do it," she said, "and I regret it to this day."

Loretta had a great sense of humour. "What did y'all do before you started singin'?" she once asked me.

"I was a teacher," I said.

"Well, what did y'all teach?"

"Phys. ed."

"Phys. ed. What's that?"

"You know—basketball, volleyball, track and field."

"Well, then, you weren't no teacher. You was a player."

After one of her performances in England, a reviewer described her as singing like she had "overalls on her tongue." The next night she told her audience about the review, which had been written by a man named Peter.

"Peetah," she drawled, trying to affect a British accent, "are you out there tonight? 'Cuz if you are, I'm gonna whup you all over the state of England!"

Needless to say, the crowd laughed uproariously at her constitutional faux pas. Loretta, recounting the story to me, added plaintively, "How was I to know there was no states in England?"

⌒

I HAD BEEN A SPORTS NUT FROM CHILDHOOD, and the passage of time had done nothing to blunt my interests.

My father and brothers taught me well. I closely followed the fortunes of the Toronto Maple Leafs and the Montreal Canadiens, and every season kept an eye on the leading players' goals and assists. For several years I was the proud owner of four gold-section seats at Maple Leaf Gardens and went as often as I could. Each spring at playoff time, the equally hockey-obsessed Lyman organized an elaborate pool for Balmur employees and friends, with three-hour meetings during which we carefully "drafted" our slate of players. I won the pot—about $1,500—a couple of times.

Hockey wasn't just a diversion for me. In 1984, on my behalf, MacInnis held informal talks with then Leafs majority owner Harold Ballard about acquiring the team and the Gardens for $40 million. Our plan was to assemble a consortium of investors to buy majority control; my personal stake would have been about 25 percent. Ballard initially indicated an interest in discussing it further, but later he changed his mind. The issue came up again briefly in 1989, but again it collapsed, wrecked on the shoals of the complicated ownership share structure, the ongoing battle between Canada's two largest beer companies, Molson and Labatt, and a vastly inflated price tag.

On the road I'd sometimes get updates on the progress of key playoff games via hand signals flashed to me from the wings by the technical crew. We generally tried to stay in hotels that carried feeds of the games. When that failed, we repaired to sports bars. In one such bar in Atlanta we were watching a playoff game when two other patrons spotted me with the band and sent a bottle of champagne to our table. I waved a thank you, and they came over. We weren't drinking but agreed to join them for one glass of champagne.

They had obviously been drinking for some time, because one of them was slurring his words. I'd seen that before, but I was shocked when at a certain point he announced that he had to leave—he was a neurosurgeon and was scheduled to operate early the next morning.

Later, when VCR technology arrived, we carried a video player and a TV with us. The crew would jerry-rig the box to my TV and I'd tape key games, ordering everyone not to disclose the results until I'd had a chance to watch them, usually after a concert. At home in Toronto I was an early adopter of satellite technology; Bill and I had a dish installed in the backyard that allowed us to access seven NHL games at once.

Over the years I have enjoyed skating with Gordie Howe at the old Montreal Forum, eating lobster with Jean Béliveau in Prince Edward Island, sharing dinner with Wayne Gretzky and his parents (lobster again) at my home in Toronto, golfing with Bobby Orr in Florida, trading quips with Doug Gilmour and Börje Salming, hoisting an ale with Lanny McDonald, signing the cast on New York Ranger Ron Duguay's broken right leg, and performing at more than one NHL All-Star Game gala dinner. Hanging on a wall beside my swimming pool are two hand-painted ceramic hockey jerseys, replicas of the original sweaters worn by the Toronto Maple Leafs and Montreal Canadiens; they were a sixtieth-birthday gift from Bruce Allen. And I own two now-antique arena chairs, one from the old Montreal Forum and one from Maple Leaf Gardens—further proof of my eastern neutrality.

And that's just hockey. When baseball's Toronto Blue Jays were formed in April 1977, I was invited to sing the national anthem at their home opener at Exhibition Stadium. It was a miserable day, freezing cold. I sang bundled up in a red parka—a gift from one of the northern communities I'd visited five years earlier. Snow blanketed the entire field and the wind was howling, but forty-four thousand pro-baseball-deprived fans turned out to mark the historic event. The Blue Jays even won the game, beating the Chicago White Sox 9–5. It was a victory to savour, since the team would finish that debut season ignominiously, with 107 losses. I sang the anthem at two other Blue Jays games: the opening of their new stadium, the SkyDome, in 1989, and at their first World Series game in 1992. On the latter occasion I could barely perform; that same morning I'd received word that my old friend Karen Oxley had passed away from complications associated with multiple sclerosis. Everyone else in the building was bursting with excitement, but I was in mourning. That song felt like the longest two minutes of my life.

When it was possible, I'd work local sports references into my act. Appearing on the campus of Purdue University in Lafayette, Indiana, I performed the day after their football team, the Boilermakers, had been walloped to the tune of 52–6 by the Fighting Irish of Notre Dame. I came onstage draped in a long T-shirt that I'd had printed with the words *Notre Who?* The crowd loved it. Sometimes, however, I courted trouble. I was in Atlanta in the late 1980s when that city and Toronto were competing to host the 1996 Olympic Summer Games. Cheeky as ever, I invited the crowd to come visit Toronto when the Games were being held. A loud chorus of (good-natured, I think) boos filled the room.

In later years I have developed similar passions for tennis and golf, and I try to ensure that I'm free to watch the Masters, Wimbledon, the U.S and British Opens and other major tournaments in both sports. For years on tour we made a point, when we could, of organizing golf and tennis matches, developing some fairly intense rivalries between various members of the entourage.

Until I injured my rotator cuff in the early 1990s (throwing seashells into the Atlantic Ocean), tennis was my sport of choice to play. It took less time than golf, so we booked courts in every town we could. At one tour stop in Seattle we met lawyer and former Wimbledon-ranked tennis pro Trish Bostrom, who showed us a few handy tricks of the trade. As it turned out, Trish was also an Anne Murray fan, so she'd occasionally take a weekend off and fly down to Reno or Vegas if we were playing there, to see the show and put us through our paces in tennis clinics. One year she made Canadian Thanksgiving dinner for about twenty of us at her beautiful waterfront home.

I've been fortunate enough to have played some of the finest golf courses in the world, including Pebble Beach (in a pouring rainstorm), St. Andrews and Keltic Lodge's Highland Links. I had golfed only once in university and didn't really learn how to play properly until I started golfing with my brother Harold during my summers in Pugwash. (Bill never played much, though on one memorable outing at a course in Las Vegas, he put about six consecutive drives into the water on a par three, angrily threw down his clubs and then waded waist high into the water in search of his lost balls.)

In Palm Springs we organized the inaugural Anne Murray Road Show Invitational Putting Tournament. I won by two strokes, but Cynthia unilaterally decided that the winner would get only $5 and the golfer with the highest score would get the rest: $33. It was during one of those road trips that I broke 90 for the first time, shooting 88. During the concert that night I somehow managed to let it slip that I had established a new personal best. The next night, a fan presented me with a special gift—a pewter letter opener with golf shoes on the handle and the inscription *88—Anne Murray Oct. 28 1994.*

That achievement paled, however, beside my first (and, alas, only) hole-in-one. In October 2003 I was playing the 109-yard, par-three seventeenth hole at the Kaluhyat Golf Club—designed by Robert Trent Jones Jr.—at the Turning Stone Resort and Casino in New York State. The tee was elevated and I remember thinking that it would be a perfect hole for a hole-in-one; I even visualized the route the ball would take. To be perfectly honest, it didn't follow the path that I had imagined. Instead it hit the rough at the edge of the green and took a rolling, circuitous route—*plonk!*—right into the cup. In his excitement my drummer, Gary Craig, almost crushed my ribs hugging me. Needless to say, I've practised similar visualizations at dozens of par threes since then—to no avail.

I've always been fit, but now, as I prepare for the challenge of my senior years and with my scoliosis asserting itself more forcefully, I work even harder at staying strong and in shape. I try to do something physical virtually every day: swimming, aerobics, fitness training with weights and bands, or brisk walking. I even hope to play some tennis again now that the shoulder has been strengthened. It's not restlessness— I can veg out with the best of them—but I need to be active. I'm up early and I like to keep moving.

MY TENURE at the Riviera's Versailles Theatre in Las Vegas ended in 1984. By that point I was among the highest-paid acts on the Strip, earning $250,000 a week, the same as Kenny Rogers, Dolly Parton and a few others. That was serious money, so serious in fact that the hotel eventually decided it was a losing proposition. But then, as I understand it, Dolly (or her managers) raised her asking price—to $300,000 a week—and the Riviera balked. Pretty soon, hotels all over town had decided to scale back on high-priced talent and started booking different and much cheaper acts. The Riviera would have kept me at the same wage level, but by then I could no longer tolerate the debilitating two-shows-a-night format.

A few years later the Hilton invited me to perform on my terms: one ninety-minute show a night. Comparatively, that was a cakewalk. It was in the same venue that I had made my Vegas debut, opening for Glen Campbell in 1971. At that time management had warned me not to offend its clientele by wearing hot pants onstage. On this occasion I worked a mocking homage to that contretemps into my act, making an onstage costume change from a tearaway skirt to a pair of white sequined hot pants.

It was customary for the hotel to offer headlining stars accommodation in what was known as the Elvis Suite. The King had played—and sold out—the hotel's two-thousand-seat showroom for six years (eight hundred consecutive shows) in the 1970s, not a shabby record. When there, he lived in a thirtieth-floor penthouse that had been built expressly for him, a five-bedroom monster of a suite, outlandishly decorated, where he entertained friends, practised karate and sang gospel songs. In one bedroom the wallpaper was made out of pigskin. When I tried to open the drapes to let some light into the living room, they were so thick and heavy I couldn't move them. The windows didn't open either, but there was a door to the rooftop patio that brought in some fresh air. The Hilton must have had a colourful past; there were still bullet holes in the elevator, apparently the work of Elvis or one of his gang. My only complaint was that the hotel did not carry a feed from ESPN, the U.S. cable sports network, so I couldn't watch the NHL playoffs.

On my first stay they offered me the suite and I declined, always preferring windows that opened. But when I returned for my second appearance near Christmas that year, I reluctantly took it. I had invited my mother and her friend Arlene Moffatt to stay with me, so we all had plenty of room to spread out. After a few days, however, Leonard called me. A recession had badly hurt earnings on the Strip and a group of high rollers was due in from Japan. Could the hotel move our party from the penthouse to another suite in the hotel and give Elvis's quarters to the high rollers? So we moved, finding two adjoining suites in which the windows opened. Leonard discreetly suggested to the hotel management that I might be entitled to some compensation, a small gesture to offset the inconvenience of relocation. They agreed, and gave me $5,000 to spend anywhere in the hotel.

So Mom, Arlene and I quickly repaired to the jewellery store, where an attractive ruby and diamond ring caught my eye. The cost was $4,500.

"But you still have five hundred dollars left," said Mom. "Let's look at earrings."

Of course, there were two pairs I liked.

"Take them both," said Mom.

"But then I'll be over my limit."

"Well, call them and see if it's okay."

So we did. The hotel raised the limit and I bought both pairs. The truth is, I would have been happy to move out of the Elvis Suite for nothing. Later it turned out that I had given a Christmas present to the hotel staff as well as to myself. The high rollers from Japan left behind so much money for the house that their Christmas party, which had been cancelled as an economy measure, was rescheduled.

Christmas in my own home was something of a schizoid affair, a private family celebration and a public, televised one. In 1988 I'd shot a Christmas special for the CBC with guests Glen Campbell, Alan Thicke (who wrote most of my other specials as well as this one), then up-and-coming country singer George Fox and Canadian figure skater Brian Orser, as well as Bill, Will and Dawn, whom I actually persuaded to sing with me. The show drew almost 4.5 million Canadian viewers, making it the network's highest-rated variety program in the past ten years. The CBC was so pleased with those results that they reran it every Christmas for the next few years, always with good ratings—much to the chagrin of my kids, who invariably took a good ribbing about their appearances from school friends.

Despite the popularity of my Christmas special, I was under no illusions. Getting mainstream radio play was becoming harder all the time. A younger generation of Canadian singers was emerging, including k.d. lang and Celine Dion, to say nothing of the American powerhouses—Whitney Houston, Mariah Carey and Reba McEntire, to name a few. At forty-five I had to recognize that my career was entering a different phase and, while my backlist of albums continued to sell briskly, I would have to adapt accordingly. The road ahead would be more difficult; I knew that. But I never bargained for just how challenging, both professionally and personally, the nineties would become.

CHAPTER EIGHT

AFTER TWENTY-FOUR YEARS IN THE MUSIC BUSINESS, I had seen just about everything, or so I sometimes thought. I was wrong. In 1992 I experienced something completely new—and it was an unwelcome shock—the first in a series of events that would make the nineties my most challenging decade, both professionally and personally: Capitol Records dropped me from its roster of recording artists. I recorded twenty-seven albums on their behalf, I sold 30 million records and I earned them tens of millions of dollars, but none of that mattered. My last three albums—*As I Am, You Will* and *Yes I Do*—had failed commercially, if not artistically, and the nabobs of Nashville were no longer sure what to do with me. The last two, not incidentally, were produced by one of the nicest guys in Nashville, Jerry Crutchfield and, despite their failure to generate the hoped-for returns, I am still proud of the work we did together. But the cost of my upkeep was beginning to outpace the projected returns. I knew this was how the music business operated.

Thank you for your efforts today, Ms. Murray. Now, what can you do for us tomorrow? Still, the blow stung.

Jimmy Bowen was in charge of Capitol's country music operation. He'd started as a singer/songwriter and in the late fifties had scored a hit record with "I'm Stickin' with You." Then he went into production and worked with Frank Sinatra, Dean Martin and Sammy Davis Jr., among many others. In Nashville he would ultimately help engineer the careers of the Oak Ridge Boys, Reba McEntire, George Strait, Suzy Bogguss and Garth Brooks—not a bad little résumé.

At any rate, Capitol and I were at something of an impasse. Lyman and Leonard flew down to Nashville to discuss the issue, but after Bowen left them cooling their heels for ninety minutes, they left. The next day another Capitol executive told Lyman that the company was not interested in renewing my contract, which was soon due to expire. The matter was still in limbo when Leonard and I met with Bowen a few weeks later. Their story had changed a little. Now, Bowen suggested, they were prepared to underwrite the costs of another album, if Bowen himself produced it. I had reservations about working with him—more instinct than anything else—and hedged on my answer, saying I would give it some thought.

Of course, I had already given it thought. I knew exactly the album I wanted to record—*Croonin'*, a collection of great songs from the fifties, including "Secret Love," "Allegheny Moon," "Old Cape Cod" and "The Wayward Wind"— all recorded by artists whose music had been seminal for me. I wasn't about to turn that project over to Jimmy Bowen, and in fact I never told him about it.

Eventually we let Bowen know that I was not interested in being produced by him. Capitol responded with a formal offer proposing to demote me from the main label to a junior affiliate, with a dramatically reduced advance. As Leonard later observed, it was an offer I could not *not* refuse. And so, for the first time in twenty-four years, I was without a musical home.

With or without Capitol, I was determined to make *Croonin'*, even if it meant paying for it myself—which I did, to the tune of $300,000 in production costs. My producer was the affable Tommy West (né Picardo). Tommy had produced dozens of artists, including the man who had been his best friend, the late Jim Croce ("Time in a Bottle" and "Bad, Bad Leroy Brown"), and he'd been a fan of mine since he'd heard "Snowbird" playing on a Chicago radio station one day in 1970. The first few times Tommy heard it, he later told me, the station had never announced my name. Typically DJs gave the name of the artist after a record had finished playing; "Snowbird," he explained, was one of those songs that DJs could use to fill a two-and-a-half-minute window that took them right into a newscast. Eventually Tommy got hold of my album and said to himself, "My God, what have we got here?" Someday, somehow, some way, he promised himself, he was going to get that woman into a studio.

We eventually met in L.A. during tapings of a Helen Reddy summer replacement TV show in 1974 and talked for two hours. Tommy said even then that I reminded him of Patti Page, and that my voice would lend itself to an album of pre-rock 'n' roll hits. Later Tommy was one of the small group of producers whom Leonard and I considered after cutting professional ties with Brian Ahern. But he was then affiliated with CBS Records, and his managers didn't want him working for Capitol. When "You Needed Me" was released, someone played it for Tommy and he wrote me a note. Paying what must surely be the best compliment I've ever received, he said that "it was the best thing ever to come out of one human's throat."

We met again briefly a few times after that, but it wasn't until 1992, during rehearsals for my performance with the Boston Pops Orchestra, that we had a chance to have a serious conversation. Despite the long hiatus, Tommy hadn't forgotten me. He'd been "stalking you in my dreams," he said, following my career closely. Mine, he said, was the quintessential alto voice. Most women lose part of their lower register—the ability to hit the D below middle C—after puberty, he explained. My comfortable range extended from there to A above middle C. What helped my material to work, Tommy maintained, was that men and women could sing along in the same octave.

I told him I was thinking seriously about going ahead with a fifties album, but he was way ahead of me, having already assembled a tape of the old songs. He sent the tape, but it unaccountably languished for months in Leonard's desk. When it finally reached me, we called Tommy and agreed to co-produce the album. I recorded it in January 1993 and sold the finished album to Capitol's Canadian affiliate, EMI Music Canada, in April.

The making of *Croonin'* ranks among the most rewarding recording sessions of my life; among all my albums, it ranks near the top of my favourites. We had a very hard time picking songs—there were so many from which to choose. We knew the material was unlikely to garner much radio play, so we tried to counter that by adding value—nineteen tracks in all—a strategy I would be urged to pursue on later albums as well. We also knew that the finished product had to be better than good, because my versions would inevitably be judged against those of the original artists, many of whom were still alive. Those singers had made these songs seem effortless—trust me, they're not—and it's not until you try to record something like "Old Cape Cod" that you realize how hard it is to sing well.

Tommy had to talk me into recording "Cry Me a River," because Julie London's rendition was, in my judgment, flawless. I felt the same about Peggy Lee's signature song, "Fever," originally recorded by Little Willie John. I'd already laid down the vocal track when, one day in the studio, my keyboard player, Doug Riley, suggested calling Peggy and playing it for her (he'd worked with her a few times and had her number). I wasn't there at the time; otherwise I would have protested. Apparently she loved it, and was concerned only that she be credited for rewriting some of the lyrics, which she was.

When the album was complete, I arranged for copies to be sent to Julie, Peggy, Gogi Grant ("The Wayward Wind"), Perry Como ("Wanted"), Jo Stafford ("You Belong to Me"), Patti Page ("Old Cape Cod"), Eddy Arnold ("I Don't Really Want to Know"), Doris Day ("Secret Love") and Rosemary Clooney ("Hey There"). Almost all of them responded, writing warm and appreciative notes of thanks. I was deeply gratified.

I sent another copy to Charles Koppelman, then CEO of EMI Music in New York. An EMI affiliate company, SBK, had agreed to distribute the album in the United States, but its marketing enthusiasm had been conspicuous by its absence. Trying to light a fire, I made an appointment to see Koppelman during a trip to New York that fall. He told me that he loved the album, had it loaded on his car stereo and played it all the time. So far, so good, I thought. But then he made a point of saying, "This album wasn't my idea." I think my jaw must have dropped a few metres. While he didn't say so expressly, it was a clear signal that, because it hadn't been his idea, he had no intention of throwing any marketing muscle behind it.

Koppelman was faithful to his unexpressed word—he did absolutely nothing. A month or so later I wrote him to express my disappointment, saying that I had "handed the label probably the best album of my life and they have received it with an indifference that is incomprehensible. They have no idea who I am or what I'm about and, what's worse, they don't seem to be interested in finding out." Their short-sightedness was costing us both. In Canada the album had already sold 150,000 copies—platinum and a half—and it would sell many more. On the road in the U.S., the response from audiences was unprecedented. But without hard work and a solid promotion plan, most Americans would never know the album existed. I closed my letter by telling Koppelman that he could make a difference if he chose, but until that time "I would remain disgruntled and dispirited." And disgruntled and dispirited is exactly how I remained.

THE *Croonin'* ALBUM was in its final stages when I received one of the great honours of my lifetime: induction into the Canadian Music Hall of Fame. It was a memorable evening. Bill, Will and Dawn attended and I was awash in generous tributes from Gordon Lightfoot, Celine Dion, k.d. lang, Jerry Seinfeld, Alan Thicke, Gene MacLellan and Glen Campbell. In turn I used my thank-you speech to acknowledge the enormous debts I owed, not only to the obvious circle of managers and agents but also to a group of remarkable but largely uncelebrated Canadian female performers who came of age before it was possible to enjoy the kind of career I had enjoyed: Juliette, Shirley Harmer, Gisèle MacKenzie, Joyce Sullivan, Joan Fairfax, Sylvia Murphy and others. Although I was often labelled a pioneer in the field, the truth is that others came before me. Who knows what they might have achieved if they had had more opportunities? As a young woman growing up, these were the women I watched on Canadian television, and they had inspired me.

About the same time, my business manager, Lyman, was being courted by rival organizations. One of them was the National Hockey League, which was considering him as a possible commissioner. At one of our regular meetings he told Leonard and me that he had to work either full-time for Balmur or full-time for someone else, and that if he stayed with us, he wanted to take Balmur into other areas of the music business, particularly publishing, and develop some non-music activities as well. Thus did we embark on what was then a limited and fiscally prudent corporate expansion. For a time it showed considerable promise. Balmur signed Rita MacNeil and Michael Burgess to management contracts and we opened a new office in Nashville, buying and refurbishing a house on 18th Street. Tinti Moffatt, who had been managing country star George Fox for us, moved to Nashville to head the operation. Tom Long, already resident there, became head of music publishing. There were other items on the expansion wish list, including TV production, executive coaching and management of professional athletes. But it wasn't long before most of our plans had to be temporarily shelved. Leonard Rambeau was dying.

I first became aware that he was sick—exactly how sick I didn't know—around 1993. He was losing weight and having periodic attacks of stomach pain, so acute that at one point I saw him writhing in agony on a hotel-room floor.

"Leonard," I said, "what is wrong with you?"

"It's colitis," he said. "I'll be fine." His wife, Caron, had colitis, so Leonard had self-diagnosed and decided that he must have it too.

Some months later he seemed to improve—the result, I learned much later, of a round of chemotherapy he had said nothing about—and was well enough to accompany me on a promotional trip to Europe. Because he seemed better, I suggested it might be a good time to hire a fitness trainer to help him get back in shape—a well-intentioned recommendation that later made me feel like a complete fool. The man was still very sick and I didn't see it—or want to see it. Leonard knew only too well what was going on, but, as ever, he wanted to protect me and said only that he was on the mend.

Lyman too recognized that Leonard, who looked drawn and ashen, was ill. At one of our regular Balmur meetings he asked him, "Leonard, are you okay?"

And Leonard said, "I'm just a little rundown."

"Well," said Lyman, never one to mince words, "you look like a dying man to me."

"I'm fine."

But Leonard wasn't fine, and he kept that to himself. Perhaps he was as much in denial as we were. I know that he was planning ambitious trips and projects even as the life began to ebb out of him, talking about all the things we still had to do. But he was also finding it increasingly difficult to deal with Lyman, who had a tendency to be very forceful in his opinions and who fought every issue, big or small, with tenacity. A lawyer for Capitol who once sat across the table from Lyman told him, "You have every attribute of a dog, except loyalty." Not a fair characterization, since Lyman was never less than loyal. But he did negotiate everything with pit-bull ferocity.

The conflicts with Leonard were mainly over Balmur's spending and staffing levels. At one point Leonard called me, literally in tears, complaining that he just couldn't deal with Lyman anymore. His authoritarian streak was wreaking havoc with people whose support we needed—producers and musicians. Leonard said we had to find some way to carry on without him. Matters came to a head in the summer of 1994. Before he went to the Maritimes that June for his vacation, Leonard called to give me the grim, irreversible diagnosis: Stage IV colon cancer. It was a devastating blow.

Meanwhile in Nashville, Tinti Moffatt was finding it difficult to sign new acts. The best prospects, it seemed, were women, and Leonard was opposed to managing another Nashville-based country female singer, fearing it would further erode my standing. Indeed, despite his deteriorating condition, Leonard was focused almost exclusively on trying to revive my career, leaving little time to execute the expansion agenda. In August, projecting reduced cash flows for the next few years and after talks with my lawyer, Dave Matheson, Lyman decided to step down. In his letter of resignation he said he did not think it was in Balmur's interests to undertake further expansion then, but that without it he would soon find himself restless.

One answer to the cash-flow squeeze was to accept more endorsement contracts, so I signed a deal with the Hudson's Bay Company, the venerable Canadian department store usually known as "the Bay," to appear in a series of commercials. These were shot in Florida, in a store designed to look like the Bay. Part of the advertising campaign involved life-sized cardboard cut-outs of me placed prominently in Bay stores. That fall, while playing a gig in Vancouver, I spent some time hanging out with my old university friend Jenny (Adam) Villard. Needing to buy a baby gift for a friend, Jenny and I went to the Bay. I picked out an outfit and handed my credit card to the salesgirl. It was a brand new card with my married name, Langstroth, on it.

"Could I see a piece of ID, please?"

"No, I'm sorry," I said. "I left it all at the hotel. But this is my married name. I normally go under Anne Murray."

"Do you have any ID on you to verify that you are Anne Murray?"

"No," I said. I was a little dumbfounded, since in those days I usually couldn't go ten feet without being recognized in public—to say nothing of my being the store's spokeswoman.

"Just a second," Jenny suddenly interjected.

She left us, returned a minute later carrying one of the life-sized cut-outs, and set it right beside me.

"Here," she said to the clerk. "Is this good enough?"

The poor girl just about had a fit.

There was a problem with the cut-outs, however: the photos had been reversed and didn't look quite right. We contacted executives at the Bay, but they maintained it was too late to change them. Then the ever-resourceful Leonard came up with a scheme. In the photos I was wearing my Order of Canada pin, which is traditionally worn on the left, over the heart. Because the cut-out pictures had been reversed, the pin now appeared on the right. Leonard told the Bay that he had received a call from the government Protocol Office in Ottawa. They'd seen the posters and were troubled by this unforgivable faux pas—Canada's oldest company appeared to be wilfully engaging in very un-Canadian behaviour. Leonard covered his tracks by actually calling a friend in the Protocol Office, just in case the Bay contacted them. That was all it took; the offending poster boards were yanked immediately.

In January there was more distressing news. Gene MacLellan, the man whose song had launched my career, was dead by his own hand at the age of fifty-six. We had always been friendly but never particularly close. Gene treasured his privacy, shunning the limelight that his songwriting talent had brought him, as if it were as much a curse as a blessing. The money he earned in royalties from "Snowbird," "Put Your Hand in the Hand" and other songs made him uncomfortable. In fact he stopped recording after 1979, retreating to Prince Edward Island and turning his attention to God. He travelled the gospel circuit through most of the eighties, performing frequently in penitentiaries. But he had started to write again in the early nineties. Then he too was felled by illness, and the black dogs of depression gnawed at him. I will remember Gene not only as a hugely gifted songwriter but also as one of the most naturally soulful singers I've ever heard. He was a sweet, shy man of uncommon humanity, with a wonderful sense of humour.

Meanwhile, Leonard was declining. In January he was placed in palliative care, where I visited him several times— very difficult meetings for both of us. The next month, at the annual Juno ceremonies, the organizers gave Leonard a special lifetime achievement award. I accepted the award on his behalf and, knowing that he was watching from his hospital room, spoke directly to him—one of the toughest assignments I'd ever been given. I didn't want to do it, but I knew I had to. In my remarks I said that Leonard Rambeau had been the only really indispensable person in my career. We'd been together for almost twenty-five years, bound by nothing—never a written contract—but mutual trust and respect.

The next day I took the award to him. Silly, he called it, and laughed. But that was Leonard: always modest about his achievements. A month later he was dead, only forty-nine years old.

His strategic managerial skills were generally acknowledged, but Leonard's human gifts were greater. It wasn't widely known, but Leonard Rambeau was an adopted son. His parents subsequently had four more children of their own, but they always treated him the same—specially, in fact. He returned that love with his own, which was abundant and unqualified. He loved his parents, loved his siblings, doted on his mother, his wife, Caron, and his children, Derek (my godson), Scott and Julia. He was meticulous, attentive and wise. His memory was encyclopedic—he never forgot a name, a date, a place; he remembered everything and everyone. If relatives of mine or of the band members lived near any concert venue, he'd always arrange for complimentary tickets to be available. At Christmas his list of recipients of seasonal gift baskets numbered in the dozens. As a human being he was a model of modesty and genuineness. I miss him to this day. When later that year I was awarded the $10,000 Governor General's Performing Arts Award, I donated the money to Leonard's alma mater, St. Mary's University, to help fund a scholarship in his name.

With his passing, my first instinct was to quit the business, immediately. He was so valuable to me, so in synch with my thinking, so protective of my interests that I simply couldn't imagine carrying on without him. But I had an American tour to complete, and the show, as they say, must go on. When it was done, I decided, I would take some time off and determine whether I wanted to continue performing, and if so, how.

I spent my fiftieth birthday—and my twentieth wedding anniversary—without Bill and the kids. We were in Livermore, California, starting the new tour on the grounds of the Wente Brothers Winery, which was nestled in a beautiful valley an hour east of San Francisco, an idyllic setting for an outdoor concert. The surrounding countryside offered a vista of rolling hills blanketed in parched grass the colour of gold and dotted with big shade trees. My dressing room was filled with balloons, flowers and gifts, including boxes of golf balls and every golf knick-knack yet invented.

Ten minutes before show time, I was still in my bathrobe fixing the bathroom plumbing. A malodorous pong was being emitted by the drain, and I concluded there was probably no water in the trap, so I poured a bucket of water down the pipe—and it worked. Not long into the show the audience broke into a rousing rendition of "Happy Birthday" and a steady parade of fans bearing flowers or presents made its way to the stage. Afterwards we had champagne and a huge birthday cake in the dressing room. I immediately plunged my hand into the cake, grabbed a handful and shovelled it into my mouth, smearing my face like a two-year-old. The band and crew raised their glasses in a celebratory toast and then proceeded to get a bit toasted themselves.

The next day Cynthia and I flew to Carmel to meet Doris Mary Anne von Kappelhoff, better known as Doris Day. I'd sent her a copy of *Croonin'*, on which I'd recorded "Secret Love," her Oscar-winning song (from *Calamity Jane*) that was number one on both the Billboard and Cashbox charts in 1954. She wrote back in thanks and gave me her phone number. My natural inclination would have been not to call, not wanting to impose, but she had been such an idol to me that I did, and she invited me to Carmel for lunch. Not wanting to make the trip alone, I'd invited Cynthia to join me—she was as big a fan as I was.

Doris was waiting for us at the restaurant alone, seventy-one years old and looking beautiful. It took her a very long time to order, so I said to the waitress, "You must be really glad when she finally decides." That drew quite a chuckle out of her, but otherwise I found her demeanour quite serious, unlike the ever-bubbly persona we knew from her films and later TV shows. At one point I told her that I didn't think she'd ever received the credit she deserved for her singing ability. "You have one of the best voices ever."

She acknowledged the compliment, tears welling up in her eyes. "When someone I respect admires what I've done," she replied, "it really touches me."

Doris was reluctant to revisit the past. When I gently probed, she invariably turned the conversation back to her house or her animals—her many cats and dogs. But she did recount the story of recording "Secret Love." She was living in Hollywood at the time and rode her bike to the Warner Brothers studio. The orchestra was warmed up and ready to go, so she went into the recording booth, sang the song once, and that was it. The producer said, "Well, we can't do any better than that." So she hopped on her bike and rode home. The recording process had taken all of three minutes.

She seemed a little reserved at first, but as she grew more comfortable, her natural warmth eventually shone through. After lunch—Doris insisted on buying—she invited us back to her estate, a beautiful house with about twenty rooms on fifteen spectacularly landscaped acres, situated on a 500-foot (152-metre) bluff overlooking a golf course. She'd acquired the property in 1983, when it was just a dirt farm, and gradually developed it, adding a carriage house and a magnificent guest house. The interior of the main house was decorated tastefully in reds; there was even a bright red piano.

Doris lived in a semi-reclusive state—she had divorced her fourth husband, Barry Comden, in 1981—and doted on her animals. One of them, Butch, a pit bull, expressed great interest in having me for lunch. The yard was completely fenced off and divided into dog runs. Each dog had its own bed and the cats had an area all their own. There were doggie doors and cat doors and toys for all. Doris had never bought an animal; they were all strays or from shelters. She was part-owner of the Cypress Inn in Carmel—the only hotel that allows pets—and had helped set up two foundations for the sheltering and spaying of animals.

It was clear that Doris had essentially cut herself off from her former life. The house contained few clues as to what she— one of the biggest box-office stars in history—had achieved. There were no pictures of the glamorous Hollywood life, no gold records, and just a hint of memorabilia from the thirty-nine films, seventy-five hours of television and hundreds of songs to her credit. The visible souvenirs were a framed piece of music from Motown's Berry Gordy—the first song he ever wrote, expressly for her—and a winding staircase (from the set of *Please Don't Eat the Daisies*) that led to her bedroom.

Doris was someone who liked to get up at five in the morning and go to bed by eight, so the movies suited her perfectly. She rode her bike to the studios every day. "I could never do what you do," she told me.

Although I'd met many stars over the years, most of the contacts were casual or incidental, brief conversations backstage at an awards show or TV talk show. On this occasion I'd been able to spend five uninterrupted hours—a genuine privilege—in the company of one of the greatest stars of the modern age. I was able to get a sense of the underlying innocence and vulnerability that had endeared Doris Day to me and to millions of others.

WITH LEONARD'S DEATH AND LYMAN'S RESIGNATION, I faced a double dilemma: a sudden vacuum in my career and business management. My first call was to Lyman. Would he consider coming back to Balmur, if only temporarily, to sort out the confusion? He agreed, staying about six months, and was enormously helpful.

Then I took some time off and, celebrating my fiftieth birthday for the second time, went to Scotland for two weeks with the Chicks with Sticks. We played several challenging layouts—Troon, Turnberry and Gleneagles, as well as historic St. Andrews—and made a tournament of our various matches, which I ultimately won. For the birthday party we rented the Walkway, a tiny Chinese restaurant in Glasgow, and spent the better part of the night carousing, drinking, dancing on both floor and tables and singing karaoke. The room was dimly lit but I managed to videotape the whole thing. It was, hands down, the party of a lifetime, and as we boarded the plane for Toronto the next morning, we had the hangovers to prove it.

When I returned home, I called Bruce Allen. One of his clients, rocker Bryan Adams, had co-written (with Gretchen Peters) a great song, "What Would It Take," for me. I called Bruce to see if Bryan might sing it with me on my next album. In passing, Bruce said simply that if he could ever do anything for me, just to let him know. Some months went by and I called him back, suggesting we talk further. I still had a career, and I couldn't pretend to manage it myself. He quickly got to the point. *Shy* is not a word often used to describe Bruce, and while he would never say anything expressly critical of Leonard, he did not understand the way I had been managed. He respected Leonard's protectiveness but thought it had been carried too far, that I'd been kept too much in a bubble, without a close-enough connection to day-to-day issues. If he was going to represent me, he said, things would be dramatically different. I would have to take on more responsibility and be fully involved in decision making. That was the only way the relationship could work.

Not everyone was convinced that Bruce and I would get along, but Bruce thought my upbringing—having to survive in a house with five brothers—would help, that I'd know how to deal with his assertiveness and volatility. My line at the time was, "I'll leave the four-letter words to him and save mine for the golf course." I was impressed by his enthusiasm, his conviction that we could find a way to end my long drought on the charts.

I remember one amusing telephone exchange I had with Bruce. During a previous conversation I'd told him in no uncertain terms that I wanted to have July and August off, and would not play Billy Bob's in Fort Worth, Texas, which he had tentatively booked—the venue was simply not my type. This time he was calling to tell me that my publicist, Marlene Palmer, would be joining a planned promotional tour for an upcoming PBS special.

"Oh, no," I said. "There's no point. I've already got my road manager, Darlene Sawyer, and my hairdresser, P'tricia Wyse. I hate it when there's a bunch of people following me around."

"But she's already made all the reservations," Bruce protested.

"Well, she'll just have to unmake them."

There was a slight pause. "Okay, Anne, have it your way. Marlene stays here. You have July and August off. You're not playing Billy Bob's. Oh, and by the way, we've renamed the company."

"Really? What's it called now?"

"Eunuch Productions."

Bruce's blunt approach was a shock, but it was a healthy and necessary shock. I learned a lot from him, more perhaps than I ever had from anyone else. By putting me in charge of my professional life, he ultimately made me stronger.

Understandably, Bruce did not want to inherit the old Balmur machine. To the extent that they got along, Lyman and Leonard had functioned as an attraction of opposites. Lyman and Bruce, both cut from precisely the same cloth, would not have survived a week together. With Bruce's arrival, Lyman again stepped aside, and his protégé, Tony Baylis—the son of Paul Baylis, who had produced and directed *Let's Go* thirty years earlier in Halifax—assumed the top management job at Balmur.

There was one other casualty of that transition: Fred Lawrence, my agent of twenty years. Bruce maintained that if he was going to resurrect my career, some new thinking and new personnel were required. I handled this leave-taking badly, I'm afraid. What I should have done was talk to Fred personally and explain the situation. Instead I delegated that assignment to Bruce. When I finally did work up the courage to call Fred after the fact, he refused to take the call. Fred was a loyal, diligent agent and a genuine fan. To my continuing regret, we still haven't managed to heal the breach. Since then, two agents at New York–based ICM have looked after me well: Terry Rhodes and Scott Morris.

When Bruce took a closer look at Balmur, he was appalled. By the mid-1990s the cost of its infrastructure was out of all proportion to my ability to generate income. To reduce expenses, I enlisted help from my friend Cynthia McReynolds. Although she had no formal training, she possessed a remarkable business head. Growing up, she'd been very close to her grandfather, Ralph Johnson, the man charged with running the former Birks jewellery store empire for the Birks family of Montreal. Their dinner-table conversations were all business, and from the age of ten or eleven Cynthia was attending company board meetings. She knew her way around a balance sheet, and she didn't like the looks of mine. She came in—as a favour, unpaid—and, working with Bruce, started tightening my fiscal belt. It was at that point, for example, that I ended the retainer system I had maintained with the band; the income stream could no longer justify that level of overhead. She also connected me with wealth-management experts whom she trusted. Later, for a couple of years, Cynthia served as our road manager. It wasn't a task she particularly enjoyed, but she did it to help us out. On the road, as in Toronto, she was the proverbial life of the party.

Meanwhile, Bruce Allen was trying to resurrect my career. "The broad needs a hit," was the line he liked to use when talking about taking over the managerial reins. "She's a household word, but we have to make her viable again. We have to get her back on the radio."

He was right, too. But making it happen would prove more difficult than we knew. My next album, simply titled *Anne Murray*, was produced by Ed Cherney, who'd worked with Bonnie Raitt and Jann Arden. Almost a year in the making, it featured duets with Bryan Adams (on his song) and with Aaron Neville ("That's What My Love Is For"). It took a year to complete because, in midstream, when it was virtually finished, I decided it had too many ballads, and we went back into the studio to record a few more upbeat tunes. I dedicated it to Leonard because, even in the long and desperate months of his illness, he had been planning it with me.

When I played the rough mix of the Adams tune for my mother, she said, "Very nice, Anne, but I can hardly hear that young Bryan fellow." So we went back and remixed that as well. We had high hopes for that track, and audiences hearing it for the first time loved it. But we were disappointed once again. Number seven on the Canadian charts was as high as it went, and it did poorly in the U.S. market.

I toured the album that fall and the following winter. In the past, Leonard had always helped me plan my stage shows; now I was on my own. That was part of the new deal with

Bruce. When I played my first U.S. gig after he signed on—at Bally's in Las Vegas—he called to wish me luck. His parting and characteristic advice was, "Don't choke on me now, Anne."

One stop on that tour was Montreal's Place des Arts. We were taping the show for a later TV special and DVD release (*An Intimate Evening with Anne Murray*) and had invited Celine Dion to appear as a guest, singing "When I Fall in Love" with me as a duet. On the day of the show, she'd just arrived from Europe and was jetlagged, so she sent her backup singer, Elise, to the theatre to rehearse with me. Elise held a mobile phone to her ear while Celine sang the part to her, then Elise sang with me. Not ideal, but manageable; I was grateful that she was even on the show. "From now on," I joked, "I'm sending my backup singer Debbie to all my rehearsals."

In a flourish of hair, fur and perfume, Celine breezed in at about 8:45 that night for the live show, accompanied by her husband/manager, René Angélil, a 300-pound black body-guard and an extensive entourage. Our song was part of a medley from the *Croonin'* album. Just before it started, I turned around to my drummer, Gary Craig, and mouthed the words "I'm scared." After all, a live duet, taped for TV in front of three thousand people, with no rehearsal and with Celine Dion, no less. When she walked onstage for the second verse, the room erupted in applause and the crowd jumped to its feet. Behind her always cool façade, I thought I detected a glimmer of apprehension as well. What unnerved me was wondering what she might do with the song during the actual performance. I was singing the harmony; if she decided to improvise, which she can do as well as anyone in the world, I'd be thrown off. But she was a complete pro and stayed within the confines of the melody. We did three takes—

no one in Salle Wilfrid-Pelletier was complaining—and used the first one. When it was over, I turned to my band and crossed myself—a symbolic *Thank you, Lord*. A decade later I put our recording of that song on my final album, *DUETS*.

A few years later, my mom, Dawn and I went to see Celine perform at an outdoor venue in Florida and we met with an unfortunate incident. We went backstage afterwards to congratulate her, but instead of being escorted into a private holding area—the normal courtesy for other performers— we were ushered into a room crowded with about five hundred people. That was a nightmare. In seconds they were all over me, asking for photographs and autographs. Had it been for only ten or twenty minutes, it would have been tol- erable, but we waited for an hour, besieged, and finally left, more than a little upset. I couldn't really blame Celine—she very likely had no idea this was happening—but her handlers ought to have known better.

IN 1997 BRUCE ORGANIZED a month-long tour of Australia, my first trip there in fifteen years. We received a warm recep- tion and played sold-out concerts in Perth, Melbourne, Canberra, Coolangatta, Newcastle and Sydney. In fact, the trip was so successful that I went back two years later and did the same circuit again.

Before we left, I took the kids to Florida for the March break. One day Dawn asked me to take her window shopping on Palm Beach's famous Worth Avenue, the city's shopping mecca. The Chanel store was displaying a fetching little cotton shirt-and-shorts ensemble. "Oh, Mom!" she said. "It's so cute!

You have to try it on!" So in we went, my first mistake of the day. None of the off-the-rack versions fit, but the patient saleswoman unpinned the outfit on the store-window mannequin; on impulse, without bothering to check the price, I decided to buy it.

Dawn went off to sample some nail polish and I proceeded to the cash register. As the garment was being wrapped, I noticed a price tag peeking out of the paper: $847. I swallowed hard, stunned, but could hardly change my mind at that point. As they say, "If you have to ask . . ." What I wanted to ask was, "How do you have the nerve to charge $847 for a pair of pink cotton shorts and a blouse?" But I didn't. I signed the slip and made my escape.

"Do you have any idea how much this cost me?" I said to Dawn when I found her. She was as shocked as I. Back at the condo I unwrapped my purchase, and only then noticed another price tag, for $500—attached to the shorts. Surely this was a mistake. Alas, no. When I checked the credit card receipt, I was forced to absorb the grim news: I had spent $1,347 for a summer ensemble. Several moments of deep breathing followed. When I returned home, I called up my designer, Lee, and had him move the Chanel label, hidden at the back of the shorts, to the front—in full view, where everyone could see it.

Back in Toronto, I was packing for the Australian tour and noticed an unsightly accumulation of dust on the wall safe we'd installed in our bedroom. Concealed behind a panel, it was never actually locked—to avoid the inconvenience of having to use the combination every time.

"Look at this, Bill," I said. "This thing is filthy. It's caked in dust." And with that I drew a disgusted finger across the offending dial, inadvertently spinning it.

"What are you doing?" cried Bill. "You just locked the safe!"

We looked at each other with alarm. Neither one of us had the faintest idea what the combination was, or, for that matter, where it was. We searched the house from top to bottom—nothing. So we called Chubb, who told us that the charge for opening the safe would be $500, plus additional costs for first removing it from the house, then reinstalling it. Ouch. I then flew off to Perth. Bill got another estimate and went back to Chubb, and they agreed to lower their price by $200.

The whole project wasn't completed until the Australian tour had ended and I was in Vegas. Workmen extracted the safe from the wall and returned it a few days later, opened and ready for service.

Calling home one day from Vegas, I spoke to my house-keeper, Mary McNally.

"Oh, by the way, Anne," she said. "We found the combination to the safe."

"You mean we went through all that for nothing?"

"Not really. It was in the safe!"

So there's the lesson in home security: either never leave the combination inside the safe, or never dust it.

⌒

ONE NIGHT WHEN I WAS JUST BACK FROM AUSTRALIA, my eighteen-year-old daughter crawled into bed with me, pale, drawn and literally shaking. "Mom," she said, "there's something really wrong with me."

I had been aware for a few years that Dawn's eating habits were unusual, but I had put it down to typical teenage behaviour. She also had food allergies, which served to mask a more serious problem. I had grown more concerned when I found magazines in her bedroom with earmarked articles about eating disorders. When I confronted her about the issue, she denied that anything was wrong. I confronted her again after a teacher to whom she had confided called me. Again Dawn insisted that everything was fine. The signs were there, but I was too busy or too myopic to see them.

By her middle teens Dawn was already a tall, striking young woman, and her friends, family and even some of my professional colleagues were encouraging her to consider a career in modelling. I wasn't among them; I vehemently opposed the idea, having endured enough photo shoots to comprehend just how empty and boring such a profession could be. But Dawn was determined to pursue it, and eventually I relented. She then set up meetings at various agencies. She was five-foot-ten and weighed a mere 130 pounds, but their first piece of advice was to come back to see them when she had lost fifteen pounds.

At that point she pretty much stopped eating altogether. In two months she had shed the fifteen pounds and was wearing size 5 blue jeans, and still she thought she was too heavy.

At least I recognized her late-night appeal in my bed for what it was: a serious cry for help. By the next morning she was back in denial, but I was adamant. The very next day we saw a Toronto psychologist, who quickly diagnosed anorexia nervosa. We went as a family to see the psychologist, and some of those conversations were wrenching.

All of this occurred just as I was about to embark on a U.S. concert tour. We rescheduled some bookings so that on June 18 I could help Dawn enrol at an eating disorder treatment centre in Naples, Florida. One of the first things the staff said to Dawn was, "You've walked through the door. Now the hardest part is behind you"—reassuring words for everybody. When I left, Dawn said she'd call me at the hotel at 7:00 p.m. It was nine o'clock before she called—two of the longest hours of my life. But she was settling in and seemed fine.

It would be nice to be able to say that that was the end of the matter, that her two months in treatment cured her of the disease. In fact, it was just the start. Anorexia, like many other psychological diseases, is a pernicious syndrome and it requires constant vigilance. Although Dawn made significant strides, there would be occasional relapses and other treatment centres in the years that followed—including the controversial Montreux Clinic in Victoria, B.C.—sometimes for long periods of time.

At one point, thinking she was largely recovered, we were asked to do a benefit for Sheena's Place, a Toronto community support centre for people with eating disorders and their families. Public awareness of our situation led to a round of media interviews on the subject—joint appearances on several American talk and news shows, including sessions with Jane Pauley, Donny and Marie Osmond, Diane Sawyer and Oprah Winfrey. In retrospect, that media campaign was a mistake. Although our sole intent was to inform as many people as possible, we weren't ready for it. It was too much, too soon. By the end of it I felt I'd been violated, thrown into the media's insatiable jaws and chewed up.

One interviewer went so far as to ask me if I was doing this media blitz to promote my *What a Wonderful World* album. I was appalled. Pauley, I remember, interviewed us for more than three hours—for a fourteen-minute segment; at the end of it, Dawn was literally curled up on the floor crying. Then *People* magazine ran a long feature trumpeting the news that I had saved my daughter. But I had never said anything like that. In fact, I had said just the opposite—that no one can "save" someone in that situation. On the positive side, we did receive hundreds of letters and emails from grateful sufferers, parents and friends who said they had indeed been helped.

A decade later, I'm happy to report that Dawn is doing very well. I won't use the word *cured*, because anorexia is, like diabetes, a condition you control more than you cure. And for all the trauma the illness caused, it definitely brought mother and daughter closer together, emotionally and musically. One night she came home from an evening of karaoke with a tape of her performance and played it for me. I had always known she could sing and harmonize, but I had no idea just how good she was. I was stunned. After that I recruited her to do backups and a duet on *What a Wonderful World* in 1999 and to tour with me on the road occasionally. In 2008 we did fifty-seven shows together.

In the past few years Dawn has launched a solo career as a singer/songwriter. She's written and recorded an album, *Highwire*, fusing her glorious voice with her natural gift for poetry. Music is a very different business than it was when I was starting out forty-one years ago. Not many record companies, agents or managers are clamouring to invest time and money in young talent the way they were in the late 1960s and early 1970s. I was surrounded by people who pushed, promoted and encouraged me; otherwise I'm sure I would have given up. These days you have to be driven and an aggressive self-promoter. Dawn definitely has the talent. Time will determine the rest.

I'm no less proud of my son, Will. After several years of working for the government, he decided to return to an old love—classical languages—and re-enrolled in a university program. He's also an avid cyclist and a Brazilian jiu-jitsu (capoeira) enthusiast.

IN FEBRUARY 1998 we embarked on an American tour, starting in Green Bay, Wisconsin. For my merry little band of twenty-three it was the start of a new adventure on the road. For the first time we would, when necessary, be sleeping on buses. There was a fleet of three in all—one for the girls (predictably dubbed the "chick bus"), one for the guys and one for the show equipment and everything else—amazing vehicles, nicely appointed with bunk beds, TVs, VCRs, a fridge and microwave ovens. Each bus was 45 feet long, weighed 42,000 pounds and boasted 470-horsepower engines. These beasts didn't come cheap, either; including charges for the bus, driver and gas, the price tag was $4,350 for each day on the road. One thing the buses could not accommodate was defecated waste; number twos, therefore, were strictly verboten. As my bass player, Peter Bleakney, later put it, they can put a man on the moon, but if one of us had an overwhelming need to evacuate, we had to stop the bus—go figure. Inevitably there would later be some violations of the rule. But compared to flying, especially to some of the far-flung hamlets on our itinerary, the bus was a quantum leap forward. I wished I'd done it earlier.

The chick bus was widely acknowledged to be the superior environment—soft mood lighting, flower arrangements, scented candles, the fridge stocked with fresh, healthy foods and fine wine. The guy bus featured Kmart lighting and the space was littered with half-eaten bags of Cheetos, empty bottles of Corona beer, desiccated brownies and stale tortilla chips. The fridge was another disaster zone: a bottle of vodka, a jug of sour milk and three-day-old barbecued ribs rapidly mouldering into a high school science experiment.

On party nights—birthdays, holiday celebrations, etc.— we'd all climb aboard the same bus and swap stories of the road. I enjoyed recounting a few of my own: the time, for example, that my guitar player Georges Hébert and bassist Garth Proude jumped me the night before a scheduled photo shoot in the Maritimes and deliberately gave me a hickey on my neck. Or the day we played Pebble Beach Golf Course and a seagull swooped down and stole the camera belonging to my conductor and arranger, Steve Sexton, right out of his golf cart. The mental picture of us chasing that seagull down the fairway, madly flailing our golf clubs at it, still makes me laugh (the bird finally did drop the camera).

One of my favourite stories concerned the late Andy Cree. Over many drinks, the other members of the band had told him that he was the only one of them who hadn't slept with me. Andy was very put out by this, so one night after a show, and after a few drinks to fortify himself, he knocked on my hotel-room door and said there was something he had to talk to me about. I invited him in and he said, "Oh, Anne, I feel terrible! I don't understand why I'm the only one in the band who hasn't had sex with you."

"Andy, what the hell are you talking about?" I said, barely able to contain my laughter. I quickly set him straight and sent him off to bed with his self-esteem restored. It was weeks before the others stopped teasing him about it.

That first night on the buses, the highway out of Green Bay was a sheet of treacherous black ice, with cars sliding off the road at an alarming rate. Most of us had recently seen the movie *Titanic*, so encountering ice on our maiden voyage was not exactly an encouraging omen. It didn't help that it was also Friday the thirteenth. But we made it safely to our next stop, Saginaw, Michigan. There Cynthia energetically bounded off the bus at 4:00 a.m. to organize hotel-key packs, then returned, announcing, "I just gave every guy in the lobby a Happy Valentine's Day kiss! Judging by the looks on their faces, I probably should have brushed my teeth first."

Later that year I finished a two-week run at Bally's in Las Vegas—my favourite of all the venues I've played in the town that makes you appreciate all the other towns. On our last night, management wheeled a big thank-you-and-farewell cake into my dressing room. But the evening ended on a bizarre note.

A fellow Canadian, Broadway and Vegas star Robert Goulet, came backstage after the show. Sporting jet-black hair and wearing a pair of oversized gold aviator glasses, he barged in and greeted me but didn't say a word about the show (actually, I wasn't entirely sure he had seen it). A friend of his, the entertainment director of the Flamingo Hotel, then said to me, "Of course you know Mrs. Goulet," gesturing to Bob's wife. Her name was Vera, but we'd never met.

"Well, Anne," said Bob, in his bellowing theatre voice, "I bet around '55 and '56 you used to watch me all the time on TV, when I was on constantly from coast to coast. And you probably said to yourself, 'That's what I want to do!' And here you are. You made it, kiddo. Way to go!" Then he gave me a good swat in the ribs. "In fact, you probably made more money than I did, kid!"

"Maybe," I replied.

Then Vera countered, "You made a lot of money, Robert."

His friend added, "And you got to keep all of it." I didn't know what he meant by that.

Vera asked me if I still lived in Canada.

"Yes, I do. I've found that since mine was mainly a recording career, I could stay in Canada. It's not like doing Broadway musicals, where I assume you'd have to live wherever the show is playing for quite a while."

"Not that long," she shot back.

"Oh, yes," said Bob. "Recording! When you record, you can buy a house overlooking the lake. You can buy the lake! You can buy the whole country! I didn't sell that many albums, really."

"You sold quite a few records," corrected Vera.

"You could buy a house wherever you want, Bob," said the friend.

Then Cynthia asked Bob if she could take a picture of us together.

"Oh, okay!" he hollered. "As long as you take your clothes off!" With that, he grabbed me for the photo. Then he headed out of the dressing room and disappeared down the stairs, bellowing all the way. I was in a state of shock for the rest of the evening. (At the airport the next day, my stage manager, Bob Groza, told me that Elvis Presley once saw Goulet singing on TV, promptly reached for his gun and shot out his set.)

For memorable Vegas experiences, the Goulet visit ranks up there with the earthquake that struck during my 1999 run at the Orleans Hotel and Casino. About 3:00 a.m. the entire building started to sway back and forth, waking everyone up, a completely disorienting and scary experience. The higher the room, the more shaking you feel, and my suite was on the twenty-first floor. The curtains were dancing and water was sloshing out of the toilet. When a huge vase fell over and smashed on the marble floor, I was convinced my life was over. Cynthia came running from her room, ashen white, hanging on to the doorframe for dear life. The tremor lasted for only about twenty-five seconds, but it felt like an eternity. A security person knocked on the door to give us the all-clear and told us to stay put. Hundreds of frightened people poured out of the build-ing and gathered outside. We turned on CNN and, sure enough, they were reporting the earthquake, which had reg-istered 7.0 on the Richter scale. Its epicentre was miles away, in Joshua Tree Park, midway between L.A. and Vegas. Needless to say, most of us were too much on edge to go back to sleep, especially once the aftershock had hit about half an hour later. But the quake was apparently good for casino business as patrons tried to parlay their survival luck at the blackjack tables.

THE DEVELOPING CRISIS WITH DAWN served as the cata-lyst for exposing an equally serious domestic fault line—in my twenty-three-year marriage to Bill. In fact it was Dawn who, with a few well-chosen words, forced us to begin to confront what we had so long avoided confronting.

"What's going on with you two?" she asked.

And the truthful answer, alas, was nothing. Not for a long time. Bill and I might have been good entertainers, but we were not good communicators. Instead of addressing issues, we tended to ignore them and allow them to fester, a very unhealthy approach. That fundamental weakness—and it was a weakness—was critical.

At the time, had anyone suggested to me that Bill and I, separately or together, might benefit from professional counselling, I'd have scoffed and rejected the idea outright. I mistakenly thought that only weak people needed such help, and I didn't consider myself weak; in fact I prided myself on my strength. Now, having been through many therapy sessions with Dawn, my views have changed by 180 degrees. I believe now that most people could use therapy from time to time.

Had I known then what I know now, I would have behaved and acted quite differently. I would have worked to confront Bill's drinking problem, which had been evident for some time but to which I turned a blind eye, hoping it would go away. I dropped hints and even chastised him from time to time, but there was never that heart-to-heart that should have happened. Rather than tackle the problem head-on, I would instead sit and have a drink with him.

Typically, few marriages dissolve without joint blame, and we were, I suspect, pretty typical. I have no intention of conducting a marital audit or apportioning degrees of culpability— we both share responsibility.

Of course, Bill had known from day one of our relationship that I wanted children. And he signed on for that, even though he already had two kids of his own, and even though he would turn fifty with two toddlers under the age of five. But the concept of late fatherhood is one thing and the reality quite another; I'm sure it was a shock to him. He wasn't always as patient as he might have been, and understandably so.

The truth is, Bill essentially sacrificed a good career for me. He was forty-four when we married, still at the peak of his creative powers, a born entertainer and a talented producer sidelined by the burden of late paternity. And although we had a housekeeper and a succession of nannies to help with the mundane household chores, the inescapable fact remained: Bill became precisely what I had once prophesied the husband of a touring performer would become—Mr. Anne Murray.

From time to time there were projects that engaged Bill's talent and interest that could be developed from home on a part-time basis. He produced a John Allen Cameron show for CTV out of Montreal, as well as retrospectives on *Don Messer's Jubilee* and *Singalong Jubilee*. He used his extraordinary skills in photography to do stills for film location shoots. And he served as a creative consultant for Balmur, supervising the art for my albums. But many of these projects were one-offs; they didn't begin to approximate the career he had had.

Symptomatic of his boredom, I think, was his later involvement with the International Croquet Association, a volunteer job that often took him away when I was at home, and Amway, the network marketing organization. Bill became a distributor for Amway, and though I recoiled from the very notion of it, I said nothing, thinking that it would at least keep him busy. I said nothing even when he started holding Amway meetings in the house. Again I was culpable: more evidence of my reluctance—my failure—to communicate what I honestly felt.

Looking back, I think I expected too much of him, expected that he could provide the mothering that I was unable to give and that Will and Dawn needed and were missing. I did my best. I made sure things were looked after;

I provided the nannies and I provided the house. You can do all those things, but you can't replace not being there.

Perhaps I took too much away from him, didn't leave him with enough to do, or was too controlling, which I have a tendency to be. And too often people would use Bill simply to get to me, which must have been another demoralizing blow.

The end did not happen suddenly. It seldom does, but it seemed that way at the time—the realization that the deep connection just wasn't there anymore. We both knew the marriage was dying and we couldn't seem to talk about it. It must have been devastating for him; it certainly was for me.

I didn't talk to anyone about it, not until the marriage was well and truly on the rocks, though people must have sensed it. Leonard was dead. My mother was almost ninety. My brothers and sisters-in-law would never ask unless I offered, and I wasn't offering. And though Cynthia was a close confidante, we never talked about our collapsing marriages; she and Ken would later separate as well. Of our merry little gang, Chicks with Sticks, the golfers and tennis players, six of the twelve marriages ended in rupture—the statistical norm—four over the same period, but marital problems were discussed very little. It was as if an invisible and inviolable circle of discretion had been drawn around those most private matters. Never once did I hear any of the women say a single negative word about her spouse.

Dawn's ordeal, terrible though it was, did have at least one positive consequence. At one of our first family sessions, the therapist asked Bill what he was prepared to do to help Dawn.

"Anything," he said. "Absolutely anything."

"Really?" asked Will. "Are you prepared to stop drinking every night?"

That got his attention. Bill stopped drinking almost immediately and checked himself into Homewood, a therapy centre for alcoholics. That process was hard, involving weeks of critical self-examination. When he entered the program, Dawn gave Bill a blank diary book to record his thoughts and feelings. He has since filled seven volumes of diaries and writes every day. I also sought professional help, and found it hugely constructive.

But as a couple we were forced to recognize that the marriage was over. The fundamental ground had been shaken. The bonds of trust and respect had been eroded and could not be restored. Eventually Bill said that perhaps it would be best if he moved out and we parted ways; soon afterwards we did. It was not acrimonious. The details were worked out without the rancour and combativeness that often attend divorce. And though he has since remarried and moved back to Nova Scotia, we have remained friends. Fortunately, freed of the dark albatross of alcohol, Bill has also been able to repair his relationship with his children.

⌒

DAWN'S ILLNESS AND THE DIVORCE weren't the only problems I was wrestling with. Balmur was spiralling out of control. For our operation in Nashville, on top of the townhouse we already owned, we bought a house, renovated it, installed a recording studio and hired (at its peak) eleven songwriters, plus support staff. Then in 1998 we bought and merged two animation studios, one in Toronto and one in

California, the premise being that we would expand into that field, creating animated TV series based on *There's a Hippo in My Tub*, my children's album, and other properties. We added a book publishing division, then bought another house in midtown Toronto, gutted it and, at huge expense, converted it into offices. All of this seemed like a good idea at the time, but in fact we were ill-equipped to realize these dreams. At one point, needing to raise more capital for the expansion, we tapped $3.2 million in private equity. Suddenly I was sitting on a board of directors with a group that included investment fund managers, former senior CHUM Ltd. executive Fred Sherratt and Charlie Allen, a chartered accountant with a background in telecommunications. I had always viewed Balmur as something I could have fun with in my retirement, but I hadn't retired and I wasn't having any fun. Something had gone terribly wrong.

I allowed this runaway train to get away from me, and though I sensed disaster looming, I was unable to apply the brakes. It was my own fault, but with Lyman gone, I had no one telling me, "You can't or should not do that." And Balmur CEO Tony Baylis, well-intentioned though he was, was in over his head, just as I was. It took me two years to get the mess sorted out. In 2001 we finally sold Balmur, lock, stock and recording studio, to Corus Entertainment. "The sale gives me the opportunity to continue what I do best—recording," I said at the time, "while keeping my hand in the business on a consulting basis." I became honorary chairperson of the merged company and, with Bruce Allen, sat on the board of directors. After thirty years, that marked the formal demise of Balmur Ltd. To be honest, I was glad to see the end of it. I had lost millions.

In all of this—Dawn's frightening continuing saga, the bitter acknowledgment of a failed marriage and the expensive unravelling of Balmur—there was but one silver lining: *What a Wonderful World*. Released in 1999, it was an album I had to be coaxed into recording. The idea actually came out of our Nashville office and Sparrow Records, which had Amy Grant and other Christian and gospel singers under contract. The original concept was for only religious songs, many of them taken from the Baptist and Presbyterian hymn books, a prospect that made me, a Catholic, a little uncomfortable. Tommy West suggested that we also include inspirational songs from the secular canon, such as "Let It Be," "I Can See Clearly Now," "Bridge over Troubled Water" and "Let There Be Love." The latter was a duet with Dawn written expressly for us by Canadian singer/songwriter Amy Sky after she'd seen us interviewed on television about anorexia. Tommy produced the album and also sang with me on a track that combined "Just a Closer Walk with Thee" and "Take My Hand, Lord Jesus." We ended up with twenty-six tunes.

Bruce Allen's marketing mavens sprang into action and we soon had a *What a Wonderful World* cottage industry: a companion hardcover book of colour photographs of Nova Scotia and the song lyrics that included a twelve-track version of the CD; a CBC and PBS TV special on the same theme, also sold in DVD format; and a songbook, with sheet music for all the tracks. The album itself went platinum in both Canada and the United States—my first penetration of that exclusive territory in almost twenty years.

On the boys' bus that June, I notified the band and the crew that I planned to take the next year off. The band joked that it was because I had a new car (an Audi A6) and a new dog (my first, a West Highland Terrier named Mikey) and was tired of buying expensive watches for all the people who had been with me twenty years—Aidan Mason, Georges Hébert and Debbie Ankeny, with more to follow.

But the new millennium was approaching, an opportune time for stock-taking. I was fifty-four years old, and while my voice was still in fine form, the previous five years had been physically punishing and emotionally wrenching. I needed a break. On one level, touring was good for me—a distraction from the pressing and complex domestic issues I was facing—but it was also enervating. I discussed the R-word with Bruce Allen; while he didn't endorse the notion of retirement, he did encourage me to take some time for myself. Indeed, he wondered why I hadn't done so a lot sooner. It might, we reasoned, even be beneficial to the career; on the premise that less is more, a year off might actually help build demand.

But Bruce was convinced it would not last. "Anne," he declared in his soft-spoken way, "you'll be bored of playing #%&! golf in six *%#*! months and want to get back on the #&**! road. We've got money on it." And, of course, he was right.

CHAPTER NINE

WHEN THE CLASS OF 1962 GRADUATED from Springhill High School, we were asked to write a kind of last will and testament for the yearbook—one of those adolescent flourishes that many years later often seem so revealing of character. I wrote the following: "I, Anne Murray, bequeath to my friend Chuck Merlin my ability to sing the hit songs between periods and to keep the beat on the desk." I suspect I must have driven people half-crazy with my constant singing. In fact, I know I did. My chief academic rival, Helen Gilroy, wrote for her will: "I bequeath to anyone who sits near Chuck Merlin my ability to keep my sanity when Anne Murray starts to sing." Above my photograph in that yearbook is a quotation chosen by the editors. It's a line from "Let Me In," that infectious 1960s song by the Sensations, about hearing music and wanting to be let in. I was sixteen years old and music was already my life.

A little later, while still in my teens, I was invited to perform at a Catholic Women's League Convention at the

Colonial Inn in Amherst, the little town parked on Nova Scotia's border with New Brunswick. When it ended, a woman from Cape Breton approached, thanked me for the concert and asked me to sign my name on a small rain hat that she'd been given in a loot bag. It was the first autograph I had ever signed. Upon receiving the signed hat she said, "You know, you're going to be famous one day." I'm not sure what that woman saw in me—my talent was still pretty raw. Of course I would have liked nothing better even then, but the idea of fame seemed downright laughable. In those days I was playing to audiences that rarely numbered more than a few dozen for fifty bucks at best.

Besides, for a teenage girl from blue-collar Springhill, the very notion of attaining stardom was absurd. We might aspire to careers in the professions—nursing, teaching, law, perhaps—but seldom anything further afield. No one seriously contemplated show business, no matter how talented they might be. Indeed, a more disparaging view predominated, one succinctly encapsulated in something my Aunt Ethel said to my mother a few years later, after "Snowbird" started soaring on the charts and just before I left Halifax for big, bad Toronto. "Well, Anne might be able to make it here in the Maritimes," she said, "but Toronto—that's a whole other kettle of fish." She was right too; Toronto is a very different kettle of fish.

Aunt Ethel was only one of many observers who insisted that, whatever my vocal abilities, I would never last in show business. I would never last because I was ill at ease with fame and happiest in seclusion, my core personality a complete opposite to the very notion of celebrity. I would never last because I couldn't decide what I wanted to be—a country singer, a pop singer, a folksinger or a middle-of-the-road adult contemporary singer, whatever that is. I would never last because I declined to play the celebrity game and to court constant attention. I would never last because I refused to leave Canada and move to Malibu or the Upper East Side and didn't party relentlessly on Sunset Strip or in SoHo. I would never last because I declined to put my career and earning potential ahead of my family and remained loyal to a single label instead of selling myself to the highest bidder. I would never last because my musical choices were too bland and my delivery was too restrained. I would never last because in an era that celebrated singer/songwriters, I never wrote my own material. I would never last because I wasn't essentially a chanteuse, or a torch singer, or a Broadway singer, or a message singer, or a hard rocker. If I was anything, it was probably a crooner in the fifties style, the style that shaped my earliest appreciation of popular music, but one that had largely gone out of fashion by the early 1960s—and thereafter couldn't have been relied upon to sell out a suburban backyard tent, let alone the Houston Astrodome.

I endured all these wise critiques and trenchant analyses—and then some—and just kept singing. Forty years later, I have sold in excess of 50 million albums and have been showered with awards and honours, far beyond anything a young girl from hard-luck Springhill could possibly have imagined. A few years ago they even put my likeness on a Canadian postage stamp. Not too shabby a career for a musical anomaly, for someone who couldn't decide what she wanted to be. Luck, talent, drive, support, hard work, a unique timbre to the voice that conferred almost instant recognition—all of that was mine, and you probably can't make it without it.

But I think my achievement also testifies to a simple but

enduring truth: there is ultimately no substitute for good singing, honestly rendered. It's why the estates of Sinatra, Como, Clooney and Fitzgerald, among many others, are still enjoying robust royalties. And it's why audiences kept buying my records and coming to my concerts—to hear good and sometimes great songs, well sung.

Of course, that may not always be the case. Today an array of high-tech tools allows engineers to "correct" vocal imperfections (too flat, too sharp, etc.) not only in the studio but in live performance as well. There are already dozens of pop singers—and there will be many more—whose success owes nothing to their actual ability to sing. They need their other gifts, of course: songwriting, good looks, showmanship, personality, a good choreographer. But when people are exposed to good singing, they still recognize and respond favourably to it.

⁓

I DISCOVERED SOMETHING ABOUT RETIREMENT in the year 2000—I wasn't ready for it, just as Bruce Allen had predicted. I enjoyed the time off immensely. I stayed home, reconnected with my children, wintered in Florida, read books, went to Spain on a glorious golf holiday with the Chicks with Sticks (Cynthia won that tournament) and generally used the time to decompress and unwind. My only professional commitment that year was a three-week Christmas tour, which, as always, I enjoyed.

But I knew at the end of it that I couldn't retire. It wasn't a matter of having new empires to conquer or more gold records to sell. I was under no illusions about that. It was more a question of what I would do with myself. I needed to be active, moving, goal-directed. Besides, retirement shouldn't be decided simply on the basis of age or income. You have to be mentally prepared for it, and I wasn't. So the following year, I again answered the siren call of the road.

My band by that point was a lean and mean machine, led by the calm and steady hand of keyboard player and band leader Steve Sexton. As one symphony conductor we worked with put it, "You guys are tighter than a bull's ass in fly season." Having succeeded Pat Riccio in 1987, Steve oversaw a septet that was thankfully a good deal tamer than the ragtag, if no less talented, group I had hopscotched across three continents with three decades earlier. As a rule, I no longer had to worry whether any of this more buttoned-down ensemble would turn up too drunk or too stoned to play.

Almost inevitably, our touring band of troubadours became something of a family. We commiserated with and administered to each other's colds and flus, toothaches and gastric upheavals. We mourned the deaths of loved ones, celebrated birthdays, weddings and the births of children, and made sure our parties included everyone, bus drivers and truck drivers alike. And in that loving way that families have, we relentlessly ridiculed each other's golf games, haircuts, wardrobes and personal peccadilloes. One of our favourite targets of abuse was guitarist Aidan Mason, who was notorious for losing things. On every tour he seemed to misplace either clothing or reading glasses, or his passport, his boarding pass, his hotel key, his itinerary. His misadventures became our longest-running soap opera. Aidan was my longest-serving band member—thirty-two years.

My pianist, Brian Gatto, also managed to get himself into

the odd scrape. Perhaps the most memorable one was during a 796-mile overnight bus trip from Turlock, California, to Orem, Utah. Cynthia and I had opted to fly, but everyone else was riding the bus. They had gone to sleep—except Brian, who wandered up to chat with Jim Dallas, our new driver. The highway they were on passed right by Reno, and Brian persuaded Jim to take an exit into town and drop him off at the Silver Legacy Casino so he could try his luck for half an hour. No one would mind, he reasoned; they were all fast asleep.

But Jim had to find a parking spot, and when Brian finally came out of the casino, the bus was nowhere to be found. It was three hours before they found each other and the bus was back on the road. The next day, everyone was checking their watches, trying to figure out why they were still so far from Orem—including Brian, who cleverly feigned puzzlement. It wasn't until after they arrived at the hotel that Driver Jim fessed up about his little detour. Brian, incidentally, was still in junior high when he was asked to write an essay about what he wanted to be when he grew up. His declared ambition—to be a piano player for Anne Murray. He was with me for twenty-one years, and has the gold watch to prove it.

For a while, we were quite literally a family. My hairdresser, P'tricia Wyse, travelled on the road with her infant daughter Mercer for almost three years, and with her next child, Sloan, for a few months as well. P'tricia was far more than a hairdresser. She was, as her mother had told me when I hired her, a ray of sunshine. She was an organizer who took charge of my whole dressing room operation, and she introduced me to the manifold joys of manicures and pedicures— a luxury I had never experienced until she came on board in

1993. She could hardly believe that I was (then) forty-eight years old and had never had a manicure or pedicure.

P'tricia had taken over from Shiela Yakimov; both of them worked in tandem with George Abbott, who was my makeup guru. Beginning in the late seventies and for more than twenty years thereafter, he did all of my TV shows and photo shoots. While he worked his magic we'd often reminisce about old movies and performers. He was always generous with his considerable knowledge of the art, and taught me how to apply stage makeup properly so that I could do it on my own, out on the road. He was, and remains, a good friend.

I attended two weddings for members of the group, both of them performed in Las Vegas. At Steve Lewis's nuptials in the late 1970s, our group sat on one side of the aisle while the Helen Reddy entourage sat on the other. Steve was working for Helen at the time, so he had two Vegas headliners witnessing the event. Pat and Don (D.T.) Thompson played the music and we all sang "Goin' to the Chapel." Steve's mother sat beside me at the ceremony and held my hand so tightly she almost cut off the circulation. She knew that she was watching a disaster in the making, and she was right—the marriage lasted about a year.

Bassist Peter Bleakney married Claire Toth at the Candlelight Wedding Chapel in 1993. Cost of the affair: $150, including the organ. Vern Dorge rented a scooter and zoomed up with his saxophone slung on his back. Steve Sexton served as best man, Gary Craig was "maid of honour," Aidan Mason played videographer and road manager Maurice Cardinal did the stills. Brian Gatto played the organ, with Vern on the sax. After the brief ceremony—the facility was rented by the half-hour—the happy couple signed the marriage certificate in the lobby, under the watchful gaze of numerous celebrity photographs, including Whoopi Goldberg. As we emerged from the building onto the Strip, people were bungee jumping across the street at Circus Circus. Only in Vegas. That night after the show, I threw a small reception in the green room at Bally's. I had ordered a big carrot cake with Mr. and Mrs. Bugs Bunny on top and gave the couple $500 mad money to rent a convertible, which they did. Peter and Claire, I'm pleased to say, are still together.

We went back on the road several times in 2001. One warm summer night in June, at the outdoor amphitheatre in Hinckley, Minnesota, my professional life came full circle. My opening act was Glen Campbell—sixty-seven years old, a little grey around the temples, but still singing with that pure, rich sound. I hadn't seen him in seventeen years, not since he appeared on my TV special in Quebec City. That time, I think, may have been a bad period for Glen. As he candidly recounted in his autobiography, *Rhinestone Cowboy*, he was drinking and using cocaine pretty regularly. I remember one group session in my hotel room during which Glen was singing selections from his next album and strumming on an air guitar; he kept excusing himself to use the washroom— to snort cocaine, we were pretty sure.

Glen had been so thoroughly immersed in music from such a young age—he was on the road in bands from his late teens—that he never had the opportunity to go to university. As a result he developed something of a complex about his lack of education. When he was with me, he seemed able to only play his music or tell jokes, never to conduct a real or sustained conversation. On the road, whenever I dropped by his hotel suite to chat, the first thing he did was play his new album or recount some amusing anecdote. We never were able to just sit down and talk, and it puzzled me for a long time. Then, one night in the seventies, I met him and his friend, song-writer Jimmy Webb—who wrote many of Glen's great hits—for dinner in London. During the evening I finally confronted Glen about the issue. He said that he was uncomfortable because both Jimmy and I had college educations, and he didn't. We quickly assured him that having a degree conferred no exalted status or special ability. Besides, anyone who could sing and play like Glen Campbell didn't need a college education.

Glen eventually did tackle his dependence problem. He turned to God and within a month had ostensibly managed to give it all up—smoking, drinking, other drugs. On stage that night in Hinckley, he joked about it with the crowd. "Since I quit drinking, this is all I have," he said, lifting a water bottle. "Although my daddy told me you can get just as drunk on water as you can on land." Glen's oldest daughter, Debby, no slouch herself in the music department, did a couple of numbers as well.

When I came onstage, I explained to the audience how important Glen had been to me early in my career and how lucky I had been to have that support. Then he came back on and we sang two Everly Brothers duets—"Let It Be Me" and "Dream"—and brought the house down. I've enjoyed a lot of special nights on stages all over the world, but this one, given our shared history, was particularly magical.

Our fall tour that year began only ten days after what was perhaps the defining moment of the past forty years—9/11. The venue was Yavapai College in Prescott, Arizona. So soon after the attacks, we weren't quite sure what to expect from an American audience, but it seemed prudent to take

"What a Wonderful World" out of the medley portion of the show. During the unplugged portion—a segment in which I sang four or five songs suggested by the audience—I sang "A Little Good News" and was amazed at the crowd's enthusiastic response. It happened again the next two nights as well, in Bakersfield and Jackson, California; both audiences gave us standing ovations and started to chant, "U.S.A.! U.S.A.!"

During a tour stop in Reno I had lunch with an old friend, comedian R.G. Brown. He and I were regulars on the *Glen Campbell Goodtime Hour* in the early seventies, although we actually met on a flight to Hawaii to tape one of the shows. I took to R.G.'s outrageous sense of humour immediately and visited him frequently during subsequent trips to L.A. R.G. visited Bill and me in Toronto a few times as well. Once, after picking him up at the airport, we arrived home just in time to interrupt a burglary in progress. As we opened the door, we heard things crashing to the floor and the thieves hustling out the back door. The front foyer was filled with their prospective loot—guitars, etc.—and there was a getaway car parked up the street. R.G., no stranger to heists from his days living in New York and L.A., leapt into action and chased the culprit down an alley. He didn't catch him, but the perp, afraid he was about to be caught, threw away the bag he was carrying , allowing R.G. to recover all my jewellery and valuables.

A few years later he came to Toronto for the Christmas holidays. Cynthia and Ken McReynolds were hosting a New Year's Eve gathering, but R.G., knowing no one besides Bill and me, declined to go. But then he crashed the party— dressed up like a cleaning lady. He said nothing, just breezed in and started going through the house with a vacuum cleaner, dusting and tearing down Christmas decorations, emptying the dishwasher, generally creating havoc and even breaking a dish. He was gone in five minutes. People were dumbfounded. No one except the four of us had any idea who "she" was, and we thought it was hilarious. He is one of a kind.

———

AFTER THE U.S. TOUR we flew to Vancouver to tape the "What a Wonderful Christmas" special at the Orpheum Theatre. One of my guests was Canadian jazz singer and pianist Diana Krall. Discussions between her managers and mine initially proved difficult. First they weren't sure whether she wanted to do the show, then whether she could do it because of her schedule, then whether the song we had chosen would be to her liking. We proceeded to make our plans while awaiting her answer, but the clear impression they left was that Diana was difficult.

Finally she agreed to appear, but didn't show up until all the other segments had been taped. By that point I was pacing anxiously in my dressing room backstage; after all the build-up about how difficult she could be, I was more than a little nervous about meeting her. I stuck out my hand to greet her, saying, "Hello, I'm Anne. Nice to meet you." She immediately started to cry.

When she had finally composed herself, Diana said, "You don't know what this moment means to me. I grew up on your songs."

"Well, thank you very much," I said. "Now tell me, what would you like to sing?"

"Oh, I don't know."

"Oh. Okay. Well, do you know 'Have Yourself a Merry Little Christmas'?"

"Of course."

"You wouldn't mind singing that?"

"We can sing anything you like."

It couldn't have been easier. Either she was on her best behaviour that day or it was a case of "her people" talking to "my people" and blowing things out of proportion. That seems to happen a lot in this business.

⁓

CYNTHIA CONTINUED TO TRAVEL WITH US as road-manager-cum-bon-vivant—her hijinks could probably fill a book on their own. One cold December day we found ourselves in Peekskill, New York. Looking for some lunch, Cynthia and I decided to raid the pantry on our tour bus. Unfortunately it was cold and the power was off, so we couldn't even boil water. Undeterred, Cynce went to the front of the bus and promptly started throwing every switch she could find. "One of these has got to turn on the power," she grumbled. And one of them did—but another one emptied the contents of the bus's bathroom all over the hotel parking lot. Cynce wisely avoided the bus driver for the rest of the day.

It was during that 2001 tour that we first noticed her cough, the disturbing kind that doesn't go away. She had smoked for years, and while the Chicks had encouraged her to quit, she couldn't seem to muster the necessary will—or wouldn't. Since I was among those encouraging her to stop, I had to quit too. When I was in my twenties, I smoked ten or twelve cigarettes a day. In my thirties I cut back to three or four a day, fewer when I was performing on the road or recording. I also stopped smoking in public at that time,

embarrassed and feeling guilty that such a filthy and dangerous habit had a hold on me. I had quit for a year here and a
year there but had always eventually weakened. This time
I knew I had to do it for keeps, and I did.

The following year, Cynthia consulted a physician and
he found a spot on her lung: the dreaded modern curse, cancer.
It was horrible. When she got sick, you could feel the life
draining out of us as a group. She was our glue, our captain,
the centre without which we could not hold. Initially the
doctors thought she had developed large-cell lung cancer,
which they deemed treatable with surgery. However, the tests
proved just the opposite: it was small-cell cancer.

That was it. There was nothing they could do surgically.
Cynthia's marriage was long since over by then, and she had
gone to live with her brother for a time. But when she became
ill, she did not want to be a burden to him or her children. So
she came to live with me for the last two years of her life, during
those long, debilitating rounds of chemotherapy and radiation.
I was happy to have her—she was my best friend. When I was
touring, my housekeeper, Virginia Gallego, looked after her.
Cynthia's kids came frequently to visit, but it was a very tough
time. She wasn't a particularly good patient. She wanted to be
left alone, so you had to wait for her to come to you. She didn't
want to see any of her friends, although they did drive her to
and from treatments. She fought on like that for two years and
lived to see her younger son, Drew, married.

In January 2004 I went down to Jupiter, Florida, and
took Cynthia along with me. She'd finished her regimen of
chemo and radiation, and the doctors, amazingly, had given
her a clean bill of health. As far as I knew and as far as she
knew, there were no signs of cancer in either her lungs or her

brain. For weeks she seemed fine. But in mid-March I noticed that she was a little unsteady on her feet. On the Thursday of that week, she was dizzy and nauseated. The next day, incredibly, we played a full round of golf at Heritage Ridge—I don't know how she did it. On Saturday, at about 5:00 p.m., she called to me that she couldn't see properly.

I called 911 and we went to the hospital, where they did scans and too quickly reported the grim results: the cancer had metastasized to her brain. The doctors thought surgery might be possible if a neurosurgeon could be found, but it would have meant moving her to Miami, and that seemed a mistake to me. I wanted her home with her family. She slipped into a coma soon afterwards; typically, her last words and last thoughts were about her children. I called them and then I called Darlene Sawyer, my assistant, and we arranged a medivac flight to airlift Cynthia and me back to Toronto. The plane, due to leave Jupiter at 6:00 a.m., had mechanical difficulties and did not arrive there until 3:00 p.m. I spent those long hours with her in the hospital in silent prayer.

An ambulance met the plane in Toronto and she was taken on life support to a hospital—I can't even remember which one. Her son Drew was out of the country, but Shane, daughter Sloan, Ken, her mother, Vena, and brother John were there. The doctors told them that surgery was out of the question. They could keep her alive, but there was no hope for recovery. The family took the hard decision right then to let her go.

There was no formal funeral or burial—Cynthia had asked to be cremated—but we did hold a memorial service in her honour, on St. Patrick's Day, a great day for a party, as Sharon Bright noted in her moving eulogy. It was more like a celebration of Cynce's extraordinary life. In her remarks, Sharon, her close friend, recalled some of Cynthia's finer moments . . . the time she left a Thanksgiving turkey roasting in the oven, went outside to play catch with her kids, burnt the bird to a crisp, ordered chicken from Swiss Chalet, dressed it up on plates and pretended the cuisine was hers . . . the time, as president of the Thornhill Golf and Country Club, she led a club excursion to the racetrack. It was an oppressively hot day, and when we boarded the steamy, non-air-conditioned school bus for the return trip, Cynce, losing her patience, removed her pantyhose and tied them to the window, allowing them to flap in the breeze like a flag from the side of the bus . . . the time she was entertaining friends for an elegant lobster dinner and, when one of the guests—whom she had just met—requested a bun, she sent it hurtling down the table like a rocket. He was afraid to ask for another . . . the time she and I returned from a golf game to find Dawn's Grade 6 class cavorting in the pool. Determined to welcome our guests properly, we both shook hands with the teacher and then walked straight into the pool with all our clothes and our golf shoes on. Even the eleven-year-olds were lost for words.

After the service, family and friends were invited to my home, where—in true Cynthia McReynolds style—her boys were soon dancing enthusiastically on my big marble coffee table, which subsequently collapsed and broke into many pieces. It was a helluva goodbye party, what Bill used to call a hullit. We all miss her terribly, including my children, for whom she had become like a second mother. Cynthia was sixty-two when she died. Later that year I recorded and dedicated to her memory what I thought would be my last album, *I'll Be Seeing You* (titled *All of Me* in the U.S.).

I'll Be Seeing You HAD BEEN PRECEDED by another hit album, *Country Croonin'*. Produced by Tommy West, it featured thirty classic songs from the country repertoire, including the old Everly Brothers single "Let It Be Me," done as a duet with Vince Gill. For the album cover photograph, we went for the glamour look: a shot of me lying on my side propped up on one elbow, wearing a long, slinky, sleeveless black dress. Everyone loved it except Time Warner, which was involved in the distribution. They felt it didn't look country enough and expressed their concern to Bruce Allen.

"So let me get this straight," Bruce said. "You want me to call Anne Murray and tell her that her CD cover is too classy? Tell you what, you make the fuckin' call! You call her up and tell her she looks too classy. And while I'm at it, why is it you guys are always trying to lower the f—ing bar? We deliver this great shot and you want her to look like a f—ing hayseed!" That, needless to say, was the end of the discussion.

Later, when Bruce opened his first copy of the CD, he found two stickers on it. One advertised the duet with Vince Gill and the other said *two CDs for the price of one!* Bruce immediately called EMI. "Yeah, I've got Anne's new CD here. What's with the f—ing 'two for the price of one' sticker?! This is not a f—ing discount album! Who authorized this? Next time I go to the music store, I'm not going to see this f—ing sticker, am I?" The offending label was quickly removed.

MY FATHER HAD LEFT A MODEST ESTATE, and my mother, with her careful spending habits (a legacy of the Depression era) and my brother Daniel's astute investment counsel, eventually became a reasonably wealthy woman. In her last few years she gave generously to her family, the Church, the hospital and Springhill's new community centre, which was named in her and my father's honour (the Dr. Carson and Marion Murray Community Centre). She also served as honorary chair of the board of directors of the Anne Murray Centre, from the time it opened its doors in 1989 until her passing. She occasionally came to Toronto to visit, flew south every winter to my condo in Jupiter, Florida, to enjoy the sunshine, and once even accompanied me on a three-week concert tour in the western United States.

The friction that had marked our relationship during my adolescence had long since passed. At one point in the early eighties she was angry with me about something—I didn't know what the cause was—and she had retreated into a zone of passive-aggressive silence. Finally I could take no more of it and said, "Mom, what is it? What have I done wrong?" I forget now how that contretemps ended, but it marked a turning point for me; after that I stopped reacting to her criticism, spoken or implied. I simply decided not to let it bother me. That changed our dynamic and we got along much better as a result.

On the road or in Florida, Mom was always a lot of fun. She'd been blessed with good health and high energy, and even in her nineties at my summer home in Pugwash, you would see her striding vigorously across the lawn between the cottages of her respective children. For her ninetieth birthday we held a huge family celebration at Ron Joyce's Fox Harb'r Resort.

When we returned to my place in Pugwash at 2:30 a.m., she insisted on looking over all the gifts she had received. Mom and her brother Wilfred, then age seventy-nine, were the last ones to bed—at 4:00 a.m.

Sometimes, when she needed the attention of any one of her children, she would quickly recite all our names aloud until she found the one she wanted—"David, Daniel, Harold, Stewart, Bruce . . . Anne!" And she still invoked her many favourite phrases, such as "upon my word," "without a word of a lie," "mark my words" and "there'll be no detour for her," which meant that the person she was talking about was going straight to Heaven.

Disliking attention as I did, I'd often have to remind Mom not to call me by my name in public places, but she just ignored me. We'd be shopping for groceries in the supermarket in Florida and she'd shout from another aisle, "Anne, you won't believe what they're charging for cantaloupes here. Five dollars! It's outrageous!" At other times she would point to me and say to the salesclerk, "Do you know who this is?" If the answer was no she'd say, "This is Anne Murray, and I'm her mother!" I could have died. She'd often make a point of going into record stores to check that they had plenty of my albums on hand. If they didn't, or if the ones they had were not prominently displayed, she'd let them know about it.

Florence Massey was our neighbour in Jupiter, and she and Mom became good friends over the years. They were both widows and had been born in the same year. Driving back to the condo one night after I'd done a show in Fort Lauderdale, Mom said, "You know, Florence, sometimes I think it would be nice to have a man around. You know, just for the company. Have some coffee, a little conversation. No hanky-panky—

I wouldn't want him pawing at me or anything—just a man for a little company. Of course, you wouldn't want him around all the time."

"Well," said Florence, "the trouble with finding men at our age is that you have to look after them. No, Marion, the only reason that I can think of for having a man now is if he can drive at night."

A few years later Mom and a friend drove from Springhill to Bangor, Maine, to attend one of my shows. On a day off we all trooped to the mall for some Christmas shopping, then repaired to a seafood restaurant for dinner. Several band members had just received their twenty-year watches and were busy showing them off when Mom offhandedly mentioned that the last time someone had bought her a watch had been sixty-six years earlier—a gift from Dad—when she was twenty-three. That remark got my attention. In all these years I'd bought watches for many people, but never one for my mother. A month later, when Mom came down with flu and was bedridden, I bought her a beautiful Raymond Weil watch with a card that read: *Sixty-six years is long enough to wait for a new watch.*

Mom was just shy of her ninety-third birthday when she started experiencing occasional dizzy spells. She consulted doctors, who discovered an arterial blockage. Telling her she had the body of a seventy-year-old, they recommended an aortic valve replacement, a five-to-six-hour open-heart procedure. I was performing in Grand Forks, North Dakota, but I called her at her Halifax hotel the night before the surgery. Everyone in the family who could be there was with her, and she said that she was getting quite the send-off. She was very matter of fact. "I might not come through this," she said, "but I've had a great life and you'll just have to go on without me."

The operation itself was a success, but the procedure loosened some deposits of plaque, which reached her brain and caused a couple of strokes. When she still hadn't awakened after twenty-four hours, I cancelled the remaining four shows on the tour. Getting to Nova Scotia was not simple, but sweet Van, our tour bus driver, volunteered to drive us back to Toronto. We made the long trip in a day and I caught the next flight for Halifax. We were all there when she died, children and grandchildren. Marion Murray is buried beside her husband and her parents in Springhill—a great, smart, loving woman I was blessed to call Mom.

AFTER FORTY YEARS ON THE ROAD I sometimes feel there isn't a venue I haven't played: tents, arenas, opera houses, hockey rinks, grand palaces, smoky casinos, amphitheatres, charming theatres-in-the-round, less charming bingo parlours and, on my fifty-seventh birthday (how's this for a coincidence?), Pittsburgh's Heinz Hall—a spectacular theatre named for the famous family that created the slogan "Heinz 57."

I've slept in some of the world's finest hotels and some of its worst, which were invariably (with my windows open) situated next to a bustling railroad siding, a busy parking lot, a trash compactor or a building under construction. Outdoors I've sung in torrential rain, blistering heat and wicked lightning storms. At state fairs I've had to compete with fireworks displays and ostrich races held near the stage. I've sung in theme parks with roller coasters running non-stop in the audience's sight lines, with noisy choirs of crickets determined to give their own concerts, and at one place where a guy hanging by his teeth from a helicopter flew over the crowd right in front of the stage. "Couldn't you at least have waited until I'd finished the damned song?" I shouted up at him. More than once I've been targeted as a tasty late-night snack by swarms of angry gnats—just try singing "I Just Fall in Love Again" with those pernicious flies biting you under your blouse or fluttering up your nose.

In the Houston Astrodome, a venue packed with forty thousand people where I played three times, I was the diversionary act sandwiched between the main event—chuckwagon races. I had to be driven to the stage (at roughly second base) in a convertible, and the nearest spectator was at least a hundred yards away. The sound system was a doozy: it fed back a vibrating echo of every line I sang just as I started the next one. In Yakima, Washington, local teenagers were using the street outside the old theatre—it had thin wooden walls—for drag racing, an unwelcome orchestral accompaniment. In Toledo, Ohio, I was streaked—by a naked woman, just my luck. At Disney World I've played with the monorail whooshing by, and somewhere (a location I've forgotten) I was performing on a revolving stage when the damn thing got stuck and started to smoke. I quickly climbed atop the piano while they fixed it.

There was no smoke at Toronto's Roy Thomson Hall, but the fire alarm did go off on the hall's opening night, while I was in mid-song. And in the same city's O'Keefe Centre, with my mother in the audience, I kept getting interrupted by some yahoo shouting, "Show us your tits!" I couldn't quite believe what I had heard, so I said, "Pardon?" He shouted it out again and I still wasn't sure, so he did it one or two more times. It's no wonder that in those days I used to say, "There's no such thing as the big time."

The nadir of small time, I think, was in Reno, Nevada, at John Ascuaga's Nugget. There my opening act was a pair of performing elephants, Bertha and Tina. Together they weighed eight tons. Just before show time the handlers would prompt them to evacuate their bowels, achieved by virtue of a Pavlovian command—"Bertha, shit!" and "Tina, shit!"—to which they responded instantaneously. The results looked like organic cannonballs. Then their co-star, a twenty-five-year-old woman known as "The Lovely Barbara," would put them through their pachyderm paces; she had them dancing and bowing down while she hung gymnastically from a bar they held in their trunks. Bertha and Tina were housed behind the casino in a huge stone paddock with a pond in the centre. Pat Riccio and Peter Cardinali liked to visit them and give Bertha cigarettes. She would take the cigarette gently from your hand with her trunk and put it in her mouth, all the while looking at you with her huge, soft eyes. She loved cigarettes.

I never actually saw the elephants do their act—I was always getting dressed and warming up when they were on—but I could smell them. It was unbelievable. One night Pat and Peter snuck into the lovely Barbara's dressing room just to sniff one of her costumes. It was, Pat said, like a punch in the face. The clothes smelled exactly like an elephant, which may explain why she kept largely to herself.

My audiences have been as varied as the venues. I've sung for the hyperkinetic and the comatose, the clever and the obtuse, the falling-down drunk and the all too sober, the adoring fans and the excessively adoring fans, the very young and (in a line my stage manager Steven Lewis usurped from Martin Mull) "old people and their parents." My most faithful fans—dubbed Snowbirds—seemed to compete with each other to see who could attend more of my concerts; some of them have been to hundreds. They and others have showered me with enough flowers, balloons, teddy bears, perfume, chocolates, knick-knacks and golf paraphernalia to fill a good-sized Wal-Mart. It's been more than a decade, I think, since I've actually had to buy a new golf ball.

At least three times over the years, marriage proposals were made in the middle of my show. The prospective groom would always write to me beforehand so that I'd know what song he wanted to use. At the opportune moment, we'd beam the spotlight on the unsuspecting girl while he went down on bended knee. Afterwards I'd always ask, "What did she say?" Then the audience would cheer and the young woman would cry.

Sometimes an audience can be quite sharp. I was in Houston once when someone called out for me to sing "Amazing Grace."

"Hmmm . . . 'Amazing Grace,'" I mused. "I'm not sure if I remember all the words. It's that menopause thing, you know." To which a quick-witted woman added, "Amazing grace—that's what you get when menopause is over!"

And sometimes they can be a little thick. At intermission once in Branson, Missouri, someone sent me a note saying: *Dear Anne Murray, I was at my Air Force base in Fresno, Calif. in 1944 when you entertained us. You have been my favorite lady singer ever since. You shook hands with me. Sincerely, Charles Conkle.* Naturally the crowd got a big laugh out of that. I was quick to inform Charles that, even though I'd been singing a very long time, I wasn't even born in 1944.

Beginning in the 1970s and more frequently in recent years, we arranged to play with local symphony orchestras.

At first it was a novelty and a thrill, but later we did it to give the show a different look and feel. Some orchestras evinced a certain disdain for our (or any) brand of popular music, as if appearing with us was more a matter of obligation than of pleasure. In subtle (or less subtle) ways they let us know it, too. In general we found American symphonies much less snobby and more fun than the Canadian ones, perhaps because of a longer tradition of incorporating pop into their classical programs. But the quality level was hugely uneven. There were several first-class ensembles—among them Pittsburgh, Dallas, Los Angeles, the Boston Pops and the Nashville Symphony—many mediocre ones, and quite a few that were simply amateurish. In Maryland once, my guitarist Aidan Mason struck up a conversation with the lad next to him, who was playing cello. On hearing that he was in university, Aidan asked, "Are you taking music?"

"No," the boy said. "Biology."

Quite often after a show I'd meet and greet members of the audience. At one such event in Las Vegas, I met a woman who had travelled by bus from Vancouver—a forty-nine-hour journey—to see the concert. We shook hands and exchanged a few words, after which she immediately got back on the bus for the return trip. A fellow from Belgium had won a contest to fly to Vegas and meet me. "I was crying the whole show," he confessed, "and I don't know why."

Every once in a while I'd look up at one of those events to discover someone from my past—a girl I'd gone to school with in Springhill or a woman I'd known in university. She'd say, "Hello, Anne, I'm sure you don't remember me, but . . ." This kind of remark always puzzled me, as if becoming a celebrity somehow carried with it a high risk of serious memory loss. "Why wouldn't I remember you?" I'd say. "We were in school together for three years!"

⌒

THE TITLE OF MY THIRTY-THIRD ALBUM, *I'll Be Seeing You*, was appropriate. After that, I thought, I was done. That was all I had in me. There'd be no more albums, no more tours. Although I could still work the voice to where it needed to be to perform, that was getting increasingly harder. At long last I felt ready to retire. I adopted the line old hockey players use: "You have to know when to hang 'em up." This was my moment.

Then Bruce Allen called me one day and said EMI wanted to talk to me about making another album. I could hardly believe it.

"Forget it," I told him. "I'm done."

"Now hold on, Anne," he said.

"Bruce, I'm not doing another album."

"Just do me one favour, please," he said (although, being Bruce, he probably didn't say please). "Go to the meeting. They have some good ideas."

"What ideas?"

"Go to the meeting and find out."

Some meeting. It was more like an intervention. Half the world seemed to be there, including Bruce, all in league to make me change my mind. EMI's president, the always genial Deane Cameron, chaired. Deane's is the proverbial mailroom-to-CEO story. He'd started working for Capitol at eighteen, in 1972—just a few years after I signed with them—unloading albums from trucks in the warehouse and stocking the shelves.

EMI's good ideas turned out to be one idea, but it wasn't a bad one: an album of duets with about a dozen big-name artists, men and women. Deane's people had already drawn up a roster of possible A-list producers. Still, I was skeptical. I'm known for having something of a stubborn streak, and it was on bright display that day.

"I'm not doing another album, Deane."

"Just listen to the list."

"I don't want to do another album. What's the point? It won't get played and therefore it won't get bought."

"If we do this right, it might actually do pretty well."

I didn't share his optimism. My only contribution was to suggest that if such an album were made, why not do it with women only? The idea was dismissed out of hand.

The meeting ended inconclusively, but just to appease them, I said that they could make some inquiries and see what producer might be willing to take on such a project. One name at the top of the list was Phil Ramone. If there's a major recording artist of the past fifty years that he hasn't worked with, I'd be surprised: Barbra Streisand, Michael Jackson, Elton John, Ray Charles, Paul McCartney, Frank Sinatra . . . well, you get the idea. A child prodigy on the violin—he performed for Queen Elizabeth at age ten—Phil later studied at Juilliard and might well have had a concert career. Instead he went into recording, and five decades later he was still playing at the top of his game.

Phil called me in Pugwash to tell me how much he loved the basic album idea and to do a little lobbying. I was still the reluctant bride, but did agree to test the waters by sending emails or hand-written notes to different singers to ascertain their interest. Several said yes immediately, including k.d. lang,

Olivia Newton-John and Shania Twain. The first one to jump in was k.d. She's been a fan of mine—I think I was her first crush—since childhood. In fact, back then she actually sent me a song she'd written; it never reached me, and as a result I never responded to her. Today we like to joke about whether she'll ever forgive me for the oversight.

Once I'd surrendered to the inevitable, I suggested to Phil that we try to include a track with the late Dusty Springfield. The only song I knew that we had both recorded was "I Just Fall in Love Again." But we had no idea how to find it or what condition it might be in. EMI's Fraser Hill finally tracked it down, only to be turned down by the agents for Dusty's estate. So then I sat down and wrote them a personal letter, explaining that Dusty and I had been friends, had admired each other's work and performed together, and that I'd been one of the few to whom she wanted to say goodbye before she died. They wrote back immediately, giving their consent. Phil then did elaborate conjuring tricks in the studio to make it seamless, as if we'd been recorded together. It gave me chills to be singing a duet with her when she was no longer with us.

With three or four artists on board, I again raised my women-only proposal and this time won some backing, particularly from Phil. I thought it would make the task of finding duet partners easier by narrowing the field and would serve to set my album apart from all the other duet albums, which included both men and women. Picking the songs to record with each partner was trickier. To avoid competing claims on the same tune, I asked each singer separately which song they wanted to sing. Shania immediately started bidding for "You Needed Me"—a song, she said, that called to her—and we conducted a long and delightful email exchange. Eventually we had a lineup of seventeen singers and songs. Dawn would be singing one of the songs with me, and I also hired her to sing with me on the demo tracks that we sent to all the participants.

Because I was working with such great singers, making the record was as much fun as I'd had in a studio for a long time. Sarah Brightman had just finished shooting a movie in Toronto, and she breezed into the studio completely without makeup. We were paired on "Snowbird"—not Sarah's typical musical fare, but she worked very hard at getting it right. Olivia Newton-John was, as always, the consummate professional, fully prepared, warmed up and ready to sing from the moment she entered the room. She's so good.

I'd met Jann Arden a few times and knew of her wicked sense of humour. Once, shortly after a Juno Awards ceremony, she was interviewed by Peter Gzowski on his CBC radio show. She reported to him that her dressing room had been next to mine and that I was really drunk. Then she said, "And Anne's got a secret nobody knows. You know those great legs of hers? Well, she screws them on—she keeps the legs in boxes."

The next thing I knew, my mother called and wanted to know if I was drunk on the Junos. Some girl on the radio had said so.

"What girl, Mom?"

"I don't know. Some singer."

"Mom, surely you know me better than that."

"Well, I suppose so."

I checked around, got the full story and had a good laugh. And when Jann had her next album release party, I sent her a little present: a flower box into which I'd put a mannequin leg. She later had it mounted in her house. I invited her to play golf at my Toronto club; she turned up in jeans, boots and a lumberjack shirt—and then had to spend a small fortune in the pro shop getting properly outfitted for the course.

DUETS was special for another reason: for the first and only time, I was singing with both my children on an album. Being in the studio with them as we laid down vocal tracks was a great thrill for me and a special memory for all of us. Will, a wonderful singer in his own right, joined us on "You Won't See Me," and I've heard from many people that Dawn's duet with me, "Nobody Loves Me Like You Do," is their favourite cut on the album.

DUETS surpassed all my expectations for it. By the middle of 2009 it had sold almost 400,000 copies. Unfortunately I made no money on it. At a total cost somewhere north of $650,000, it was by far the most expensive album I had ever made. It was recorded in three separate locations, Toronto, L.A. and Nashville, with shared royalties on every song and teams of videographers recording the whole thing for a subsequent TV special. Yet I hardly had grounds for complaint. Its success laid the foundation for my last tours—twenty-nine dates in the U.S. and twenty-seven in Canada in 2008—which were virtual sellouts. It was critically important to me that I make my final exit from the stage to packed houses, with audiences on their feet asking for more, and it was that album that made all of that possible.

The Canadian leg of the tour was, understandably, one that stirred deep emotions, nowhere more than in my Maritime home. In Charlottetown I had a post-show reunion with eight of my former students from Athena Regional High School. Some of them are now grandmothers, but when they sang a team song I had taught them more than forty years earlier, it was as if time had stood still. The next night, in

Halifax, when we sang Allister MacGillivray's ballad "Song for the Mira," the entire audience sang along—3,500 voices and mine, choking back tears.

My final concert, on May 23, 2008, was at the Sony Centre in Toronto. It would be the last time I'd be singing so many of those songs, and again I was more than a little choked up. Then, just as we approached "You Needed Me," I looked down into the audience and saw a guy in the front row yawning widely. Well, that deflated my sentimental balloon in a hurry. But the ovation at the close was warm and sustained and very moving. We'd covered 11,000 miles and played fifty-six shows in twelve weeks of work. Amazingly, there'd been no hiccups—no illness, no arrests, no attempted murders. And the old voice actually held out for the entire tour.

One interesting footnote to the *DUETS* story is that it was nominated, at virtually the last minute, for a Juno award as album of the year—the result of a recount of sales by the auditors. When they notified me about it, they said that, as a result, an album by Calgary recording artist Feist would have to be dropped from the list of nominees. I suggested that instead of bumping her, they just make it a list of six albums. So Feist remained a nominee and went on to win the Juno in that category (and several others).

WITH THE END OF THE 2008 TOUR, I knew that my "hang 'em up" moment had finally and irrevocably come. It was time to retire.

My son, Will, ratified my decision in typically amusing fashion one night when we were watching the Grammys together. Commenting on the performances of some of my peers, he quipped, "You see, Mom, you're doing the right thing—quitting before you suck."

Of course there's always a little voice inside that keeps insisting, "You don't really want to stop. You're still fit, still having fun and, with enough effort, you can still get the voice to where it needs to be for performance." And all of that is true. On the other hand, there's also a genuine satisfaction in knowing that I won't ever have to work quite that hard again—not to worry about rehearsals, not to fret about costumes or buses breaking down, not to run the endless gauntlet of media interviews. Part of me will certainly miss it; who wouldn't? It's been a rewarding career in every possible sense. But I can still sing: sing at parties, sing with family and friends, sing in the shower, if I choose. And I will—I don't need a stage to sing. All in all, I feel very good about the decision.

When I started singing as a child, it was just a spontaneous act that I never thought about. Later, as a teen, singing became something I somehow needed to do; some irresistible force within me needed to be expressed musically. When I turned professional, I continued to enjoy performing, even with all the challenges of the road and of the business. Still, I saw my music, and indeed all pop music, as simply a form of entertainment, a way to please audiences for an hour or two, in live concert or on an album. What I failed to understand then, but came to learn again and again, is the incredible power that music possesses—the power to heal, to shape destiny, even to change lives. A popular song may just be three minutes of not terribly profound poetry, but the right combination of words and music can touch people at their very core. The testimony of this truth can be found in the hundreds, indeed thousands, of letters and emails I've received over the years from fans. I know I'm not alone. I'm sure the same has held true for most performers—Dusty, Barbra, Ella, Mahalia—take your pick.

Not long ago I received a letter from an American woman. She'd lost her husband and two young children in a tragic car accident and had fallen into a deep depression. A church pianist and vocalist for twelve years, she could no longer bring herself to perform. Indeed, she was so despondent, she wrote, that she was planning to take her life. One day she went into a Christian bookstore and happened upon *What a Wonderful World*, the album of inspirational songs I'd made with Tommy West in 1999. She put it into her car's CD player on her ride home, started to listen to Joie Scott and Richard Wold's "The Other Side," and started to weep. As she wrote, "I played it over and over as my tears poured down . . . and began to feel peace washing over me." Instead of driving home, she went to her church and told her pastor what she had been planning to do. She prayed, then went home, sat down at the piano and played and sang for hours. "I cannot describe the joy I felt . . . I am surprised at the amount of power your music had inside of me. I truly believe that if I had not listened to that song on that day, I would not be writing this."

Even more recently, I received a letter from an Ohio woman. The daughter of missionaries, she'd been raised in a strict religious environment without access to secular music— except for my music, which her father and the family listened to every night. In effect, she said, I sang her to sleep. While her schoolmates were listening to Bon Jovi and Journey, she was listening to me. She eventually wore out the tape. "Gosh, how I hated taking away your voice," her email said, "because then

all of the other destructive voices would bellow in upon me."
Today, at thirty-five, she still finds herself crawling under the
covers with my music. "I am not a needy woman—but on
the occasions when I need comfort . . . you are there . . . For
me, you are a comfort. You are the voice of my young, young
childhood. You are the voice of my adolescence. You were my
safety blanket. And while I no longer depend upon you, I am
still glad to hear your voice."

What the music of Anne Murray does for her, the music
of hundreds of other artists is equally capable of doing. Such
letters confirm that a song isn't always just a song. It's a connection, forged in the universal language of music, perhaps
the only language that carries such potent emotional and
psychological subtext.

⁓

In 1999, when I sang at EMI's fiftieth birthday bash, it was
brought to the company's attention that I had been with them
for thirty years, considerably longer than anyone working
there at that time. Given the anniversary (and the minor detail
of having by then sold over 40 million albums), they decided
to give me a gift. The offer was carte blanche—I could have
anything I wanted. But what could I want? Then I had a brain-
wave: a custom-made golf cart for my summer home in
Pugwash. It had to be classy, but also roadworthy, able to get
me from the cottage to the golf course, and preferably loaded
with accessories.

"Maybe I'm lowballing them," I wondered aloud at one
group dinner. "Do you know how much money I've made for
EMI in thirty years?"

"Why don't you throw in a set of golf clubs too?" someone suggested.

"Good idea."

In the end I was presented with a silver fibreglass cart lined with carpet (big mistake—I later had it replaced with rubber matting). The vehicle has headlights, turn indicators, rear-view mirrors, a cooler in the back and a small storage trunk in the front. Oh, yes, and there was a new set of TaylorMade clubs.

Now that I'm officially retired I'll be making increasing use of these fine toys. Indeed, while I wasn't entirely sure I would enjoy retirement once I actually took the plunge, I've been pleasantly surprised. I seem to have no shortage of friends, activities and challenges to fill my time.

Since my divorce I have been on my own, and the truth is, I like it that way. While various friends have occasionally tried to play Cupid, I've resisted these well-intentioned initiatives. I don't feel ready at this point to make the compromises that a relationship would inevitably require. Perhaps, as I settle more fully into retirement, my attitude will change. But for the moment, I feel content.

My mother, who aged beautifully, used to bemoan her neck. "I hate this old neck!" she'd say. I feel the same about mine, although, contrary to the assumptions of at least one journalist, I've never had a stitch of cosmetic surgery. My scoliosis slows me down on occasion, but if a wrinkled neck and a sore back constitute the full bill of physical complaints, I will count myself lucky and meet the other challenges as they come.

I look back on my forty years in show business without any major or lingering regrets. Others will make their own assessments, but I feel I achieved as much as I could have dreamt, and then some. Would I have had a bigger career if I had taken the advice of my first manager, Nick Savano, and others and moved to Los Angeles or New York? Perhaps, but I certainly don't lie in bed at night wondering what might have happened if I had. And I don't think I suffered terribly from not uprooting myself. Staying put allowed me to maintain those aspects of my life that were far more important to me than any gold or platinum album—my ties to home and family.

If I regret anything, it's that I didn't take enough time for myself, Bill and the kids. It took me a long while to see that I worked harder than I needed to. Bruce Allen certainly agreed. Before he came along, Leonard, Lyman and I operated on the assumption that to capitalize on every hit record, we had to maximize my exposure—the enduring make-hay-while-the-sun-shines principle. At the time, none of us knew any better. But as I later discovered, the laws of supply and demand apply as much to performers as they do to crude oil and pork bellies—a little less can sometimes yield a lot more. It wasn't just performing, either. Were I to do it all again, I'd record fewer albums—perhaps twenty studio albums instead of thirty-four (not to mention all the compilations)—and make each one of them count. Too often our decisions were driven by bottom-line instead of artistic or creative considerations.

But all of this is hindsight, and I don't dwell on it. Looked at in its entirety, mine was a remarkably stable and, by conventional show business standards, almost quiet career—one that didn't make the kind of spectacular waves that often lead to burnout. Instead it just rolled evenly along, year after year, album after album, making connections with audiences. Although I did my share of performing in the entertainment meccas of New York, London, Las Vegas and L.A., my core and most loyal following ultimately resided elsewhere, in the markets of middle America and Canada. It was there that I could always count on a warm reception, there that I spent the most time, and there, to be honest, that I always felt most comfortable—away from the fanfare and the intense pressure, among ordinary, down-to-earth, not terribly flashy people— "just plain folks" sorts who are not (I think) much different from me.

Of course it's true that, by virtue of my success, I enjoyed a better quality of life than is the norm. And it's true that I occasionally had the privilege of meeting and performing for presidents and prime ministers, princesses and queens— experiences I enjoyed immensely. But you can't fundamentally change the person you are, regardless of the neighbourhood you live in or the kind of car you drive or where you buy your clothes. As I used to say at concerts about my sometimes fancy threads, "You can dress her up, but . . ." It always won a laugh, largely because it was true.

Scrub off the makeup, discard the beaded gowns, and you're left with what I was and will always essentially remain: lucky, hard-working and blessed with a good set of vocal cords, yes, but in the end—as my brother Harold suggested that memorable night at Radio City Music Hall—"just Anne." Just a girl from Springhill, Nova Scotia.

ACKNOWLEDGMENTS

My heartfelt thanks go to the following people:

Bill Langstroth: For the hundreds of pictures you took over the years and your support of this project and every other project I've ever done.

Bruce Murray: For sharing your remarkable memory of people and events, and for the family history you so painstakingly and meticulously compiled.

Bruce Allen: For your insightful guidance, enthusiasm and encouragement in the last fourteen years.

Peter Bleakney (my scribe): For your wonderful road journals, which were invaluable to us.

Darlene Sawyer: For being my "right arm" in every step of the process of writing this book, for your hours of research and your staggering attention to detail. You're the best!

Pat Riccio: For putting together the best band in the world in the early '80s. For tracking down so many band and crew members from my past and collecting stories and data from all of them. For being such a good sport in allowing me to tell "tales" about our years on the road together.

And finally, thank you to all of my fans for your incredible support throughout the years.

DISCOGRAPHY

1. What About Me (1968)
2. This Way Is My Way (1969)
3. Honey, Wheat & Laughter (1970)
4. Straight, Clean and Simple (1971)
5. Talk It Over in the Morning (1971)
6. Anne Murray/Glen Campbell (1971)
7. Annie (1972)
8. Danny's Song (1973)
9. Love Song (1974)
10. Highly Prized Possession (1974)
11. Together (1975)
12. Keeping in Touch (1976)
13. There's a Hippo in My Tub (1977)
14. Let's Keep It That Way (1978)
15. New Kind of Feeling (1979)
16. I'll Always Love You (1979)
17. Somebody's Waiting (1980)
18. Where Do You Go When You Dream (1981)
19. Christmas Wishes (1981)
20. The Hottest Night of the Year (1982)
21. A Little Good News (1983)
22. Heart Over Mind (1984)
23. Something to Talk About (1986)
24. Harmony (1987)
25. As I Am (1988)
26. Anne Murray Christmas (1988)
27. You Will (1990)
28. Yes I Do (1991)
29. Croonin' (1993)
30. Anne Murray (1996)
31. An Intimate Evening with Anne Murray . . . Live (1997)
32. What a Wonderful World (1999)
33. What a Wonderful Christmas (2001)
34. Country Croonin' (2002)
35. I'll Be Seeing You (2004)
36. DUETS: Friends & Legends (2007)
37. Anne Murray's Christmas Album (2008)

These are all available in digital or CD format, wherever you choose to buy your music.

AWARDS

CMA AWARDS

1985   Vocal Duo of the Year: Anne Murray and Dave Loggins,
"Nobody Loves Me Like You Do"

1984   Single of the Year: "A Little Good News"
Album of the Year: *A Little Good News*

CANADIAN COUNTRY MUSIC ASSOCIATION AWARDS

2002   Induction into the Canadian Country Music Association Hall
of Fame

1986   Single of the Year: "Now and Forever (You And Me)"

1984   Single of the Year: "A Little Good News"

ACADEMY OF COUNTRY MUSIC AWARDS

1978   Song of the Year: "You Needed Me"

COUNTRY MUSIC ASSOCIATION OF GREAT BRITAIN AWARDS

1974   Country Female Vocalist of the Year

BIG COUNTRY AWARDS

1988   Top Country Female Vocalist

1987   Canadian Country Artist of the Year
Best Country Single: "Now and Forever (You
and Me)"

1986   Top Country Female Vocalist
Best Country Single: "Nobody Loves Me Like
You Do"

1985   Top Country Female Vocalist
Top Country Single: Anne Murray with Dave Loggins,
"Nobody Loves Me Like You Do"
Top Country Album: *Heart Over Mind*
Canadian Country Artist of the Year

1980   Best Country Album: *I'll Always Love You*

1979   Top Country Female Singer
Canadian Country Artist of the Year

EAST COAST MUSIC ASSOCIATION AWARDS

2001   East Coast Music Association Directors' Special Achievement
Award

1990   Video of the Year: "If I Ever Fall in Love Again" (duet with
Kenny Rogers)

ACTRA AWARDS
1986   Best Variety Performance in Television: Anne Murray, "Anne
        Murray's Sounds of London"
1973   Best Variety Performer

GEMINI AWARDS
1993   Best Performance in a Variety Program or Series: "Country
        Gold"

HONOURS

2009   Honorary Doctor of Laws, University of Prince Edward Island
2008   Howie Richmond Hitmaker Award, Songwriters Hall
        of Fame (American)
2007   Anne Murray Canadian postage stamp
2006   Canadian Songwriters Hall of Fame Legacy Award
2002   Order of Nova Scotia (inaugural year)
1998   Star on Canada's Walk of Fame (inaugural year)
1997   Canadian Association of Broadcasters Hall of Fame
        Award (inaugural year)
1995   Governor General's Performing Arts Award
1984   Companion of the Order of Canada
1982   Honorary Doctor of Letters, Saint Mary's University
1980   Star on the Hollywood Walk of Fame
1978   Honorary Doctor of Letters, University of New Brunswick
1975   Officer of the Order of Canada
        Country Music Hall of Fame Walkway of Stars (Nashville)

The Anne Murray Centre, located in Anne's hometown of Springhill,
Nova Scotia, is open May through October. The Centre displays the
history of her extraordinary career.

PHOTO CREDITS

Page i Photo courtesy of the author's collection, and unless otherwise indicated, all photos are from the author's collection

Page vi (top) © CBC Still Photo Collection; (bottom) © Bill Langstroth

Page vii (top) © CBC Still Photo Collection/Robert Ragsdale; (bottom) © CBC Still Photo Collection/David Carr

Page viii (top) © Wamboldt-Waterfield/Clark Photographic; (bottom) © CBC Still Photo Collection

Page ix (bottom) Courtesy of Capitol Records, a Division of EMI Music; (Robert Wortham photographer)

Page x (top) © C. Fred Ruggles; (bottom) © Hope Powell

Page xi (top) © Courtesy of Capitol Records, a Division of EMI Music Canada; (bottom) © Bill Langstroth

Page xii (top) Photo courtesy of The Recording Academy ®; Stephen Morley © 1975; (bottom) © John R. Rowlands

Page xiii (top) © John R. Rowlands; (bottom) © Ebet Roberts

Page xiv (top) © Bill Langstroth; (bottom) © Bill Langstroth

Page xv (top) © Sherman Hines; (bottom) © Bill Langstroth

Page xvi (top) © Bill Langstroth;
(second from top) © Ebet Roberts;
(second from bottom) © Bill Langstroth;
bottom) © Bill Langstroth

Page xvii (top) © Courtesy of Capitol Records, a Division of EMI Music Canada; (bottom) © NBC Universal / NBCU Photo Bank

Page xviii (top left) © 1983 by Don Putnam;
(bottom left) © Judy Mock;
(bottom right) © CBC Still Photo Collection/Raj Rama

Page xix (top) © Bill Langstroth;

Page xx (top right) © Courtesy of John Ascuaga's Nugget Casino Resort;
(bottom) © CBC Still Photo Collection/Peter Parsons

Page xxi (top left) © Markham Theatre for Performing Arts;
(top right) © Andrew MacNaughtan;
(bottom left) © CBC Still Photo Collection/David Roark;
(bottom right) © ABC News/Good Morning America

Page xxii (top left) © Library and Archives Canada. Reproduced with the
permission of Library and Archives Canada. Source: Library and
Archives Canada/Credit: John Evans/John Evans collection;
(top right) © Denise Grant Photography;
(bottom) © CBC Still Photo Collection/Wes Raymond
Photography

Page xxiii (top) © Bill Langstroth;
(bottom) © Government of Canada. Reproduced with the
permission of the Minister of Public Works and Government
Services Canada (2009). Source: Library and Archives
Canada/Credit: Robert Cooper

Page xxiv (bottom) © Canada Post Corporation 2008. Reproduced with
permission.

Page xxv (top) © Barry Roden

Page xxvi: (top left) © George Bush Presidential Library and Museum;
(top right) © LASZLOMONTREAL.com
(bottom) © Government of Canada. Reproduced with the
permission of the Minister of Public Works and Government
Services Canada (2009). Source: Library and Archives
Canada/Credit: Sergeant Bertrand Thibeault

Page xxvii: (top) © Photo provided courtesy of Insight Production
Company Ltd. (Denise Grant, photographer)

Page xxix (bottom) © Courtesy of Capitol Records, a Division of EMI
Music (Barry Roden, photographer)

Page xxxi (top) © Denise Grant Photography

Page xxxii (top) © Mike Gillan

*Every effort has been made to contact the copyright holders; in the event of
an inadvertent omission or error, please notify the publisher.*

PEOPLE IN GROUP PHOTOGRAPHS

Page vi, top of page: *Singalong Jubilee Gang*
Back row, left to right: Michael Stanbury, Toni Hollett,
      Vern Moulton, Marg Ashcroft, Ken Tobias, Patricia Anne
      McKinnon, Edith Butler, Lorne White
Front row, left to right: John Allen Cameron, Jim Bennet, Bill Langstroth,
      Anne, Fred McKenna, Hal Kempster, Karen Oxley

Page xxviii, bottom of page: *The "Chicks" in Scotland*
Back row, left to right: Rosemary Anderson, Sandy Saley, Audrey Killer,
      Ruth Gray, Helen Simpson
Front row, left to right: Barb Turner, Cynthia McReynolds, Sharon Bright,
      Wendy Wright, Dorothy Patterson, Joan Ball, Anne

Page xxxi, bottom of page: *My band, crew, bus drivers and Dawn on the
2008 Canadian tour*
Back row, left to right: Hoot Borden, Darlene Sawyer, David Elmer,
      Joe Jackson, Van Youngblood, Kevin Smith, Thomas Stehle,
      Johnny Barnhardt
Third row, left to right: Sandy Bloos, Anne, Debbie Ankeny,
      Dawn Langstroth, Derek Rambeau, Bob Groza
Second row, left to right: Brian Babineau, Georges Hébert, Gary Craig,
      Billy Anderson, Thomas Gall
Front row, left to right: Aidan Mason, Steve Sexton, Peter Bleakney

INDEX

NOTE: Titles of albums by Anne Murray are in italics followed by the release year. Titles of other artists' albums, books, films and TV series are also in italics. Song titles are enclosed in quotation marks.